SMALL ISLANDS, BIG POLITICS:

THE TONBS AND ABU MUSA IN THE GULF

EDITED BY

HOOSHANG AMIRAHMADI

MACMILLAN

First published by
MACMILLAN PRESS LTD
Houndmills, Basingstoke, Hampshire RG21 6XS
and London
Companies and representatives
throughout the world

ISBN 0-333-68019-7

A catalogue record for this book is available
from the British Library.

10 9 8 7 6 5 4 3 2 1
05 04 03 02 01 00 99 98 97 96

Printed in the United States of America by
Haddon Craftsmen
Scranton, PA

Table of Contents

Notes on Contributors

Hooshang Amirahmadi, a Cornell Ph.D., is professor of planning and international development at Rutgers University. He chairs the Department of Urban Planning and Policy Development and is director of the University's Middle Eastern Studies program. He helped found the Center for Iranian Research and Analysis (CIRA) and served as its executive director for many years. Professor Amirahmadi is the author of *Revolution and Economic Transition: The Iranian Experience* (Albany: State University of New York Press, 1990), and editor or co-editor of seven other books, including: *The United States and the Middle East: A Search for New Perspectives* (Albany: State University of New York Press, 1993); *Post-Revolutionary Iran* (Boulder: Westview Press, 1988); *Iran and the Arab World* (New York: St. Martin's Press, 1993); and *Reconstruction and Regional Diplomacy in the Persian Gulf* (London: Routledge, 1992). Dr. Amirahmadi has also published over a hundred journal papers, book chapters, and review articles. A frequent contributor to many conferences in Europe, North America, Asia, Latin America, Africa, and the Middle East, Dr. Amirahmadi has lectured in over 20 countries and has served as consultant to the UNDP, the World Bank, the Aga Khan Foundation, a number of private corporations, and several developing nations.

Davoud H. Bavand is professor of law and international relations at Imam Sadegh University in Tehran and a legal consultant to international organizations. He received his Ph.D. from American University in Washington, D.C., in 1964. Upon graduation, Dr. Bavand joined Iran's Ministry of Foreign Affairs, first at the ministry's headquarters in Tehran, and later at Iran's permanent mission to the United Nations where he served as an expert in international law governing territorial disputes. After two decades of full-time government service, Dr. Bavand turned to full-time teaching and research. He is a frequent contributor to Iran's print and electronic media, predominantly in matters of Persian Gulf security and Iran's historical role in the warm waters. His publications include *The Historical, Political and*

Legal Bases of Iran's Sovereignty over the Islands of Tunb & Abu Musa (New York: Internet Concepts Inc, 1994).

Guive Mirfendereski is an international lawyer and adjunct assistant professor of international law at the Fletcher School of Law and Diplomacy, Tufts University. He has counseled international organizations such as the World Bank and has advised governments in matters of privatization, institution of judicial and legal reforms, and revision of business laws. From 1988 through 1991, Dr. Mirfendereski served as an associate with the law firm of Gaston & Snow in Boston. Dr. Mirfendereski holds a Doctor of Laws (J.D.) degree from Boston College Law School and a Ph.D. in international law from the Fletcher School of Law and Diplomacy. His writings have appeared in *Denver Journal of International Law and Policy, Boston College International and Comparative Law Review,* and *Fletcher Forum.*

Pirouz Mojtahed-Zadeh is senior research fellow at the Geopolitics and International Boundaries Research Center at the School of Oriental and African Studies, University of London, where he received his master's and Ph.D. in political geography. He is also chairman of Urosevic Research Foundation in London. An expert on the political geography of the Persian Gulf, Dr. Mojtahed-Zadeh has published extensively in both Persian and English. His writings in both languages include specialized academic pieces along with contributions to the media in Iran and the West. He has also lectured on the Persian Gulf and Central Asia in Europe, North America, the Middle East, and the Far East. His works are based on research travels to the Iranian and Arab sides of the Persian Gulf. Dr Mojtahed-Zadeh's English publications include *Political Geography of the Strait of Hormuz* (London: SOAS, University of London, 1991) and *The Changing World Order and the Geopolitical Regions of Caspian-Central Asia and the Persian Gulf* (London: Urosevic Research Foundation, 1992). His publications in Persian include several books and numerous articles. Dr. Mojtahed-Zadeh has served as a consultant to MENAS International Consultants of London and the United Nations.

Preface

This book is about one of the oldest and most persistent and recurring territorial disputes in the Persian Gulf. The object of this dispute consists of the islands of Great Tonb, Little Tonb, and Abu Musa. Although the controversy over the Tonbs and Abu Musa has a long history, no scholarly book has ever focused directly and solely on the subject.

Situated in the middle of the Persian Gulf, Abu Musa has an area of about four square miles and a population of about 700 to 1,000, mostly Iranian. Located near the Iranian coast, Great Tonb is uninhabited on any permanent basis and Little Tonb is even more desolate. Each of the Tonbs has been referred to by many different names. The name *Tonb* used herein has many variations, including Tunb, Tomb, Tanb, Tamb, and Tumb.

From a geopolitical standpoint, the subject of the dispute has been control of the islands overlooking the approaches to the Strait of Hormuz through which pass some 20 percent of the world's oil and tens of billions of dollars in goods. From a legal point of view, the subject of controversy has been the issue of ownership of the islands. Prior to 1971, the parties to the dispute had been the governments of Iran and Great Britain. Presently, the disputants are the United Arab Emirates (UAE) and Iran.

The significance of this book goes beyond the countries involved or the peoples in the Middle East. The West, including the United States, has continued to maintain a strong interest in the dispute. The strategic importance of peace and stability in the Persian Gulf is certainly vital to economic well-being of the major players in the region. Given the increased U.S. military presence in the Persian Gulf, any attempt at changing the status quo concerning the islands will undoubtedly have major repercussions for the American people. From this perspective, it is critical that the public in the West be better informed about the dispute and its possible implications.

The title of this book, *Small Islands, Big Politics,* is supposed to capture the past and the present politics surrounding the dispute. I do not wish to imply that the future politics concerning these small islands will inevitably be big. On the contrary, I have edited this book in the hope of bringing the future politics regarding the islands in line with their size and importance. Specifically, I will consider my contribution successful if a future book on the subject were to be entitled *Small Islands, Small Politics.*

This book examines the current political context, historical origin, and legal dimensions of the controversy over the islands. The book adopts a documentary, historical, and analytical approach to the study of the dispute. The authors are scholars and policy analysts with extensive research credentials in their respective subjects and have received their education and training in Iran, Europe, and the United States. This diversity of experience and educational backgrounds has helped provide the book with a sober analysis of the complex issues that surround claims of sovereignty over the islands.

In Chapter 1, I examine the British colonial legacy and the current strategic context of the dispute. I argue that the legal and diplomatic-historical dimensions must be considered in light of British colonialism's anti-Iran policy in the Persian Gulf and the current strained relations between the Islamic Republic of Iran and its antagonists in the Middle East and the West. As in the colonial time, the dispute today is largely motivated by a desire to weaken Iran and reduce its influence in the Persian Gulf. From this perspective, the U.S. policy of dual containment pursued against Iran by the U.S. administration under President Bill Clinton is very much the same as the British colonial policy in the Persian Gulf.

In Chapter 2, Pirouz Mojtahed-Zadeh provides perspectives on various aspects of the territorial history of the three islands as a key to understanding the issues discussed in the subsequent chapters. Among the topics he examines are the islands' geography and economic activity, the emergence and extent of the Iranian state in the Persian Gulf, the evolution of the sheikhdoms from tribal polities into territorially defined entities, the strategic and political reasons underlying the British colonial efforts to grab one Iranian island after another, and the examination of the factors leading to the eventual negotiated settlement of the dispute in 1971. The chapter concludes with the dismissal of the UAE's assertion that the 1971 Anglo-Iranian Memorandum of Understanding over Abu Musa had been obtained by duress. The text of the memorandum and exchange of various notes among the interested parties are reproduced in Appendix 1.

In Chapter 3, Davoud Hermidas Bavand examines the basis for Iran's sovereignty over Abu Musa. In so doing, he reviews the historical origins of Iran's claim to the island. Next, he examines the circumstances that surrounded and the consequences that followed from the Anglo-Sharjah occupation of Abu Musa in 1903-1904, which was in contravention of an agreement between Iran and Great Britain to maintain the status quo relative to the island so that the differences could be sorted out by negotiation. Following a brief enumeration of the parties' actions with respect to the island in the period between 1904 to 1971, the chapter concludes with an analysis of the Memorandum of Understanding. Bavand presents a cogent argument demonstrating that Abu Musa belongs to Iran.

In Chapter 4, Guive Mirfendereski examines the legal claims put forth by Iran and Great Britain in support of their respective claims to the Tonbs. The chapter states the arguments and presents the evidence for each claim, evaluates the evidence and weighs the arguments in reference to international legal standards, and determines the ownership of the islands at the time of Iran's repossession of the islands in 1971. Following a probing review of the political history of the Tonbs from ancient times, the chapter shifts its focus to the nature and the extent of cartographical evidence depicting the status of the Tonbs as Iranian territory. The consideration of the Anglo-Qasimi claims based on occupation and adverse possession extends into an extralegal review of the evidence supporting the "common understanding of mankind" as to the Tonbs' appurtenance to Iran. The chapter concludes that the weight of the evidence supports the Iranian claim to the islands.

In editing this volume, the biggest problem I faced was to identify appropriate authors. After some searching I was fortunate to find the contributors to this volume in the United States, England, and Iran. I am grateful to them for being cooperative and prompt. Because their points of view tend to support the Iranian perspective on the islands, I offered Arab scholars from the UAE an opportunity to submit chapters for the book, which unfortunately they did not, although I waited long to receive their contributions.

I have received support and encouragement from many of my students, colleagues and friends. Among them, however, Dr. Guive Mirfendereski, Alidad Mafinezam, and Pooya Alaedini deserve special mention. Alidad helped in the research and writing of the first chapter, and Pooya assisted in the reviewing of the manuscript. Guive's contribution was especially important as he helped rewrite and edit the chapters, undertook new research, and assisted in the preparation of the bibliography. His role in editing the book was indispensable particularly because of his knowledge of international law and the legal aspects of the dispute. Needless to say, I alone remain accountable for errors and shortcomings of the volume.

Hooshang Amirahmadi
New Brunswick, October 1995

1

The Colonial-Political Dimension of the Iran-UAE Dispute

Hooshang Amirahmadi

The history of the Persian Gulf is replete with rivalries and wars. Ever since Cyrus the Great founded the world's first empire in Iran 26 centuries ago, the Persian Gulf has been a battleground of cultures and soldiers. The arrival of European colonialism in the Persian Gulf in the sixteenth century intensified and expanded the power-play and, consequently, calm and harmony became even more elusive thereafter. Over the past five centuries, Iranians, Arabs, local pirates, the Dutch, the Portuguese, the British, the Germans, the Russians, and most recently the Americans, have competed and clashed for influence in the Persian Gulf. The discovery of vast oil reserves in the Persian Gulf in the early twentieth century sowed the seeds of the gulf's current instability. The two recent wars in the Persian Gulf bear witness to this new, oil-affected turbulence. The Iran-Iraq War and the U.S.-led Desert Storm against Iraq—two of the costliest regional wars in human history—serve as recent reminders that today's Persian Gulf is as unsafe and unpredictable as ever.

Three years after Desert Storm, the countries surrounding the Persian Gulf are more divided than they have ever been.[1] Kuwait and Saudi Arabia are disdainful of Saddam Hussein. Qatar and Saudi Arabia's old border disputes have resurfaced. While Iran and Iraq currently adhere to the U.N.-brokered ceasefire agreement that ended their eight-year war in 1988, they have yet to sign a comprehensive peace treaty and free all the prisoners captured during their war. Even though the Iranian adventurism abroad has subsided, the Persian Gulf monarchies still feel threatened by their powerful neighbor and the specter of Iranian-inspired Islamic fundamentalism.

Currently, to Iran, Iraq, and Saudi Arabia, the three main powers of the Persian Gulf, lasting peace and regional cooperation seem unattainable. Ideological differences among the three states have played a key role in bringing about the current discord. The _shi'i_ Islamic and republican Iran, the secular but totalitarian Iraq under a _sunni_ oligarchy, and the feudal, authoritarian Wahhabi monarchy in Saudi Arabia have little in common. The vast differences in their ideology, form of government, and the disparate sources of their regimes' legitimacy prevent meaningful dialogue. Furthermore, distinct from ideology and system of government, the nationalistic and pragmatic concerns, bent on maximizing each state's influence in the region, fuel the distrust.

Meanwhile, Egypt and Israel have fed into this fear by a propaganda campaign that demonizes Iran as a hegemonic terrorist state incapable of peaceful coexistence with its neighbors. This campaign is aimed at convincing the West, the United States in particular, that Egypt and Israel continue to remain a "strategic asset" in the post-Soviet era. The anti-Iran crusade has been supported by the United States which seeks to maintain a presence in the region and sell arms to the oil monarchies. Iran's opposition to the Arab-Israeli peace negotiations and the rise of political Islam in North Africa and Central Asia have provided justifications for supporters of the U.S. administration's dual containment policy to weaken Iran in an attempt to eliminate its historic power and influence in the Persian Gulf.

During the Iran-Iraq War, the United States sold weapons concurrently to both countries. After Desert Storm, Saudi Arabia and other oil-rich monarchies in the Persian Gulf began buying American weapons at unprecedented rates. In the wake of these multibillion dollar arms purchases, the Persian Gulf has become the most militarized region in the world.[2] The region's new level of militarization is all the more menacing because the Persian Gulf's politics today betrays an acute schizophrenia, caused by the multiplicity of colonial powers who have manipulated the locals, arming and pitting them against each other. This schizophrenia turns the Persian Gulf into an arena of rapidly shifting loyalties; today's friends can easily become tomorrow's foes.

This book discusses a territorial dispute in the Persian Gulf. The dispute is between Iran and the United Arab Emirates (UAE) over who should own and control three small islands overlooking the strategic Strait of Hormuz. Since 1971, the year British colonialism withdrew from the Persian Gulf, Iran has regained its full sovereignty over the Tonbs and has accommodated UAE in the administration of Abu Musa. On that ground and based on past legacies, the Iranian government sees no reason to alter the status quo. Guided by its long-held distaste for the presence of foreign powers in the Persian Gulf, Iran also feels that regional problems need regional solutions. Thus, the Iranian government has extended numerous invitations to the UAE to find a local, diplomatic solution to the impasse. On the contrary, the UAE wishes to take the matter to the International Court of Justice. Confronting the anti-Iran alliance, Iran finds itself isolated once again, reminiscent of its war with Iraq when the Persian Gulf's Arabs and the West categorically supported Saddam Hussein, leaving Iran with a devastating shortage of weaponry and spare parts.

The chapters that follow provide a close reading of the legal and relevant territorial-historical dimensions of Iran-UAE dispute in the Persian Gulf and dissect the intricacies of international law and its application to territorial disputes between the two countries. They show, with objectivity, authority, and confidence, that the islands belong to Iran and that the UAE's claim is unjustified. No attempt at a comprehensive understanding of the dispute can justifiably ignore its colonial legacy and current strategic context. This chapter, thus, focuses on British colonial policy in the Persian Gulf and the current political dimension of the dispute. I will argue that the legal and territorial-historical dimensions must be considered in light of Britain's historical anti-Iran policies in the Persian Gulf and the currently strained relations between Iran and Persian Gulf monarchies and their allies in the West. Similar to the conflicts of the colonial period, the current conflict is basically caused by a desire to weaken Iran and reduce its influence in the Persian Gulf. From this perspective, the U.S. administration's dual containment policy is similar to British colonial policy in the Persian Gulf.[3]

BRITISH COLONIAL POLICY

Attempting to make sense of the current dispute, we confront a peculiar ontological dilemma: Prior to 1971, it was Great Britain, the guardian of the Persian Gulf sheikhdoms, who controlled the islands. Even though the British flag was not hoisted on the Tonbs and Abu Musa, the islands were under British occupation. When Iran finally got the islands back in 1971, the UAE did not even exist yet. Indeed it was Great Britain, and not the UAE, which agreed to give back the islands to Iran. What complicates the current dispute is that the UAE is now attempting to reclaim islands which it has in fact never owned. Nor has it ever been a legal entity in any previous arrangement with Iran concerning the islands. It is in this context that the authors in this volume adopt a historical-diplomatic, political, and legal perspective on the current dispute.

Iran exercised sovereignty over the Tonbs and Abu Musa until the Arab invasion of Iran in A.D. 623. Over three centuries later, in A.D. 945, the Buyid dynasty extended Iranian rule to the Persian Gulf and Oman and captured the islands as well. The next time that Iran lost control over the Islands was in about 1507 when Portugal dominated the Persian Gulf. Iran regained control of the islands when the Portuguese were expelled in 1622. By this time, however, Great Britain had become increasingly involved in regular shipping and trade in the Persian Gulf and had developed a political and strategic interest in the area. Indeed, a fleet of the English East India Company had assisted Shah Abbas of Persia in expelling the Portuguese from Hormuz and Qishm islands in 1622. Later, in consequence of the consolidation of the British Raj in India and a parallel rise in Britain's commercial interests in Persia and Mesopotamia, the control and security of the Persian Gulf proved all the more essential to the defense of imperial British interests against the Russian threat from the north and French influence from occupied Egypt.

As Britain's power in the Persian Gulf grew, Iran became a progressively weaker state. Iran's age of glory had ended in 1747 with the death of Nadir Shah, the last Persian king to have played a dominant regional role. In the first two decades of the nineteenth century, the English East India Company mounted a series of military expeditions against the maritime tribes of the Pirate Coast in the lower Persian Gulf and imposed upon them a general treaty of peace outlawing acts of piracy and plunder at sea. Subsequently, in the period from 1835 to 1892, the British government established a general maritime truce among the pacified tribes and exacted from the Trucial sheikhs a series of exclusive undertakings whereby the sheikhs undertook to deal with no foreign power other than Britain and not to dispose of or transact any part of their territory without the consent of the British government. By 1892, the entire lower Persian Gulf had become a patchwork of British protectorates designed to thwart the advances of Iran, Russia, Germany, France, and the Ottoman Empire. Iran lost control of the islands in 1903 when Britain occupied them in the name of the Sheikh of Sharjah.

Sandwiched as it was by Tsarist Russia to the north and a British naval fleet to the south, Iran became a victim of colonial plots and territorial expansion. Defeating Iran in two wars in 1813 and 1828, Russia annexed all of Iran's territory in the Caucasus. The British, too, waged war on Iran in 1856-1857, forcing Nasir al-Din Shah Qajar to abandon Herat. During the Anglo-Iranian war, Britain seized Iran's Kharg Island, the port of Bushehr, and occupied parts of the Iranian southern province of Khuzestan. As Iranian territory shrank in this period, so did the country's political independence and regional influence. In sharp contrast, the power and influence of both Russia and Britain increased in the region.

By the early years of the twentieth century, Tsarist Russia and Great Britain were in fierce competition over influence in the Persian Gulf, and Iran was caught in between. The Persian Gulf waterway led to Britain's prized possessions in the Indian Ocean. As Iranian territory was all that separated Russia from these warm waters, a potential alliance between Russia and Iran was the greatest threat to British interests in the Persian Gulf and beyond.

Naturally, Britain endeavored to reduce Iran's influence in the Persian Gulf. Britain would achieve this by three means. First, in 1907, Britain reached an agreement with Russia to divide Iran into two spheres of influence, with Russia in effective control of Iran's north and Britain of the country's south. As a result of this arrangement, the Persian Gulf became Britain's stronghold. Second, Britain promoted disputes between Iran and its Arab neighbors over a number of islands in the Persian Gulf. The current islands dispute has its roots in the British divide-and-conquer policy in the Persian Gulf that had begun in the nineteenth century. And third, Britain weakened Iran's influence in the Persian Gulf by establishing the so-called Trucial system, where the pirate sheikhs of the Persian Gulf's southern shores were persuaded to sign a truce with Britain during the pearling season.

A key point of contention between Iran and Britain at this time was Bahrain. Britain had become the main power in Bahrain by 1861, adding it to the Trucial system. On numerous occasions, Iran asserted its claim over the island, although it had entrusted Britain with protecting the island from foreign intervention. In the early years of the twentieth century, British power over the Persian Gulf covered the whole of the southern shores. By this time many sheikhdoms had already been added to the Trucial system, including Ras al-Khaimah and Sharjah, two small sheikhdoms now part of the UAE, in whose name the UAE claims sovereignty, respectively, over the Tonbs and Abu Musa.

In 1903, during the heyday of its world dominion, Great Britain took over the Iranian islands of Great Tonb and Abu Musa. At Britain's behest, Iranian flags on the islands, hoisted in June 1904, were taken down and replaced by the flags of Sharjah. When Iran protested, Britain threatened to use naval force. To prevent a sea battle that it had little chance of winning, Iran backed down. As the decades went by, Iran continued to verbally challenge Britain's annexation of its territory. Britain insisted that the islands belonged to the sheikhdoms. This was despite historical legacy and massive record of documents and map—mostly produced by the British themselves, showing the islands as Iranian territory.

It is striking that during the period between 1904 and 1971, Britain wanted the islands to belong to the sheikhdoms more than the sheikhdoms themselves. For example, in 1934, the Sheikh of Ras al-Khaimah decided to surrender possession of the Tonbs to Iran, as he thought that the islands were legitimate Iranian territory. The British intervened to disallow the move, forcing the sheikhdom to keep its flag on the islands. Naturally, the islands dispute helped worsen relations between Iran and Britain. British policy vis-à-vis the islands once again rested on the premise that Iranian control of the islands may have turned them into a Russian foothold. With the islands under the influence of Britain's Trucial protectorates, Britain exercised more control over them, simultaneously limiting the influence of the Persian Gulf's regional powers headed by Iran.

Allied victory in World War I added immeasurably to British power in the Persian Gulf as it almost eliminated the influence of the Ottomans and the Germans in the area. In 1918, when the war ended, Russia was still in its revolutionary transitional period, also incapable of challenging Britain in the Persian Gulf. Meanwhile, the Constitutional Revolution of 1905-1907 in Iran had caused the Iranian government not to pay enough attention to its provinces, particularly the southern ones adjacent to the Persian Gulf. Britain had made numerous local arrangements with tribal chiefs often with the effect of further undermining the power of Tehran; for example, the British armed tribes in the southern provinces of Khuzestan, Fars, and Baluchestan that had cecessionist demands. However, with the dawn of the Soviet threat following the Bolshevik Revolution, Britain saw the need for a strong central government in Tehran, one that would protect British interests in Iran against Communist expansionism.

This change of perspective led the British to welcome the prospect of a Persian Cossack commander by the name of Colonel Reza Khan who would assume power in Tehran through a coup in 1921. The British were impressed by the little-known colonel's disciplined and headstrong character. They also saw in Reza Khan a nationalist and power-hungry leader who could block the Bolshevik advance through British help. Britain's decision to support the coup rested on the premise that only a strong military dictatorship in Tehran could save the country from disintegrating and falling into Bolshevik hands; yet, Britain was not completely comfortable with a strong nationalist government in Tehran. This concern led the British to simultaneously support the mutinous tribal leaders who were opposed to the central government in Tehran. This inconsistency also characterized the way

Britain operated its possessions in the Persian Gulf. On the one hand, Britain wanted to keep the Persian Gulf safe and stable for business, a condition that required a strong Iran. Simultaneously, lest Iran side with another world power, Britain wished to curtail Iran's influence over its protectorates in the area.

British fear of Reza Shah was not without basis. The Shah's distaste for British influence in Iran, coupled with his strong nationalist stance against the possibility of Anglo-Russian military presence in Iran, made him an undesired political entity in the politics of the day. In 1941, while World War II was in progress, the British from the south and the Soviets from the north invaded Iran and forced Reza Shah to abdicate in favor of his son Mohammad Reza, who would be toppled by a revolution in 1979. Reza Shah was accused of having sided with Nazi Germany, an allegation that, no doubt, precipitated his downfall. He left Iran for South Africa and died in exile in 1944.

Oil was discovered in Iran in 1908. As a concession to Britain, in 1911 the Iranian government bestowed exclusive rights to extract and market Iranian oil to the Anglo-Persian Oil Company. In 1933, Reza Shah forced the company to improve the terms and conditions of the concession to allow for a greater Iranian share and influence. In the wake of Reza Shah's request that foreigners refer to the country as Iran—as opposed to Persia—in 1935 the company was renamed Anglo-Iranian Oil Company.

The dispute over the Tonbs and Abu Musa was the main focus of Anglo-Iranian relations in the 1930s. Other disputes involved oil, control of Persian Telegraph, Duzab Railway, Imperial Airways, Imperial Bank of Persia, and the Persian debt. In the Persian Gulf, Tehran and London were at odds over British presence on the Iranian islands of Qishm and Henjam, the presence of the British political resident in the Persian Gulf at the Iranian port city of Bushehr, and the status of Bahrain, the Tonbs, and Abu Musa. The British government adamantly opposed Iran's claim of territorial sovereignty over these islands. Bahrain had fallen out of Iranian control in the previous century and was a British protectorate, while the Tonbs and Abu Musa had been taken over in the years 1903-1904 by the Sheikh of Sharjah upon the encouragement of the British government.

In the aftermath of World War II, Great Britain relinquished its colonial dominion in India. Even though Britain's presence in the Persian Gulf had been an outgrowth of its presence in India, withdrawal from the latter did not imply a retreat from the former. British presence in the Persian Gulf rested on the need for oil, commitment to the local sheikhs, control of the sea lanes of communication between Aden and the East, and holding Soviet expansionism in check.

In 1947-1948, the embattled Anglo-Iranian Oil Company agreed to enter into a supplementary arrangement offering Iran more favorable terms. However, the Iranian legislature rejected the offer, and in 1951 Prime Minister Mohammad Mosaddeq nationalized the Iranian oil industry. Britain responded by imposing a blockade on Iranian oil exports. In 1953, the CIA-engineered Operation Ajax toppled the nationalist Mosaddeq government and returned Mohammad Reza Shah Pahlavi to the throne. In 1954, as an expression of gratitude to his foreign sponsors, the Shah consented to an agreement whereby the exploration and production of Iranian oil was granted to a consortium of eight multinationals; among them was the successor-in-interest of the Anglo-Iranian Oil Company, British Petroleum. Later the composition of the consortium was altered to increase the share of the American multinationals at the expense of British interests. From this period onward, the United States replaced Britain as the main Western influence in Iran. The United States would become increasingly involved in the Persian Gulf following the British withdrawal in 1971.

The intervention of Western powers in Iran's domestic affairs and their opposition to democratic and nationalistic forces in the country was reflected in British and American policy in the Persian Gulf. In 1953, at the time of the coup in Iran, all of the southern shores of the Persian Gulf (apart from Saudi Arabia, which had become a sovereign state in 1932) were under British control. The specter of Iranian-style, anti-colonialist revolutions in the Persian Gulf unnerved Britain and the United States. Britain did not wish the sheikhdoms of the Persian Gulf to follow the Iranian model. The nationalist movement that brought Mosaddeq to power was also anchored in democratic ideals. It was the first of its kind in the region. Almost 25 years later, in 1979, Iran was consumed by another revolution, this time dominated by an Islamic ideology. Much like before, the West did its best to hinder the spread of Iran's revolutionary ideology in the Persian Gulf.

In the years 1953-1954, the British troops withdrew from Egypt, which had fallen to General Muhammad Nagib and Colonel Gamal Abd al-Nasser's Arab nationalism and the Islamic Brotherhood's anti-Western ideology. In 1956, the virulent campaign against Western imperialism culminated in Nasser's decision to nationalize the Suez Canal. The military confrontation that ensued between Egypt and the Western powers—including Israel—forever changed the geopolitical alignment of power in the region. While for two hundred years it had been the British India government that had defined Western interests in the region, after 1956, the single most influential source of defining Western interests in the Middle East and, to a lesser degree, in the Persian Gulf, would become Israel. The Soviet Union, for its part, would in turn find itself hand-in-glove with the radical Arab govern-ments, especially in Egypt and Syria, opposing the U.S. and Israel. On the other hand, suspicious of Russian motives and at the same time not com-fortable with its Western partners, Iran stood strategically ambivalent in the midst of Middle Eastern politics.

In 1960, the British government failed to secure a base in Kenya. Real-izing that British interests in the region could not be served from London and Nicosia, the British government turned Aden into a base in 1961. Aden soon proved unsuitable for British purposes in the face of the advancing wave of Arab nationalism across the Red Sea. The Yemeni civil war fueled by the local antagonists, Egypt and Saudi Arabia, eventually led to the inde-pendence of Aden in 1967 as the country of South Yemen and to the British withdrawal in the same year. In the meantime, in 1959, Iraq had withdrawn from the anti-Soviet security pact known as the Baghdad Pact and therefore Britain lost the use of its bases there. The next area to break loose from Britain's patrimony was Kuwait, in 1961. By 1962, the British possessions in the Persian Gulf had come to consist of the sheikhdoms of Bahrain, Qatar, Abu Dhabi, Dubai, Sharjah, Ajman, Umm al-Qaiwain, Ras al-Khaimah, and Fujaira (which does not have a coast on the Persian Gulf proper). In 1971, however, Qatar and Bahrain became independent and Britain pre-sided over the creation of the United Arab Emirates (UAE) by uniting the remaining sheikhdoms.

In 1961, as Kuwait became independent, Iraq reasserted its historical claim over the country. British troops were dispatched to assist in the de-fense of Kuwait's borders. When Qatar became independent, Saudi Arabia claimed that it was part of its territory. Once again, British and American influence forced the Saudis to retract their claim. Kuwait, Qatar, Bahrain, and the UAE may not have emerged as independent states had British and, to a lesser extent, American policy been different. The development of these feudal monarchies into sovereign states was far from a historical inevitabil-ity. Even today, decades after their creation, these states do not have enough citizens to man their state bureaucracies and militaries. Less than half of the people living in Kuwait are citizens. In Qatar, foreigners comprise two-thirds of the population. Only one-third of the residents of the UAE are citizens.

The decision by the British government to withdraw from Aden was largely due to London's dwindling financial reserves. Since World War II, Britain had maintained its commitments in the region frugally. Britain's economic decline in 1966-1968 was the main cause of further cuts in its overseas commitments. The announcement in July 1966 to curb expenditures at home and abroad triggered a major reassessment of

British commitments in the areas east of the Suez Canal. In April 1967, Britain decided to reduce the number of its forces stationed in the region; however, following the devaluation of the pound sterling in November of that year, Britain decided to quit Aden altogether. At the time, the British government assured the sheikhdoms in the Persian Gulf of its intention to remain in the area as long as it was necessary to maintain the status quo. However, on January 16, 1968, the Labor government of Harold Wilson announced that Great Britain would withdraw its forces from the Persian Gulf by the end of 1971. The move would end 150 years of British military and political domination of the Persian Gulf. As the time for Britain's final departure approached, the local sheikhs were overwhelmed by the anxiety of independence. The Persian Gulf's sheikhs had little if any experience with statehood, and still less with nationhood. But from the beginning days of their statehood, the Persian Gulf's new states were aware that, relying on their oil reserves as a bargaining chip, they would seek the support of Western powers in their regional maneuvering. That UAE highlighted its dispute with Iran over the islands at a time when the West was attempting to isolate Iran is indicative of this phenomenon.

Britain had two main objectives in the Persian Gulf as its departure drew near: first, to unite seven of the Trucial sheikhdoms to form the UAE; and second, to create the independent states of Bahrain and Qatar. Actualizing these objectives rested on dealing with Iran. Iran asserted that the islands of Abu Musa, Great Tonb and Little Tonb, and also Bahrain were its historical property, unjustly seized by Britain in the past. Britain was well aware that its withdrawal from the Persian Gulf would create a situation in which Iran would recover its territories. Thus, between 1968 and 1971, Britain successfully negotiated a package deal with Iran over its outstanding territorial claims in the Persian Gulf and Britain's own design for the region.[4]

Accordingly: (a) Iran relinquished its claim to Bahrain and recognized it as a sovereign independent state; (b) Iran assented to and recognized the creation and independence of the UAE; (c) Iran recognized the independence of Qatar; (d) Iran repossessed the Tonb Islands; and (e) Iran and Britain, with the consent of Sharjah, entered into the Memorandum of Understanding concerning Abu Musa, which defined and regulated Iran and Sharjah's respective areas of interest and placed Iran in charge of the island's defense and security.[5] Iran also entered into a modus vivendi with the Sheikh of Sharjah regarding administration of Abu Musa Island.

Consequently, on November 30, 1971, as British forces watched passively, Iranian troops landed on the Tonbs and took possession of the islands from Ras al-Khaimah. On Abu Musa, Iranian troops were greeted by the deputy ruler of Sharjah and took up their position in the garrison on the northern side of the island. A few days later, the British ambassador to the United Nations, Sir Colin Crowe, while regretting that no negotiated settlement could be reached between Iran and Ras al-Khaimah over the Tonbs, expressed satisfaction that the independence of Bahrain and Qatar, the emergence of the UAE and the Iran-Sharjah agreement over Abu Musa "represented a reasonable and acceptable basis" for the future of peace and security in the area.[6] In the words of the British negotiator at the time, Sir William Luce, Iran and Britain had at last "sorted out their differences over the islands."[7]

CURRENT POLITICAL CONTEXT

Traditionally, disagreements over these tiny islands in the Persian Gulf have been the outward manifestation of larger local, regional, and international rivalries and provocations directed at Iran. Not accidentally, these disputes have risen at times when Iran has been isolated or pressured to modify its conduct.[8] In 1979, for example, *The Economist* suggested that the United States occupy the Tonbs and Abu Musa in order to pressure the Iranian government to release the diplomatic and consular staff detained at the U.S. embassy in Tehran and at the same time to increase the security of Western-bound oil tankers in the Persian Gulf waters.[9] In an equally provocative style, a novel published a few years later envisioned in Abu Musa a clandestine base to be used in an aerial attack on Iran to topple the revolutionary government.[10] In understanding the current dispute between Iran and the UAE, grasping the legal complexities and understanding the esoteric historical nuances are indispensable. In addition, a comprehensive understanding of the dispute requires an analysis of its current strategic context. The periodic recurrence of the controversy in recent years has been driven by factors that had determined Britain's previous concern over the islands: oil, commitment to local sheikhs, curbing Iran's influence, security of navigation, and prevention of a rival power from gaining a foothold in the Persian Gulf. No doubt, the geographic location of these islands accords them strategic value. This does not, however, justify the acrimony that has characterized the debate over these islands for more than one hundred years.

In the immediate aftermath of the Kuwait Crisis (1990-1991) and, more recently, the flaring up of the controversy over the islands again has had more to do with the realignment of U.S. interests in the region, Iranian policy in the Middle East and North Africa, the rise of political Islam, and the Persian Gulf monarchs' concern over their internal and external security. More specifically, I propose to show that the dispute between Iran and the UAE does not reflect the importance of the islands; nor does it reflect the UAE's attempt to take them away from Iran. The dispute is about much more than just the islands; it is a reflection—more than it is a cause—of the strained relations between the Iranian government and those dedicated to containing it. No wonder that the dispute and its presentation in the Western and Arab media has turned into a vehicle for the pro-Western Arab states, Israel, and the United States to further Iran's isolation from the West and the Arab world. The Persian Gulf monarchies feel threatened by the growing Islamic activism in their countries and they fear the specter of Iranian-inspired Islamic radicalism permeating their shores.

With Islamic fundamentalism on the rise in North Africa and the reported military build up in Iran, the United States, its Arab allies, and Israel are set on weakening Iran's regional influence, particularly in the Persian Gulf,[11] even if that means forcing the replacement of the current government in Tehran.[12] A lasting solution to the dispute can only come through improving relations between Iran and all of the states that currently antagonize the Iranian government. From this perspective, the following questions are relevant: How is the dispute related to the current state of Iran-Arab relations? How is it related to Iran-U.S. relations? How have the two recent wars in the Persian Gulf affected the way the dispute is being handled?

The pretext for the current Iran-UAE islands dispute came about when, in April 1992, Iranian authorities expelled from Abu Musa about 100 foreigners working for the UAE government because they did not have Iranian visas. Later that year, in August 1992, the Iranian authorities refused to allow foreigners without Iranian visas to disembark at Abu Musa, forcing the UAE vessel to turn back.[13] Iran's Foreign Minister Ali Akbar Velayati played down the incidents as isolated actions of junior Iranian officials.[14] Iran's subsequent actions have matched the foreign minister's words; apart from the two incidents, Iranian officials have not interfered with the affairs of the Arab residents and visitors.

The incidents in Abu Musa, however, soon led the UAE to demand that Iran relinquish its control of the Tonbs as well. Some Arab countries have tried to use the floor of the United Nations to echo that demand. Thus, the Security Council has received memoranda signed by the Gulf Cooperation Council (GCC) member states, Egypt, and Syria, asking Iran to "end its occupation of Arab islands belonging to the United Arab Emirates," in the Persian Gulf.[15] The GCC and other Arab governments insist on the "Arabness" of the islands and the gulf itself in an attempt to justify their intervention in a bilateral territorial matter between Iran and the UAE.

Already predisposed to anti-Iranian sentiment, Arab and Western media have transformed the narrative such that a quarrel over three small islands[16] has metamorphosed into a first-class strategic struggle for power in the Persian Gulf.[17] At the outset of the controversy, Radio Cairo went so far as to compare Iran's actions to Iraq's invasion of Kuwait, while the *Washington Post* ran a feature-length article, also likening Iran's actions on Abu Musa to Iraq's occupation of Kuwait.[18] The *New York Times* wrote, "Abu Musa is the largest of the three islands belonging to the Emirates occupied by Iranian troops in 1971,"[19] thereby implying that Iran must vacate all the islands. Lost in the rhetoric was the history of more than twenty years of joint Iran-UAE administration of Abu Musa. By comparing the Iran-UAE dispute to the Iraq-Kuwait war, the Western and Arab media wanted to achieve three aims: first, to revive the GCC fear of Iran by propagating what I call "the Kuwait syndrome"; second, to embolden the UAE in its claims against Iran; and third, to remind the Iranian government of the dire consequences of opposing pro-Western regimes in the Persian Gulf.

The ferocity of the uproar and the extent of media attention given to the dispute paint the islands as indispensable possessions. Much of the commotion, however, is misleading. Abu Musa, the largest and the most resourceful of the three islands—which Iran and the UAE share—has an area of about four square miles. It has three small oil wells and some deposits of red oxide. Its population is about 700 to 1000 people, depending on the season. Great Tonb is sparsely inhabited. It lacks fresh-water wells. The Little Tonb is uninhabited, with no access to drinking water.

The extent to which the islands have any practical importance at all is due to their strategic location at the entrance to the Strait of Hormuz. Thus, apart from their potential use during wartime, the islands offer little benefit to either country. However, this strategic value of the islands must be viewed against the liability of the burden of having to preserve their security; even if the islands were to be given to the UAE, it would not have the necessary means to protect them against a possible Iranian attack in a time of war or political crisis. Therefore, the most practical solution to the dispute, particularly from the perspective of UAE interests, is the maintenance of the status quo within a cooperative regional framework.

The Arab governments' claim that the three islands were Arab islands belonging to the UAE does not withstand close scrutiny. Iran is by far the oldest state in the Persian Gulf, and, as the authors in this book clearly show, its historical claim over the islands long predates any other state's. Besides, when Iran reclaimed the islands in 1971, following an agreement with the departing British, the UAE did not even exist as a country. Nor does the equating of the situation to Iraq's occupation of Kuwait withstand scrutiny. Iran is a vastly different country from Iraq, and, in contrast to Iraq, Iran is not known to have invaded any neighboring country in the last 150 years, while Kuwait—with a full one-tenth of the world's oil—is in no way similar to three small, largely lifeless islands, with negligible resources. Moreover, Iraq invaded and occupied a sovereign, member state of the United Nations, while Iran is maintaining a U.N.-accepted status quo based on prior written and oral agreements.

While Iran's actions on Abu Musa in April and August of 1992 may have been unjustified, the comparison with the Iraqi invasion of Kuwait is far-fetched at best. The two isolated incidents do not by themselves explain the current opinion that Iran is a war-mongering country bent on territorial expansion. While Iraq invaded both Iran and Kuwait in the span of a decade, Saudi Arabia attacked Qatar in 1992,[20] and Turkey invaded northern Iraq in March 1995. Iran, in contrast, has kept within its borders. Not a single shot was fired during the two incidents on Abu Musa and, since then, life has continued uninterrupted on the island.

The extent of the uproar is neither an indication of the islands' importance, nor a reflection of the measures Iran took during the two incidents. Further, the uproar has no legal or historical basis. Rather, it is indicative of a comprehensive and continuing attempt by the Persian Gulf monarchies, Egypt, Israel, Britain, and the United States to isolate Iran. Indeed, isolating Iran from other Persian Gulf states is the cornerstone of the U.S. administration's dual containment policy. Thus, the island dispute is about much more than the islands; it is the most recent manifestation of the continuing ideological and political rivalry between post-revolutionary Iran and its Arab neighbors and their Western-power supporters.

To appreciate this fact better, one needs to consider the situation at the time of the Shah Mohammad Reza Pahlavi. The UAE was born at the time when travellers with Iranian passports, supposed carriers of plenty of petro-dollars, were warmly greeted at Western airports and consulates; when tens of thousands of American military and civilian personnel were working in Iran, implementing the Shah's rapid modernization programs. So when Iran acted on its well-publicized intentions to reassert its sovereignty over the islands in 1971 by taking control of them, there was little uproar in the West; the sheikhdoms and Britain did not protest; the United States and Israel, both Iran's allies, saw Iran's actions as a natural manifestation of its role as the new regional power in the Persian Gulf. The pro-Western and conservative Arab regimes, including the new UAE, were comfortable with a pro-Western and conservative regional power. In 1973, the Shah's forces helped put down a Marxist rebellion in Oman's Dhoffar region, an act that met with unequivocal praise from the Persian Gulf's Arab monarchs.

In this milieu, when the cold war was at its peak, Iran kept its sovereignty over the Tonbs and accommodated UAE in the administration of

Abu Musa. The Shah was seen by everyone in the region as the ruler of a buffer zone against the spread of Communism. Imperial Iran was the backbone of the region's status quo. It possessed enough diplomatic savvy and military wherewithal to deter war. Until the end of his reign, the Shah continued pouring much of the country's oil wealth into American arms, purchasing state-of-the-art weaponry. The Shah's shopping spree was costing the country over $8 billion a year—over five times Iran's expenditure in 1993.[21] With the exception of Israel, Iran was the biggest purchaser of weapons in the world. Yet since the Shah was a friend of the United States, no one in the West talked about Iran's military build-up, nor its potential threat to its neighbors.

The revolution that consumed Iran in 1979 ended the country's pro-Western orientation and changed the strategic balance in the Persian Gulf.[22] The neighboring Arab states and the West were soon to find the shock waves of the Iranian revolution unsettling. The clerics who had suddenly come to rule Iran stepped up their anti-Western rhetoric, calling on neighboring Arabs to establish Iranian-style Islamic republics in their countries and to revolt against Western neocolonialism. Iran was no longer the stable buffer against leftist instability that the West and the Persian Gulf monarchies needed; it was now itself a source of instability, threatening conservative, pro-Western governments in the area. In 1979 Mecca's Grand Mosque was seized by *sunni* revolutionaries and the Saudi *shi'i* rebelled later that year and in 1980. The phrase "Islamic republic," whose recipe Iran was trying to export, struck the Arab monarchies as partly good, partly bad. The monarchies were undoubtedly Islamic—in the case of Saudi Arabia, to the point of fundamentalism. What they abhorred was the republic part of the recipe. Monarchs who were—and continue to be—de facto owners of their countries and all their resources and feared that revolutionary fire might embroil the people of their regions too.

Ironically, this was a time when the ruling clergy were striving to unite Muslim Iran with fellow Muslims in Arab countries. They downplayed Iran's pre-Islamic glories in favor of the country's contributions to Islamic culture. They even tried to replace English with Arabic as the second language taught in Iranian schools in an attempt to counteract the *westoxication* of the Iranian society. The Shah had tried to detach Iran from Arabs as best as he could. Glorifying Iran's Aryan and pre-Islamic past was the Shah's main tool for achieving this aim. During his reign, it became fashionable to name newborns after pre-Islamic figures in Iran's history. The Shah even went as far as changing Iran's Perso-Islamic calendar to one beginning with the year of the founding of the Persian Empire by Cyrus the Great in the sixth century B.C. It is ironic that the pro-Western, secular Shah had friendlier relations with the Persian Gulf monarchies than the Islamic clergy ever could. It was not important that the Shah was touting a secular and nationalist horn. It mattered more that he was set on preserving the Persian Gulf's pro-Western and monarchical character.

While Iranian revolutionaries were unnerving the neighboring Arab states and the West, domestically, they were faced with the challenge of establishing and maintaining authority. Almost immediately after the establishment of the new regime, a bloody power struggle ensued causing further political disorder and economic dislocation. Meanwhile, the episode of American hostages in Tehran was causing a rapid deterioration of U.S.-Iran relations, damaging and crippling the government's image and effectiveness internationally. The developments that weakened the new regime in Tehran, emboldened Saddam Hussein to invade the country in 1980. Counting on the support of the United States and the Arab states, Saddam Hussein had hoped for a quick victory and the imposition of his territorial demands on Iran. The war, however, dragged on, and this caused further anxiety among the ruling sheikhs in the Persian Gulf. About seven months into the Iran-Iraq War, in May 1981, the GCC was formed. It brought together Saudi Arabia, Kuwait, the UAE, Oman, Qatar, and Bahrain under a collective security umbrella. The council was to foster regional cooperation among the six monarchies and intertwine their economies more deeply. It was no secret, however, that the Council's main objective—albeit an implicit one— was to keep Iran's ideological fervor from permeating the members' shores. In early 1981, as the GCC was drafting its statute, Iraq seemed well on its way to a quick and decisive victory over Iran's poorly organized and divided military. But even in the face of Iran's imminent defeat and the imminent toppling of the Islamic Republic that would have followed, the Persian Gulf's monarchs remained on guard. It was not Iran's military might that unnerved them, but its contagious revolutionary ideology. At no time in their histories had the Persian Gulf monarchies' internal stability and the legitimacy of their rulers seemed so fragile.

When Iraqi forces invaded Iran in 1980, they broke the peace that Persians and Arabs had kept for centuries. Eight years later, when the two sides finally put their guns down, they had both lost, what Henry Kissinger said the United States had hoped would happen: close to a million people had died and war damage to Iran's economy alone amounted to over $600 billion.[23] Iran's religious-nationalist zeal was manifest in the Iranian human-wave tactics. While this worked to counterbalance Iraq's logistical superiority, it also put the count of the war's dead and the maimed disproportionately on Iran. While Iraq received massive military and financial assistance from the United States and the GCC (around $50 billion), Iran fought the war alone. Iran's isolation and the ensuing difficulty in procuring weapons and spare parts crippled the Iranian war effort and devastated the country.

To a large extent, Iran had only itself to blame. Throughout the war, it delivered conflicting, irreconcilable messages to the GCC. Iran tried to neutralize the GCC's support for Iraq by assuring the monarchs of its peaceful intentions toward them. Yet simultaneously, Iran worked to challenge the legitimacy of the Persian Gulf's rulers, seeking to replace them with Iranian-style Islamic republics. In the meantime, and most crucially, Iran continued its open confrontation with the United States in the Persian Gulf at a time when GCC members took refuge under the U.S. security umbrella. Revolutionary Iran became the Persian Gulf's perceived villain, giving the Arab governments a pretext to unite against it. GCC neutrality would have helped Iran's war efforts immeasurably. But Iran's attempts to export its revolution combined with its anti-American rhetoric compelled the GCC to side with Iraq.

The spilling over of hostilities from the Iraq-Iran War into the Persian Gulf had demonstrated the vulnerability of the sheikhdoms in the lower Persian Gulf. The Iranian rocket attack on the Kuwaiti coast alarmed Kuwait of the devastation that a more determined arsenal could inflict on the tiny sheikhdom. The Iraqi aerial attacks on oil tankers eventually resulted in the reflagging and escorting of Kuwaiti vessels under U.S. naval protection. While an Iraqi aircraft exacted a murderous toll on a U.S. ship, killing over twenty servicemen, the USS *Vincennes* shot down an Iranian civilian jetliner, killing 290 passengers. As the oil platforms near Iranian islands and oil fields in the Persian Gulf became launching pads for Iranian revolutionary guards' speedboats, the U.S. navy blew out of the water one Iranian oil derrick after another.

Construing the Iranian threat solely in terms of Iran's aggressive motives and the sheikhdoms' defensive response can be misleading. As the war dragged on, Iran and Iraq continued to weaken each other. Their oil production, the lifeblood of their economies, suffered substantially. Some of this was good news to Saudi Arabia. First, the kingdom solidified its position as OPEC's swing producer, filling the oil gap created by the parties to war. This brought the Saudis billions in extra revenue and cast them at OPEC's helm like never before, a trend that has continued into the 1990s and shows no signs of abating. The Saudis also used their new-found power within OPEC to cripple Iran's war efforts: in 1986, the Saudis flooded the oil market, causing a drastic drop in oil prices. Iran's projected oil income of $15 billion for that year dropped to an actual $5.8 billion. The second reason the Saudis were benefiting from the war was strategic. With Iran and Iraq at war and the GCC consolidated, Saudi Arabia—could through its leadership role in the GCC—further its influence in the Persian Gulf. The Saudi leadership of OPEC and the GCC would not have come about had Iran remained a pro-West monarchy, an ally of the United States.

In August 1990, Iraq invaded Kuwait to seize Kuwait's oil fields and to gain more access to the Persian Gulf's coastline. In January 1991, the United States at the head of a multinational force attacked, sand-blasted, and expelled Iraq from Kuwait, restoring the Al Sabah family to power.[24] While Iran's protest against the Iraqi invasion of Kuwait helped improve Iran-GCC relations, the mutual animosity and suspicion continue to exist. Iran has not forgotten the GCC's support for the Iraqi aggression on its soil; the GCC countries still fear Iran's destabilizing effect on their regimes. In particular, the small Persian Gulf monarchies consider Iran's rearmament program threatening, though it is nowhere near as extensive as Saudi Arabia's, Kuwait's, or even the UAE's. In this vein, the islands dispute reflects the UAE's fear of Iran's potential threat to its security. To some extent, the UAE's concerns are justified. When a territorial dispute has become embedded in nationalistic fervor between states in the region, a military confrontation has often followed, sometimes years later.

Typical of the UAE's position regarding the Tonbs and Abu Musa is the call on Iran to end its "occupation."[25] In response, the Iranian president Hashemi-Rafsanjani has warned that to reach the islands, the UAE will have to "cross a sea of blood."[26] The metaphor underscores the visceral nature of the Iranian view that these islands are indivisibly part of Iran. The sentiment is not peculiar to present-day Iran, however. The Shah Mohammad Reza Pahlavi believed that these islands belonged to Iran by historical and incontrovertible right. Reminiscent of Winston Churchill's admonition, "we shall defend our island, whatever the cost may be,"[27] the Shah, in September 1971, thundered, "[t]hose islands . . . are ours. We need them. We shall have them. No power on earth will stop us."[28] As he had explained it earlier, "[t]he islands were ours; but some eighty years ago Britain interfered with the exercise of our sovereignty and grabbed them and subsequently claimed them for its wards, Sharjah and Ras al-Khaimah."[29] In Iran today, the islands dispute has indeed become a national issue, making it impossible for the Iranian government to negotiate any concession.

Hypothetical war scenarios aside, Iran is going through a period of introspection, attempting to invigorate its devastated economy. During its first decade, the Islamic Republic used its radical foreign policy to deflect the

Iranian public's attention from the hardships at home. That policy has changed and ideological zeal is now secondary to bread and material well-being. Iranians are increasingly demanding that their government deliver on its promise of prosperity. The revolution's initial fervor has given way to pragmatic concerns. Having learned from the crushing defeat of Iraq in Desert Storm, Iran has no intention to invade any of the GCC countries. If the UAE understands the change in Tehran's approach and the new moderation of Iran's policy in the Persian Gulf, Iran-UAE relations and Iran-Arab relations more generally, could improve dramatically. Such a development would render the island dispute moot.

Iran-Arab relations are deeply influenced by outside powers, chief among them the United States and Israel. The West plays a leading role in orchestrating the dispute. To the liberal Western mind, the theocratic government of Iran is an anachronism, unfit to meet the complex demands of modern statecraft and international commerce. Ever since Iran's clergy took power in 1979, the Western media have continuously berated the Islamic Republic for its arcane and illiberal ideology, its violent suppression of domestic dissent, and its alleged support for anti-Western and anti-Israeli terrorism abroad. The name Iran conjures up in the Western mind images of self-flagellation, public hangings, stoning of moral infractors, and suicide bombings—all in the name of religion and God. In the age of science and information highways, Iran is seen as having reverted to the dark ages.

The United States leads the Western world in propagating this image and in opposing Iran's domestic and international policy,[30] considering it an "international outlaw." Iran and the United States have no formal diplomatic relations. Iran's relations with Germany, France, and Japan, however, continue on a large-scale and unabated. While Iran's clerical government has become more moderate and pragmatic over its sixteen-year history, it is still seen as a pariah in the West. The ideological zeal that characterized Ayatollah Khomeini's rule is no longer the dominant force in the country. Pragmatic and pro-business clergy intent on liberalizing the economy oppose the hard-line factions within the Iranian government. Today, Iran's support for destabilizing and revolutionary ideologies in the Middle East is nowhere near what it was in the early years of the revolution and during the Iran-Iraq War. Iran is changing on the inside; yet its image outside remains unchanged, particularly in the eyes of the West.

Iran-bashing also serves Israel and Egypt, albeit for different reasons. Egypt's propaganda support for UAE's claim is motivated by its desire to reestablish Egypt's leadership in the Arab world. In the post–Cold War era, both Egypt and Israel need to preserve their "strategic" significance for the

United States in order to continue receiving billions of dollars in American aid. With Arab-Israeli peace negotiations in progress, Israelis see their dream for territorial expansion reaching a complete dead end; they are now turning to a new strategy based on economic hegemony in the region. This requires maintaining military superiority and unhindered economic expansion. With Iraq in shambles, Iran remains the only country that can challenge Israel in achieving its new strategic goals. No wonder then that Iran's alleged crash program to build a nuclear bomb, its supposed involvement in terrorism against Israel, and Iran's opposition to the peace process have become the most critical factors in U.S.-Iran relations. Iran's own egomaniacal mind-set and its defiant words have helped its adversaries to characterize it as a rogue state.

In analyzing the current state of U.S.-Iran relations, most Iranians, both within and outside the government, subscribe to a conspiracy theory. This theory rests on the assumption that with the Cold War over, America needs a regional menace like Iran to legitimize the selling of billions of dollars worth of weapons to the Persian Gulf monarchies every year. In the absence of backlash states such as Iran and Iraq, what need would there be in the Persian Gulf for American arms and military personnel? While the United States is interested in the continued large-scale sale of armaments to the oil-rich Persian Gulf states, its problem with Iran today cannot be reduced to money and profit alone. Protecting Israeli security, preserving the Persian Gulf monarchies and other pro-American states, and assuring the flow of oil at a reasonable price continue to top American foreign policy concerns in the Middle East.

In terms of U.S.-Iran relations alone, however, no single occurrence in recent history provided as great an impetus to the United States for a total realignment of forces in the Persian Gulf to Iran's detriment than the picture of blindfolded American diplomats, detained as hostages in Tehran for 444 days. Arguably, not even the fall of the Shah or the rise of Ayatollah Rouhollah Khomeini had by itself as great an impact on the future of U.S.-Iran relations as the hostage crisis; which came, lest it be forgotten, at the time when President Jimmy Carter's administration had resigned itself to a new regime in Tehran and was in the process of restaffing the U.S. Embassy in Tehran and the architects of U.S. foreign policy had begun to toy with the notion of an Islamic version of the *cordon sanitaire* to contain the Soviet influence.

While the rise and fall of governments lend themselves to analytical debate and examination, images are difficult to overcome. Since the hostage crisis, U.S.-Iran relations have been marred by images that have shaped an entire American generation's perception of Iran and Iranians in the same manner that America's arrogance of power, as typified by the Vietnam War, had offered substance to the appellation "the ugly American." The United States finds much of Iranian behavior disconcerting: the rituals of flag burning; chants of "Death to America and Israel"; the label "Great Satan"; the Iran-Contra scandal; the hostage crisis in Lebanon and suicide bombing of the U.S. marine barracks in that country; the death sentence on Salman Rushdie and the assassination of the Islamic Republic's political foes abroad; opposition to the Arab-Israeli peace process; and the purchase of armaments and strategic civilian goods, including nuclear reactors, from Russia, North Korea and China. These are all linked inexorably into one ball of cause-and-effect of the present state of Iran's image in the United States, providing fodder, as it were, for the double-barrel approach to Iran first under presidents Ronald Reagan and George Bush and later under President Bill Clinton's dual containment policy.[31]

The emotion generated by the hostage crisis shifted completely the longstanding fulcrum of the U.S. policy in the Persian Gulf from the mountainous coast of Iran to the sandy lowlands of the gulf, particularly to Saudi Arabia and the UAE. With the rise of reformist Mikhael Gorbachev to power in the Soviet Union, the security of oil supplies and Israel no longer rested on a strategic cooperation between Tehran, Washington, and Tel Aviv. The brokering of peace between Egypt and Israel in 1977 by President Carter had secured the stability of the border in the Sinai. The Soviet collapse was seemingly further proof that Iran possessed little if any strategic significance for American interests in the region. Yet, the transformations that have followed Desert Storm and the break-up of the Soviet Union have created a new regional order in which Iran again has become the meeting place of the Middle East, Central Asia, and the Caucasus.

During President Bush's administration, Washington showed signs of wanting to improve relations with Tehran. Iran used its influence in Lebanon to free the Western hostages held there. The accession of Ali Akbar Hashemi-Rafsanjani to Iran's presidency in 1989 had strengthened the power of the moderate and comparatively liberal factions within the Iranian government. During the Bush presidency, Rafsanjani purged the Iranian Majlis of many hard-line elements. At this time, American oil companies replaced their Japanese counterparts as the biggest buyers of Iranian oil. About a decade prior to these developments, Republicans in the United States had benefited from the hostage crisis. The crisis had been the greatest single cause of President Carter's defeat by candidate Reagan. The fact that the hostages had been freed on the very eve of Reagan's inauguration, attested to a Democratic-Republican split on the question of Iran. As the Iran-Contra affair demonstrated later, Republican administrations in Washington have adopted a more conciliatory approach toward the Islamic Republic than their Democratic counterparts.

President Clinton's approach to Iran was evident in his choice for secretary of state. Warren Christopher had been Carter's chief envoy to Algiers in 1980. There he had met with Iranian representatives to discuss the fate of the hostages and the possibility of securing their immediate release. The Iranians did not yield; they delayed the release of the hostages until Reagan was inaugurated. The Republicans benefited immeasurably from the delay. In the wake of his perceived impotence to deal with Iran, Carter lost the election. Twelve years later, Warren Christopher became secretary of state. The Clinton administration devised the Dual Containment Policy (DCP) to counter the menace posed by the Persian Gulf's two backlash states—Iran and Iraq. The policy seeks to isolate Iran and Iraq politically and to strangle them economically, leaving them in a permanent state of underdevelopment and reduced military capability so that they no longer pose a threat to their neighbors. While Iraq's economy suffers from United Nations sanctions, the Iranian economy, already subject to a longstanding U.S. embargo, is under additional pressures by new U.S. restrictions on commercial deals with Iran.[32]

The practical application of the DCP belies its stated objectives. The DCP is actually a uni-containment policy, a policy of containing Iran. As far as the U.S. government is concerned, Iran and Iraq pose vastly different threats to American interests in the area. From Washington's perspective, Iran is the more intractable menace, more difficult to contain and discipline. In turning much of Iraq into rubble during Desert Storm and in isolating and strangling it after the war, the United States has enjoyed the support of its Western allies and the Soviet Union—now the Commonwealth of Independent States. Thus, in implementing the DCP toward Iraq, the United States relies on the consensus in the United Nations Security Council, a consensus that legitimizes America's current military presence in the Persian Gulf. The case of Iran is very different. America has had little success in persuading Russia, China, Germany, Japan, France, and Italy to join the effort to economically strangle the Islamic Republic. Large-scale trade between Iran and Western Europe and Japan continues. Much to America's distaste, Iran continues to buy arms from Russia, China, and North Korea, a trend that has already joined Iran and these three countries in military arrangements over which the United States has peripheral influence at best.

While America enjoys a post–Desert Storm carte blanche among the Persian Gulf's monarchies, it has far less influence on the fate of Central Asia. Russia, not the United States, is the main foreign power in that oil-rich and nuclear-armed region. Desert Storm succeeded in just forty days not only because of the Western, Russian, and Arab alliance to eject Iraq from Kuwait, but also because all the countries surrounding Iraq went along with the American agenda. Iran would make a more challenging enemy for the United States because of its proximity to Central Asia where American influence pales in comparison to Russia's military and political predominance. Russia would not tolerate an all-out confrontation between Iran and the United States because the repercussions may fuel further instability in Central Asia. A united and strong Iran contributes to the stability of Central Asia. After Desert Storm, the United States prevented the imminent dissolution of Iraq with great success. It is unlikely that the United States could wield similar control in a war-ravaged Iran. In addition, given the ideological antipathy of the Islamic Republic toward the United States, if Russia and China—Iran's chief suppliers of arms—wished to oppose U.S. interests in the area, the U.S. might find it difficult to discipline and mold Iran.

Apart from factors that may limit America's future maneuvering room in the Persian Gulf, a military confrontation between Iran and the United States is unlikely because Iran has neither the intention nor the capability to invade any of the oil-rich monarchies to its south. The Islamic Republic is increasingly turning inward, in search of ways to invigorate its devastated economy. Iran's attempts at fomenting trouble in the Persian Gulf are a relic of the past. Iran's revolutionary zeal has progressively given way to pragmatic and economic concerns. The main reason the DCP is ill-conceived is that instead of expediting Iran's transformation from a revolutionary state to a bureaucratic one it is, in fact, delaying the transformation. The economic, political, and military pressure that America exerts on the Islamic Republic only revitalizes the power of the most anti-American and radical factions within the clergy and generates domestic sympathy for them. Thus, the only way America can positively affect the behavior of the Islamic Republic is through increased trade, financial transactions, technological aid, and open dialogue.

What I call the *Kuwait syndrome* is complicating diplomacy in the Middle East today, particularly relations between Iran and the GCC states. Desert Storm displayed the absolute impotence of Iraq once set against the might of the U.S.-led coalition forces. The coalition's quick victory has since given the GCC states the illusion that as long as they serve American interests they do not need to heed the demands of their stronger neighbors. The unjustified demands of the UAE regarding the Tonbs and Abu Musa suggest that the sheikhdom suffers from the Kuwait syndrome as well. The perception in Abu Dhabi, much like that in Kuwait City, seems to be that as long as they have oil and are willing to spend their oil proceeds on American arms, the United States will rush to protect them from perceived or real aggressive neighbors. This perception is faulty on two grounds. First, in a confrontation with Iran, the United States may not be able to muster the same level of international support it enjoyed during Desert Storm, in which Russian cooperation was essential (and by some accounts purchased in cash). And second, such regional diplomacy and cooperation gives rise to a perpetual state of distrust and instability in the Persian Gulf, a condition that benefits none of the local states. If the UAE continues to capitalize on Iran's current troubles with the United States, Iran-UAE relations will suffer substantially.

The prevailing animosity between the United States and Iran fuels the Iran-Arab rancor. The United States is party to bilateral security agreements with the Persian Gulf monarchies, who view the United States as their sole protector against the suspected ambitions of Iran. American and Arab attempts at isolating Iran only fuel Iran's adventurism abroad, negatively affecting Iran's relations with the Persian Gulf monarchies. Conflict in the Persian Gulf serves none of the states in the region, only the purveyors of arms and reconstruction services.

In the long run, the dispute over the islands needs a diplomatic and regional solution, a solution worked out between the parties and in reference to all relevant factors and circumstances, including geography, history, economics, and law. Once Iran and its Arab neighbors find a collective security arrangement that protects their territorial integrity, domestic stability, and national interest, the islands will lose their strategic value. From this perspective, the solution to the dispute rests on improving relations between Iran and the Arab world. This will require improving relations between Iran and the United States, which is largely influenced by Iranian-Israeli antagonism. If the larger issues that underlie and drive the current dispute are not addressed, the relations between Iran and the UAE will stay the same.

The politics of exclusion pursued by Iran and the United States highlight the differences between the two and at the same time obscures their common interest in peace and stability in the Persian Gulf, Central Asia, the Eastern Mediterranean, and the Balkans. Moreover, while Iran is slow to learn the value of good public relations and good will, U.S. foreign policy has been even slower in applying the lessons of its time-honored approach to resolving seemingly unyielding ideological challenges by means of constructive or positive engagement—that is, influence through involvement. Apartheid was overcome in large measure through constructive engagement (even though some may want to give the credit to sanctions). Continuation of trade relations with Beijing is more apt to further the cause of human rights in China than mindless and arrogant chest-beating. The fall of the Berlin Wall and the demise of the "evil empire" of the Soviet Union, too, were brought about through a persistent level of engagement of the adversary. There is no legitimate, systemic impediment to Washington's adoption of a constructive engagement policy with respect to Iran other than Iran's tarnished image internationally. While the United States reaps the windfall of Desert Storm, it remains practically ineffective with respect to Russia, the Central Asian theater, and China. The key to a successful U.S. policy with Russia and beyond is in pursuing a constructive policy with respect to Iran in the Persian Gulf.

NOTES

1. On Desert Storm, its background and regional consequences *see* Amirahmadi, Hooshang, ed., *The United States and the Middle East: A Search for New Perspectives* (Albany: State University of New York Press, 1993); and Ismael, Tareq Y., and Ismael, Jacqueline S., eds., *The Gulf War and the New World Order: International Relations of the Middle East* (Gainesville, FL: University Press of Florida, 1994).

2. *See SIPRI Yearbook 1994, World Armaments and Disarmament* (Oxford: Oxford University Press, 1994); and Amirahmadi, Hooshang, "The Spiraling Gulf Arms Race," *Middle East Insight,* X (2) (January-February, 1994).

3. On dual containment policy *see,* Martin Indyk's speech at the Washington Institute for Near East Policy, published in that organization's bulletin, *Policywatch* (84) (May 21, 1993); and Drake, Laura,"Still Fighting the Last War. Dual Containment: A Cold War Policy for a Postwar Middle East," in *Middle East Insight,* X (6) (September-October, 1994), pp. 38-43. In a nutshell, the policy advocates weakening Iran as a means of changing its behavior in such areas as development of nuclear technology, international terrorism, and opposition to the Middle East peace process.

4. Interestingly, as early as the period between 1928 and 1933, Iran and Britain had considered dealing with these issues in the context of a comprehensive treaty providing for a settlement of all their disputes in the Persian Gulf. Thus, the package deal of 1971 was by no means a new formula through which Iran and Britain attempted to settle their differences in the Persian Gulf.

5. The history of negotiations which produced the above results, points to a series of micro give-and-takes, which some have referred to as a package deal, implying that the unraveling of one part of the deal may give rise to grounds for rescission of other parts of the deal. *See The Economist,* November 6, 1992 (letter to the editor). In their book, *The Foreign Relations of Iran* (Los Angeles: University of California Press, 1974), Shahram Chubin and Sepehr Zabih describe Iran's efforts to effect linkage among the various issues and to seek a package deal, but to no avail (p. 222). A similar view is held by Rouhollah Ramazani in *Iran's Foreign Policy: 1943-1973* (Charlottesville: University of Virginia Press, 1975), p. 424, and Muhammad Morsy Abdullah

in *The United Arab Emirates* (London: Croom Helm, 1978), p. 282. On the other hand, past and present Iranian officials and certain observers in the West believe in the existence of an explicit agreement. James D. McMunn in *Great Britain's Withdrawal from the Persian Gulf: An Analysis of Policy and the Process* (Master's thesis, Georgetown University, Washington, D.C., 1974), states that the fate of Bahrain, Abu Musa, and the Tonbs was decided in a bargain (p. 60). According to McMunn, a similar view has been held by R. M. Burrell (p. 60). Joseph J. Malone in *The Arab Lands of Western Asia* (Englewood Cliffs: Prentice Hall, 1973) maintains a similar conclusion (p. 239). In *The Persian Gulf: In the Light of International Rivalries & Provocations* (text of a speech at the Rotary Club of Iran on July 17, 1972), p. 3, Abbas Massoudi the Iranian senator and publisher, with an intimate knowledge of the Persian Gulf, acknowledged the existence of an explicit Anglo-Iranian agreement over the return of Abu Musa and the Tonbs to Iran. Later, in *Khalije Fars dar Doran-e Sarbolandi va Shokouh* (Tehran: Ettela'at Publications, 1973), p. 88, he wrote: "After long negotiations on the restoration of these islands to Iran, finally the matter was resolved by an agreement between and to the satisfaction of Iran and Britain." According to the Shah Mohammad Reza Pahlavi's court minister and closest adviser, Amir Assadollah Alam, Iran had been endeavoring to connect the two issues of sovereignty over Bahrain and the three islands as early as 1969. An entry from his diary for Sunday, March 23, 1969, read in part: "The British Ambassador called. I told him we can reach no settlement in respect to Bahrain until we know the fate of Tonb and Abu Musa. In that case, he declared we have all been wasting our time. `So be it,' I said." Alikhani, Alinaghi, ed. *The Shah and I: Confidential Diary of the Royal Court of Iran by Amir Assadollah Alam* (London: I. B. Tauris, 1991). Amir Khosro Afshar, a negotiator for Iran on the islands, is quoted in this book, in an interview with Dr. Mojtahed-Zadeh (Chapter 2), as having said that "[t]here was no trade-off deal with the British during our negotiations on separate issues of Bahrain and the three islands of the Strait of Hormuz." It must, however, be noted that he probably meant there was no written agreement, which apparently does not exist. Besides, he might be hesitant to acknowledge a possible deal, being concerned about his patriotic credibility. British officials, such as Sir William Luce, who negotiated the British withdrawal from the Persian Gulf; Sir Geoffrey Arthur, undersecretary for commonwealth affairs; and Anthony Reeve, the Trucial desk officer at the foreign office, have also denied the existence of a package deal over the islands (McMunn, *ibid.,* pp. 60-61).

6. U.N. Security Council, *Official Records,* 26th year, 1610th meeting, 9 December, 1971, pars. 228-230.

7. *Times* (London), November 18, 1971.

8. *See,* Mirfendereski, G. and Meshkati, N. "America's Undertow, Iran's Achilles' Heel in the Persian Gulf," in *US-Iran Review* 6 (Commentary) (April, 1993).

9. *The Economist,* November 24, 1979. *See also The Economist,* December 22, 1979, p. 4 (letter to editor pointing out the possible tactical and strategic issues attendant upon the U.S. occupation of the islands).

10. Swift, Rebecca, *Project Norouz* (New York: Tower Books, 1982), p. 269 *et seq*. According to *Books in Print Supplement 1981-1982,* the original authorship of this book is attributed to Marion Swift and Rebecca Ross. Apparently, due to its controversial subject matter and defamatory allusions, the book seems to have been suppressed and pulled from circulation.

11. *See* "Iran Military Build-up Spurs US to Consider Escalating Sanctions," *Boston Globe,* April 6, 1995; "Christopher Urges Action Against Iran," *Boston Globe,* April 3, 1995; Oliphant, Thomas, "The Next Step in Mideast," *Boston Globe,* March 19, 1995.

12. *See* "Gingrich Speaks on Iran," on *ClariNet Electronic News Service,* February 9, 1995 (Associated Press reporting on the newly elected speaker of the U.S. House of Representatives addressing a conference of military and intelligence officers in Washington, where he stated that in dealing with Islamic terrorism, the United States should pursue an overall strategy that, among other things, "ultimately is designed to force the replacement of the current regime in Iran").

13. *See,* for example, "Iran Silent on Expulsions," *New York Times,* April 16, 1992, p. A5 (reporting from foreign diplomatic sources in Iran that Iran had expelled UAE officials, Iran had suggested to the Arab residents of Abu Musa to apply for Iranian identity cards, and the Iranian president had visited Abu Musa in February); Hedges, Chris, "Iran Is Riling Its Gulf Neighbors, Pressing Claim to Disputed Isles," *New York Times,* September 13, 1992, p. A22 (reporting on Iran's emergence as the region's dominant power after the Persian Gulf War, Iran's backing of Islamic opposition groups in the Middle East and North Africa, Iran's expulsion in the spring of certain UAE citizens from Abu Musa for reasons of visa/permit and security, and the U.S. view that Iran may be seeking to gain control of the islands to counter military cooperation between the United States and the Persian Gulf nations and also expand her navy).

14. *Iran Focus,* November 1992.

15. *See* U.N.Doc. A/47/516: Resolution 5223/98/3, September 13, 1992. Similarly, at the close of the thirteenth summit of the Gulf Cooperation Council, Abu Dhabi called on Iran to "terminate its occupation of Greater and Lesser Tunb islands, which belong to the United Arab Emirates." *BBC Summary of World Broadcasts: The Middle East,* ME/1573/A/7, 29 December 1992.

16. *See,* for example, Ibrahim, Youssef M., "Iran Is Said to Expel Arabs From Gulf Island," *New York Times,* April 16, 1992, p. A5 (reporting on Iran's expulsion of Arab nationals from Abu Musa and seizure of property, including a desalination plant, and the direction by the Saudi, UAE, and Kuwaiti media to give the matter prominent attention); "Iran Silent on Expulsions," *New York Times,* April 16, 1992, p. A5; Hedges, Chris "Iran Is Riling Its Gulf Neighbors, Pressing Claim to Disputed Isles," *New York Times,* September 13, 1992, p. A22; "Iran Says Critics Are U.S. Plotters," *New York Times,* September 17, 1992 (International), p. A12 (reporting on mounting tensions

in the aftermath of Iran preventing, in August, the passengers of a UAE ship from disembarking on Abu Musa, on the Iranian view that the dispute over the three islands was a U.S. shield to mask a big military build-up and presence, the U.S.-backed denunciation of Iran, and Iran's view that the dispute has been manufactured by the United States in conspiracy with the UAE to justify the U.S. presence in the Persian Gulf); "Syria Offers to Settle Iran's Claim to Islands," *New York Times,* September 20, 1992, p. A10 (reporting on the Syrian offer to resolve the dispute over the Tonbs and Abu Musa peacefully and in accordance with international law); "Talks Break Down on Disputed Gulf Islands," *Boston Globe,* September 29, 1992, p. 28 (Reuters reporting on the failure of bilateral Iran-UAE negotiations regarding the differences over Abu Musa in part because Iran would not negotiate the ownership of the Tonbs); "Egyptian Sees Syria-Israel Pact, Threat From Iran," *Boston Globe,* October 1, 1992, p. 10 (Associated Press reporting on the Egyptian foreign minister's remarks about the escalation of tensions in the Persian Gulf due to Iran's claim to the small islands near the Strait of Hormuz, one of which is claimed by the UAE and about which the UAE is taking the matter to the United Nations Security Council); "Iran Asserts Claims to 3 Disputed Islands in Gulf," *New York Times,* December 27, 1992, p. 8 (reporting on the Iranian denunciation of the UAE claim to the Tonbs and Abu Musa).

17. *See,* for example, "GCC Targets UAE-Iran Dispute," on *ClariNet Electronic News Service,* September 18, 1994 (Associated Press reporting on the Gulf Cooperation Council urging Iran to submit the islands dispute to the World Court); "Iran still Claiming Islands," on *ClariNet Electronic News Service,* September 19, 1994 (Associated Press reporting on Iran's rejection of a statement by the Gulf Cooperation Council that the Tonbs and Abu Musa belong to the UAE and Iran's position that the only solution to Iran-UAE difficulties and misunderstandings is through continued discussions without any preconditions); "Iran puts desalination plant on disputed island," on *ClariNet Electronic News Service,* October 1, 1994 (Reuters reporting that Iran has set up a desalination plant on Abu Musa and has launched scheduled flights to Abu Musa); "Saudi Arabia wants world court to rule on islands," on *ClariNet Electronic News Service,* October 4, 1994 (Reuters reporting that the Gulf Cooperation Council is seeking a peaceful solution to the dispute, including referral to the International Court of Justice, whereas Iran is accusing the UAE and its Arab supporters of trying to internationalize the dispute); "UAE to take Iranian dispute to international court," on *ClariNet Electronic News Services,* December 5, 1994 (Reuters reporting that in the aftermath of Iran's announcement to establish a court on Abu Musa, the UAE intends to refer its dispute with Iran over the Tonbs and Abu Musa to the International Court of Justice while Iran, rejecting the notion of adjudication, seeks to settle the dispute by dialogue); "US general says Iran island defenses pose risk," on *ClariNet Electronic News Service,* February 14, 1995 (Reuters reporting on statement by General Binford Peay, commander of U.S. forces in the Middle East, to the U.S. Senate Armed Services Committee that Iran has moved sophisticated air

defenses onto Tonbs and Abu Musa); "US closely watching Iranian moves in gulf," *Boston Globe,* March 1, 1995, p. 9 (Associated Press reporting on the U.S. chairman of the Joint Chiefs of Staff stating that Iran has deployed artillery and antiaircraft missiles on islands at the mouth of the Persian Gulf); "Perry seeking US access in Gulf," *Boston Globe,* March 3, 1995, p. 12 (Reuters reporting on the U.S. seeking guarantees of U.S. access to ports and air bases in the Persian Gulf to counter potential threats from Iraq and Iran); "Iran building up navy, Perry is told," *Boston Globe,* March 22, 1995, p. 15 (Reuters quoting U.S. officials stating concern about the threat posed by Iran to shipping in the Strait of Hormuz and Defense Secretary Perry urging the Persian Gulf sheikhs to increase their defense capability); "Iran said to deploy poison arms," *Boston Globe,* March 23, 1995, p. 2 (Associated Press reporting on U.S. defense secretary stating that Iran's military buildup at the mouth of the Persian Gulf could cripple the flow of oil while the deployment of chemical weapons, including on Abu Musa, could be used to defend the three islands jointly claimed by Iran and the UAE).

18. *Washington Post,* September 25, 1992.

19. *New York Times,* April 16, 1992.

20. *See,* for example, "Saudis, Qataris clash at border; accounts, death toll are at odds," *Boston Globe,* October 1, 1992, p. 10 (Associated Press reporting on the Saudis attacking a Qatari border post).

21. *See* Amirahmadi, Hooshang, *Revolution and Economic Transition: The Iranian Experience* (Albany: State University of New York Press, 1990), pp. 17-18.

22. For a comprehensive analysis of the revolution *see* Amirahmadi, *Revolution and Economic Transition: The Iranian Experience*; and Milani, Mohsen M., *The Making of Iran's Islamic Revolution: From Monarchy to Islamic Republic.* 2nd ed. (Boulder, CO: Westview Press, 1994).

23. Amirahmadi, Hooshang, "Economic Reconstruction of Iran: Costing the war Damage," in *Third World Quarterly,* 12 (1) (January, 1990), pp. 26-47; and Amirahmadi, Hooshang "Economic destruction and imbalances in post-revolutionary Iran," in Hooshang Amirahmadi and Nader Entessar, eds., *Reconstruction and Regional Diplomacy in the Persian Gulf* (London: Routledge, 1992), pp. 65-108.

24. *See* Amirahmadi, Hooshang, "Global Restructuring, the Persian Gulf War, and the U.S. Quest for World Leadership," in Hooshang Amirahmadi, *The United States and the Middle East: A search for New Perspectives* (Albany: State University of New York Press, 1993), pp. 363-429.

25. Ibid., note 15.

26. "Iran Asserts Claims to 3 Disputed Islands in Gulf," *New York Times,* December 27, 1992 (International), p. 8.

27. Speech on Dunkirk, House of Commons, June 4, 1940.

28. Interview with the London daily *Guardian* (28 September 1971), reported in *Arab Report & Record* (London): 16-30 September 1971, p. 291.

29. Interview with the editor of *Blitz* (New Delhi), 24 June 1971, reprinted in *Kayhan International* (Tehran): 26 June 1971 (English Edition).

30. On U.S.-Iran relations in the post-revolutionary period, *see* Amirahmadi, Hooshang, and Bill, James A., *The Clinton Administration and the Future of U.S.-Iran Relations,* Policy Report No. 3 (Washington, D.C.: *Middle East Insight,* 1993); Amirahmadi, Hooshang, and Hooglund, Eric, *US-Iran Relations: Areas of Tension and Mutual Interest* (Washington, D.C.: The Middle East Institute, 1994); and Cottam, Richard W., *Iran and the United States: A Cold War Case Study* (Pittsburgh: University of Pittsburgh Press, 1988).

31. *See* Amirahmadi and Bill, *The Clinton Administration and the Future of U.S.-Iran Relations*; Amirahmadi and Hooglund, *U.S.-Iran Relations: Areas of Tension and Mutual Interest*; and Cottam, *Iran and the United States: A Cold War Case Study.*

32. The cancellation of the Iran-Chinook petroleum development project in the Persian Gulf is a manifestation of the workings of the dual containment policy. In this particular episode, the continuing Iranian involvement with groups opposed to the Arab-Israeli peace process in part served to scuttle the deal by virtue of a presidential order. *See* "Iran is said to give oil contract to US firm," *Boston Globe,* March 7, 1995, p. 9; Hunt, Terence, "Clinton to kill Chinook-Iran deal," *Boston Globe,* March 15, 1995 (Business), p. 45. The backdrop to the cancellation was painted in the months prior to the announcement of the deal by a number of stinging articles and editorials condemning Iran's role in the spread of mayhem and terror. *See,* for example, Jacoby, Jeff, "Iran's high octane blood money," *Boston Globe,* March 2, 1995, p. 11; Power, Jonathan, "How dangerous is Iran?," *Boston Globe,* March 6, 1995, p. 11; Oliphant, Thomas, "How American companies subvert US policy in Iran," *Boston Globe,* March 14, 1995, p. 13.

2

Perspectives on the Territorial History of the Tonb and Abu Musa Islands

Pirouz Mojtahed-Zadeh

This chapter consists of perspectives on various aspects of the territorial history of the strategic islands of Great Tonb, Little Tonb, and Abu Musa at the entrance to the Persian Gulf. Prior to the 1971 withdrawal of Great Britain from the region, the status of these islands had been the subject of a protracted controversy between Iran and Great Britain. Iran claimed these islands by right based on historical title, as evidenced by official documentation of British, Iranian, and third-party origin. Motivated by strategic considerations, in 1903-1904, the British government instructed the Sheikh of Sharjah to raise his flag on Abu Musa and Great Tonb. To justify this action, the British government now came to hold the view that the islands had not been a part of any country's territory. Despite Iran's repeated letters and acts of protest, the islands remained respectively in the possession of the sheikhdoms of Sharjah and Ras al-Khaimah until the end of November 1971.

The 1968 announcement of Great Britain's impending withdrawal from the Persian Gulf was followed by three years of negotiations between Iran and Britain, which resulted in the independence of Bahrain (which had been claimed by Iran) and Qatar, the establishment of the United Arab Emirates (consisting of seven sheikhdoms including Sharjah and Ras al-Khaimah), the reversion of Great and Little Tonbs from Anglo-Qasimi hands to Iranian possession, and the establishment of a regime in which Iran accommodated Sharjah in the administration of Abu Musa under the terms of the 1971 Memorandum of Understanding between Iran and Great Britain (and Sharjah) (hereinafter referred to as the *1971 Memorandum*).

This chapter is divided into twelve sections. Section one will provide a brief description of the islands' physical and human geography. Section two will provide a general survey of the origins and extent of the Iranian State in the Persian Gulf from antiquity down to the end of Safavid rule in Iran. In section three, the focus will shift to the origins and emergence of the Qasimi emirates in the lower Persian Gulf and their evolution from tribal entities into territorially defined units under the British colonial rule. Section four describes the geopolitical implications of a series of territorial losses on the part of Iran and places the loss of the Tonbs and Abu Musa, along with other possessions, in the larger historical context of British imperial and security objectives in the Persian Gulf. Section five examines Iran's efforts in the eighteenth and nineteenth centuries to reorganize the administration of her littoral, particularly of the port of Lingeh and its dependent islands, which ultimately resulted in 1887 in the termination of the hereditary administration of Lingeh by the ethnic Qasimi sheikhs residing there. Section six analyzes and rebuts the content of a letter concerning the issue of Great Tonb written by a Qasimi governor of Lingeh to the Qasimi Sheikh of Ras al-Khaimah. Section seven focuses on the Anglo-Qasimi usurpation of the Tonbs and Abu Musa from Iran in 1903-1904 in the context of the ongoing Anglo-Russian rivalry in the Persian Gulf, which led to the British policy of controlling the islands at the entrance to the Persian Gulf and the approaches to the Strait of Hormuz. Section eight discusses the place of the islands in the territorial history of Anglo-Iranian relations from 1904 through the 1960s. Section nine provides a survey of the Anglo-Iranian negotiations from 1968 through 1971, which ultimately produced the negotiated settlement whereby the Tonbs and Abu Musa returned to Iranian possession. Section ten outlines the international response to the regaining of the Tonbs by Iran. Section eleven traces the origins of the recent controversy between the United Arab Emirates and Iran regarding the status of the Tonbs and Abu Musa. Section twelve concludes this chapter by discussing the United Arab Emirates's efforts to reopen the issue of the islands and identifies the motivation behind such a policy.

GEOGRAPHY AND ECONOMIC ACTIVITY

The sea lanes of communication entering and exiting the Persian Gulf at the Strait of Hormuz are dominated by a group of six islands—Hormuz, Henjam,

Qishm, Larak, Great Tonb, and Abu Musa. Lying at short distances from one another and the Iranian mainland, these islands dot a strategic curved line close to the median between the Iranian and Arabian coasts.

Located some 17 miles southwest of Qishm, the island of Great Tonb is situated on the north of the Persian Gulf's median line. This island's distance from the Iranian port of Lingeh is 30 miles, and it is situated at more than 46 miles from the Emirate of Ras al-Khaimah. The name Tonb, in its very many variations, in the Tangestani dialect of southern Iran means "hill." Some eight miles southwest of Great Tonb is situated the 116-feet high rock island called Little Tonb. It is an uninhabitable island.

Abu Musa is situated between 55°01'E and 55°04'E in longitude and between 25°51'N and 25°54'N in latitude. It is 31 miles east of the Iranian island of Sirri and 42 miles south of Lingeh on the Iranian coast. It is some 40 miles distant from Sharjah. Almost rectangular in shape, Abu Musa measures about three miles diagonally between opposite corners. The island's relatively low land consists of sandy plains, particularly toward the south and center, with dry grass that is grazed on by domesticated animals. The surface is uneven. Hills slope upward on the northern end of the island, eventually rising to the peak of 360 feet at the sugar-cone-like Mount Halva. Abu Musa possesses fresh water, which is produced by a number of wells on the island. Date-palm plantations are a familiar sight. The island has been known mostly for its deposits of red oxide, which is used as a pigment agent in paints, and its offshore petroleum.

The Mubarak field off Abu Musa yields the best quality petroleum produced in the Persian Gulf. The three production wells are operated by Buttes Gas and Oil Company under a concession. Initially, since the island was under British occupation, Iran was not involved in the granting of the concession. However, the terms of this concession were subsequently endorsed by Iran in November 1971 on the understanding that the profit from the exploitation be equally divided between Iran and Sharjah. There existed an overlap of the island's territorial sea with the territory under concession to Occidental Petroleum Company by virtue of a 1969 grant by the Sheikh of Umm al-Qaiwain. A solution to the problem was reportedly based on the allocation to Umm al-Qaiwain of 15 percent of Sharjah's share of the receipts from Abu Musa's oil revenues. A series of correspondence among parties interested in the oil revenues of Abu Musa is reprinted in Appendix 1.

The number of Iranians working in the oxide mines at the turn of the twentieth century stood at 100 men, producing an annual yield of 40,000 bags of oxide.[1] Presently, there are about 2,000 inhabitants working on the Iranian side of the island, under Iranian sovereignty, most of whom are employed by the Governorate of Bandar Abbas. In addition, there are military personnel stationed on the island. Several development projects have been implemented mostly in connection with services for the island, including two small but modern settlements, one for the local fishermen and the other for government employees. These two settlements enjoy electricity, 16 miles of road, and a primitive airstrip. The Northern Fisheries Company of Iran has begun an industrial project on the island. Two small fruit and vegetable farms are in the early stages of development. A distillation plant provides fresh and drinkable water for the inhabitants.[2]

A settlement also dots the Sharjah side of the island. The native population residing in and about the Abu Musa village numbers about 700 people. The population here increases during the times of the year when the weather is more suitable, thus attracting visitors from the emirates. The natives consist of a group of Iranians of Lingeh origin and Arabs mostly from the Sudan tribe in the village of Khan in Sharjah. New buildings have been constructed to accommodate the newcomers and visitors. The settlement has electricity and a water distillation plant.

The 1971 Memorandum placed the native inhabitants of the Abu Musa village under Sharjah's jurisdiction, while the strategic parts of the island were put under Iran's jurisdiction. Contact between the Iranian and Sharjah populations of the island is rare, but in the event of emergencies, such as breakdown in a distillation plant, they assist each other. The small boat *Khater* ferries between the Arab section of the island and Sharjah twice weekly, whereas the Iranian inhabitants reach Bandar Abbas by air as well as by regular boat services. In 1994, the Iranian section of Abu Musa was declared a *shahrestan* (county) of the Hormuzgan Province.

THE IRANIAN STATE IN THE PERSIAN GULF

The term *state* assumed a meaning similar to the modern sense of the word in the Persian Gulf in mid-sixth century B.C. in consequence of territorial consolidation of the Iranian empire under Achaemenid rule. That empire included most of the civilized world of the time, stretching from India in the east to Egypt and Libya in the west.

The political map of the Persian Gulf in the pre-Islamic centuries was of a simple nature. The entire region of southern coasts formed the southern flanks of the Achaemenid Empire (559-330 B.C.). The Achaemenids made use of the strategic locations in the Strait of Hormuz: they sent naval fleets to discover sea routes linking India to Egypt via Persia and the Persian Gulf.[3] The original settlement of the lower coasts of the Persian Gulf by the Iranians began during the Achaemenid times, continued under Parthian rule, and then was consolidated under Sassanid rule (A.D. 224-651).

There is little evidence of major Arab settlement on the southern coasts of the Persian Gulf before the Islamic era.[4] The first Arab migration to the coasts of the lower Persian Gulf began during the reign of the Sassanid king Artaxerxes (A.D. 224). He defeated their king, Sanatraq, and regained control of these coastal regions.[5] Nevertheless, Arab encroachment on the Iranian dominions in the lower Persian Gulf continued. In the reign of Shapur II (A.D. 309-337), the Arabs of Hagar, Qatif, and Hasa began raiding the Sassanid possessions more and more, thereby necessitating a punitive expedition which was completely successful.[6]

In the meantime, in Oman (called Masun at the time), the main Shanu'a groupings of Arab immigrants from the interior of Arabia had settled in the mountains of the Musandam Peninsula and the interior of Oman, while the other Arab migrants settled in the desert and border areas of Oman and formed the Azd federation. Faced with this massive new tribal union of migrant Arabs, the Iranian rulers of the region had little alternative but to accord the newcomers a degree of autonomy under their own tribal leadership, particularly at their main port of Diba on the Gulf of Oman and at the capital Tuam.[7]

In order to consolidate Iranian control over the region, the Sassanid king Khosrow I (A.D.531-579) modified the old feudal organization and established a military landed class who were directly answerable to the Iranian governor at Rustaq in the interior of Oman.[8] The Iranian governor recognized the status of the Mawali sheikh and appointed him as julanda (leader) over the Arabs. He was accorded the right to collect taxes in Arab settlements, and was expected, in return, to maintain discipline among the tribes.[9]

The coming of Islam in the seventh century A.D. gave the Arabs of Oman the opportunity to weaken Iran's millennial dominion in Oman, Musandam, and Bahrain, but Iranian ties were not to be severed completely, as the Iranian inhabitants of northern Oman, in the meantime, continued living in the region preserving to this day some aspects of their original Iranian features.[10]

The first Arab conquest in the Persian Gulf took place at the time of the Caliph Omar. Harrirah, a companion of the Prophet Muhammad, was assigned to conquer all areas of the Persian Gulf. First, he conquered Bahrain, and from there he expanded his authority to the rest of the Persian Gulf. At the time of the Caliph (Imam) Ali ibn Abu Taleb, an Azd sheikh was assigned as governor of Oman. The Khawarij who had been in open defiance of the Caliph Ali overtook Oman, but shortly thereafter surrendered the governorate to the Marvrudi ruler of the Iranian province of Khorassan, who had been commissioned by the Abbassid Caliph Mansur to subdue the Persian Gulf.[11]

The Buyid ruler of Iran, Amir Izzad al-Dawleh, returned territories of the lower Persian Gulf to Iranian control in A.D. 977. In A.D. 1063, Imad al-Dawleh, captured Oman on behalf of the Seljuqs of the Iranian Province of Kerman. Later in the twelfth century, Abu Bakr Saad Zangi, of the Atabaks of Fars in Iran brought Oman, Bahrain, and other parts of the southern coast of the Persian Gulf under his rule.[12]

The various descriptions of the people and places in the Persian Gulf illustrate the extent of Iranian sovereignty, presence, and influence in the Gulf region. For example, the Arab historian and geographer Abul Qasim ibn Hawqal al-Nasibi al-Baghdadi (tenth century A.D.) commented: "As has repeatedly been said, the Persian Sea is a Gulf branching out of the ocean in the vicinity of China and Waqq country; and that is a sea which goeth forth from the vicinity of the countries of Sind and Kirman and Persia, and among all other countries it is named after Persia because there has been no other country around it more advanced than Persia; and, verily the kings of Persia had, from the ancient times, the strongest hold, and they have to this day, the strongest control of the places far and wide of this sea."[13] Similarly, according to al-Maqdisi, another Arab geographer and historian: "[M]ost people call it [the Gulf between Persia and Arabia] Persian Sea as far as the Yemen and indeed are most of its ship-builders and ship-captains Persian. . . . Most people in Aden and Jeddah are Persians. . . . In Sohar they call each other by Persian names and speak Persian. Sohar is the centre of Oman . . . and most of its people are Persians."[14] According to the fourteenth century geographer and historian, Hamdallah Mustawfi, too, "the islands situated between Sind and Oman and in the Persian Sea belong to Persia, the largest of which are Qis and Bahrain."[15]

The Iranian domination of the lower Persian Gulf continued until the arrival of the Portuguese in the region, and was revived later by the Safavid rulers of Iran. When the Safavid Empire emerged in Iran in 1501, the islands of Great Tonb, Little Tonb, and Abu Musa, like many other islands of the Persian Gulf including Qishm, were dependencies of the dominions of the Atabaks of Fars. Under the Safavids (1501-1722), the province of Fars and its dependencies were entrusted to Allahverdi Khan and his son Imam-Quli Khan.[16] The Safavids restored and consolidated Iran's traditional territorial dominions south of the Persian Gulf, and Iran's ownership of these islands remained undisturbed until the fall of the Safavid Empire in the 1720s.

The Safavids revived the Sassanid tradition of political administrative organization of the country and created nineteen *ayalat* (autonomous provinces) and *beglerbeg* (semi-autonomous governorates-general). The Province of Fars in southern Iran included all the ports and islands in the Persian Gulf. Affairs of districts and islands of this province were administered from and taxes paid to the capital Shiraz.[17]

An autonomous Safavid prince was in charge of the province, which effectively rendered the province an autonomous principality. This political and administrative organization of the Safavid period, vague as it was, remained in force until the late nineteenth century. Relations between the political center of the country and outer principalities and dependencies were not clearly defined. This vagueness would soon find itself in conflict with European administrative concepts based on precise territorial relationships between the center and the periphery of the state.

EMERGENCE OF THE EMIRATES

Prior to the arrival of the European concepts of territory and boundary, the Persian Gulf, especially its southern shores, constituted a zone of contact between Iran and other sociopolitical units, such as tribes or small but independent local authorities. These paid tribute and declared loyalty, as they deemed expedient, to either power situated on the two extremes of the frontier zone of the southern Persian Gulf.

In the first half of the eighteenth century, like other tribes of the Musandam Peninsula, the Qawasim tribe, which was later to rule Sharjah and Ras al-Khaimah, continued their traditionally vague connection with the rulers of Muscat, while the rulers of Muscat, in turn, had some similar vague arrangement with the Iranians across the Persian Gulf. The tribes living in these areas, especially the Qawasim, however, roamed about freely on land and at sea, benefiting from the vague and often confused state of ownership—between the Iranian and Omani rulers—of their region. In the 1720s, they migrated as far north as the Iranian territories on the northern shores of the Persian Gulf and Qishm Island, ignoring the Iranian jurisdiction.

In the 1730s, following the demise of the Safavid dynastic rule in Iran, Nadir Shah Afshar reasserted in the 1730s Iran's control over the northern sections of Oman. In the 1740s, when war broke out between Said bin Ahmad of Muscat and the Imam of Oman, the Omanis asked for Iranian support. Nadir Shah dispatched Iranian troops stationed in the Musandam area to the aid of the Omanis. This military expedition was defeated by the Sultan of Muscat but without prejudice to Iran's position in northern Musandam. Upon the assassination of Nadir Shah in 1747, Iran's control of its ports and islands in the Persian Gulf was put in jeopardy by the chaos that followed. A number of local chiefs used the opportunity to increase their autonomous activities in the region. One such figure was an Iranian admiral, Mulla Ali Shah, who managed to establish himself as the autonomous governor of Hormuz. Mulla Ali refused payment of tribute to the central Iranian government as early as 1747 and sought alliance, by marriage, with the powerful Qasimi Sheikh of Julfar (Ras al-Khaimah) on the Musandam coast.

In 1751, the Qasimi Sheikh sent some *dhows* to the northern shores of the Strait of Hormuz, seemingly to pay a courtesy call on Mulla Ali upon the marriage of his daughter, but in reality it was to expand his influence in the districts of the northern Persian Gulf. When in 1759 robbers attacked the British political agent's residence in Bandar Abbas, the East India Company sought redress from the Iranian ruler, Karim Khan Zand. This latter ordered the governor of Lar, Sheikh Nasir Khan, to establish order at Bandar Abbas and Hormuz. An army of one thousand fighters commanded by the Qasimi Sheikh of Julfar landed at Bandar Abbas in support of Mulla Ali. As the war dragged on, a branch of the Qawasim managed to establish themselves at Lingeh, Laft, Shinas, and Qishm Island. Preferring the friendship and cooperation of the Arabs on both shores of the Persian Gulf, Karim Khan showed leniency toward Arab tribes and this helped to strengthen the Qawasim tribe of the lower Persian Gulf in the subsequent period.

When there were outside threats to this region, Iranians and Omanis joined forces and defended their interrelated dominions. The best example of this was the case of Wahhabi threats at the turn of the nineteenth century. The Wahhabis established their authority in the Musandam area in 1803 and turned their attention toward Oman, where an Irano-Muscati and Omani military alliance overthrew their authority.[18] This event further strengthened the joint Iranian-Muscati and Omani authority and cooperation in the coastal regions of the lower Persian Gulf. Consequently, the rulers of Muscat and Oman entered into a series of agreements with the rulers of southern Iran, whereby the former came to administer parts of the southern coasts of Iran and imposed their power on Bahrain and other coasts of the lower Persian Gulf on behalf of the Iranian government. Ultimately, during the reign of the Shah Fath-Ali Qajar in 1811, the Sultan of Muscat leased Bandar Abbas, Bahrain, Shamil, and Hormuz Island from the Iranian government.[19] While administering the lease in 1816, the Sultan of Muscat, with Iran's consent, attacked and occupied Bahrain.

By the turn of the nineteenth century, the maritime power of the Qawasim had grown substantially. The British, who by then had established themselves as the European masters of the eastern waters, determined that their control of the Persian Gulf and Strait of Hormuz was essential for the security of India. This policy led the British to move their forces into the Persian Gulf on the pretext of eradicating acts of alleged piracy by the tribes of the lower Persian Gulf. British naval units attacked Julfar and defeated the Qasimi forces in 1819.

A treaty of truce was signed in February 1820 by the British and five tribal leaders of the Musandam Peninsula, whereby these tribes were brought under British control. Articles 3, 6, and 10 of this treaty provided some hints of recognition by Great Britain of these tribal units, for the first time, as political entities independent of one another and of neighboring states. Article 3, for instance, allowed the tribal chiefs to "carry by land and sea a red flag, with or without letters in it."[20] This was to become the flag of the independent tribes; their progress into territorial states, however, had to wait for more than a century. The delay would be caused in part by the novelty of the concept of territoriality and the exigencies of the British policy in the Persian Gulf. The British view of this is best summarized in the following: "The concept of territorial sovereignty in the Western sense did not exist in Eastern Arabia. A ruler exercised jurisdiction over a territory by virtue of his jurisdiction over the tribes inhabiting it. They, in turn, owed loyalty to him. . . . [the tribesmen's] loyalty is personal to his tribe, his Sheikh, or a leader of greater consequence, and not to any abstract image of state."[21]

The wisdom of the above-quoted passage lay, in essence, at the basis of a decision in 1864 by the British political resident in the Persian Gulf, Colonel Lewis Pelly, to oppose the suggestion—in connection with the arrival of the Indo-European telegraph line to the Persian Gulf—that the territorial boundaries of the Trucial tribes be determined. While Pelly recognized that such a measure may ensure security of the said telegraph line, he rejected the notion of territorial determination of the Trucial tribes on the grounds that implementation of these European concepts in Eastern Arabia at the time was "inexpedient" and would have resulted in great complications.[22] Similarly, one of Pelly's later successors remarked: "Before the advent of oil, the desert was in many ways similar to the high seas. Nomads and their camels roamed across it at will and, though there were vague tribal limits, there were few signs of the authority of any established government outside the ports and oases."[23]

In 1856, in the aftermath of the eviction of the Omanis from Bandar Abbas by the Iranian prime minister Mirza Agha-Khan Sadr-Azam Nouri, and during the rule of Shah Nasir al-Din Qajar, the lease of Bandar Abbas and its dependencies was reinstated in the form of an agreement between the Sultan of Muscat, Seyyid Said bin Ahmad, and the Iranian government, whereby the Sultan of Muscat was given the title *Khan* and was described therein as the lessee and governor of Bandar Abbas and a subject of the Iranian government.[24]

By 1864, the Qasimi sheikhdom of the lower Persian Gulf had become a British protectorate and its foreign relations were restricted to those with the British government only. Sharjah's political status was formulated as an emirate independent of all others in the region. However, this political status still did not establish the territorial dimension of the Qasimi dominion which, beginning in 1866, was to undergo a long process of disintegration and reunification.

Before his death in 1866, the Qasimi Sheikh Sultan bin Saqar, who had ruled since 1803, appointed his sons and brothers as his representatives in the towns of Ras al-Khaimah, Diba, Kalbah, and Khor Fakkan, urging them to obey his elder son, Sheikh Saqar.[25] However, Ras al-Khaimah was separated from Sharjah a year later (in 1867) and was reincorporated into Sharjah in 1900. Twenty-one years later in 1921, Ras al-Khaimah was separated from Sharjah for the second time and has remained so ever since. Fujaira also claimed separation from Sharjah in 1901, but was forced to continue payment of tribute to Sharjah until 1952 when its separation from Sharjah was recognized formally by the British government. The eastern district of Kalbah also had claimed independence from Sharjah but was reincorporated into that emirate in 1951. These territorial changes based on European concepts of territorial sovereignty and political boundaries resulted in bringing partial stability to the region. Exploration for oil resources further necessitated territorial and boundary divisions in the Persian Gulf region. In 1954, J. F. Walker, a British arbitrator, was assigned to carry out territorial divisions and boundary delimitation enquiries. He defined the realm of each emirate and designed boundary lines among them. The work continued until 1961 and his territorial and boundary awards became official in 1962, whereby for the first time the emirates acquired a defined territorial dimension.

The territorialization of the emirates was fraught with conceptual difficulties, in part resulting from expedient economic and political considerations rather than legal principles.[26] Territorial ownership, hitherto, had been traditional and intermingled, especially in the lower Persian Gulf and northern Oman where Iranians and Arab tribes had lived side by side for centuries without any dividing line separating them. Ownership of these territories was common to Iran and Arab tribes and Oman without any kind of written description. The offshore islands were considered by common consent as being under direct Iranian sovereignty. Yet, nothing prevented the tribes of the territories of common Iranian-Arab ownership of the lower Persian Gulf to live and work on these islands and/or in the northern coasts of the gulf. Small wonder, therefore, that the ownership of territories of southern coasts of the Persian Gulf were ill-defined without being supported by legally binding written descriptions. People from the southern coasts could freely travel to Iran and live there indefinitely even as late as 1945.[27] It was not until the 1950s that Iran came to introduce official restrictions on bordercrossings in the Persian Gulf.

The 1962 territorial arrangement among the emirates left the question of statehood still an alien phenomenon to the tribal rulers until their collective emergence as a state in 1971. The federation of the seven emirates—namely, Abu Dhabi, Dubai, Sharjah, Ajman, Umm al-Qaiwain, Ras al-Khaimah, and Fujairah—came into official existence as the United Arab Emirates on December 2, 1971, with Abu Dhabi as its capital. The entity became a member of the United Nations on December 9, 1971.

TERRITORIAL DISMEMBERMENT OF IRAN

The rise to prominence of Russia and Great Britain in the eighteenth and nineteenth centuries inevitably evolved into competition for influence over Iran, which lay to the south of Russia and to the north and west of the British Empire in India. This rivalry had an immense impact on the political geography of Iran. The two wars fought with the Russians, which resulted in the conclusion of Golestan and Turkemanchai treaties in 1813 and 1828, respectively, together with the signing of the Anglo-Persian Peace Treaty of Paris in 1857, contributed to the systematic territorial dismemberment of Iran.

Having established themselves in the Persian Gulf in the first half of the nineteenth century, the British found the Iranians with substantial influence throughout the region. Cultural, historical, and ethnic ties between Iran and the inhabitants of southern coasts of the Persian Gulf were found to be very strong. Therefore, the British began implementing the policy of severing Iran's ties in the region. The "British strategy of depersianization of the Persian Gulf"[28] involved curbing Iranian influence in the region by separating as many islands and coastal districts from Iran as was possible. Iran's traditionally ill-defined relationships between the center and its autonomous peripheries (principalities and dependencies) together with her general political weakness made the dispossession of her territories in the Persian Gulf all the more practical. The vulnerability of the Iranian state in the Persian Gulf to Great Britain was made evident already in 1837-1838. In consequence of Iranian operations against the rebellious chief of Herat (in present-day Afghanistan), Great Britain occupied Kharg Island and did not evacuate the island until Iran had lifted the siege of Herat.[29]

As a result of the British action at Kharg in 1840, the Iranian prime minister Haji Mirza Aqasi deemed it necessary to issue a declaration to the British government reminding the latter of Iranian ownership of the entire Persian Gulf and all the islands in it. As the result of the prime minister's staunch anti-British positions, the British India government now viewed him as a "mad man" and a "Russian protégé".[30]

Haji Mirza Aqasi's action in 1840 was based on the view that prior to the arrival of the British to the region, the Persian Gulf had belonged to Iran and that, in order to expand their influence and control over the Persian Gulf, the British government had deemed it necessary to limit, as much as was possible, Iran's control and influence in the region. The want of knowledge about European concepts made it difficult for Iran to rebut effectively any claim by Russia or Great Britain that a particular principality or dependency was independent of Iran. The process of de-Iranization of the Persian Gulf was soon made evident in the case of Bahrain in 1861,[31] Sheikh Khazal in 1914,[32] and the islands of Qishm,[33] Henjam,[34] Sirri,[35] Tonbs, and Abu Musa in 1904,[36] and Little Tonb in 1908.[37]

ADMINISTRATIVE
REORGANIZATION: QAWASIM OF LINGEH

Having established their control over the Musandam coast in 1819-1820, the British government also sent an expeditionary force to Lingeh on the Iranian coast in order to subjugate its Qasimi residents. The Iranian government protested the invasion on the grounds that the Qawasim of Lingeh were Iranian subjects.[38] This development left no doubt for the British that Lingeh and its dependencies were an integral part of Iran.

In 1835, in order to prevent conflicts among the Arab tribes of the lower Persian Gulf during the pearl-fishing period of the year, the acting British political resident in the Persian Gulf, Captain S. Hennell, suggested a maritime truce, which was signed on August 21. He drew a line on the map of the Persian Gulf separating possessions of the Arab tribes from those of Iran. His map specified the ports of Lingeh, Laft, and Charak, as well as the islands of Qishm, Tonbs, and Abu Musa as possessions of Iran,[39] thus recognizing Iran's sovereignty over these islands. A similar map was produced at a later date by Major Morison who introduced a new line of territorial specification in the region, which started from Ras az-Zur near Kuwait to Sir Abu Nuair island off Sharjah and continued to Ash-Shams near Ras Musandam. This line, too, showed the Tonbs and Abu Musa and the Qasimi governorate of Lingeh as within Iran's jurisdiction. A map produced by the British Admiralty in 1881, painted the Tonbs and Abu Musa in the same color as Lingeh and the rest of the Iranian mainland.

In 1885, the Iranian government decided that the old Safavid administrative organization of the country was no longer viable in the modern world. A new administrative organization was introduced which divided the country into 27 *ayalats* of which the twenty-sixth was the Ayalat of the Ports of the Persian Gulf.[40] In 1885, Sheikh Yusuf, a Qasimi, who had ruled in Lingeh since 1878, was murdered by his relative, Sheikh Qadhib bin Rashid. This event made the Iranian government decide to terminate the Qasimi autonomy in Lingeh and its dependencies and to include this district into the twenty-sixth Ayalat. Accordingly, the Iranian prime minister Amin as-Sultan adopted the policy of increasing direct involvement in the affairs of Lingeh on the part of the governor-general of the twenty-sixth Ayalat. In 1886, Prince Mohammad Mirza was appointed as governor-general of Fars, while Saed al-Molk was at this time in the lesser post of governor of Bandar Abbas and Lingeh. A year later, under the governorship of Qavam al-Molk, Bushehr and its dependencies were also included under the administrative scheme of the twenty-sixth Ayalat, while Brigadier Haji Ahmad Khan was appointed the new *daryabegi* (lord admiral) of the Persian Gulf. The latter visited Abu Dhabi and Dubai in the newly purchased Iranian naval vessel *Persepolis* and kept up his correspondence with the Sheikh of Abu Dhabi. In 1887, on instructions from Prime Minister Amin al-Sultan, Sheikh Qadhib bin Rashid was arrested for the murder of Sheikh Yusuf. He was subsequently taken in chains to Tehran where he died. The Qasimi autonomy of Lingeh was thus brought to an end and the government of Lingeh was entrusted to a new *vali* (governor) appointed by Amin al-Sultan.

In 1898, Lingeh was seized by Sheikh Muhammad, son of Sheikh Khalifah bin Sa'id, a former Qasimi governor of Lingeh. In 1899, he was expelled by the Iranian authorities and reportedly traveled to the Trucial coast, trying to muster a force that could install him in Lingeh. Consequently, the Iranian government asked the British government to prevent any act of aggression from the southern side of the Persian Gulf against Iranian territories at Lingeh and any other part of the Iranian coast. The British government accordingly issued warnings to sheikhs of the Trucial coast not to interfere in the affairs of Iran by assisting Sheikh Muhammad.

Apparently still unhappy about the recent events at Lingeh, the Sheikhs of Sharjah and Dubai intimated to the British political agent in the Persian Gulf, Khan Bahador Abdul-Latif, a connection between the expulsion of Sheikh Muhammad and a perceived Russian effort to gain a foothold in the Persian Gulf. They argued that the friendly relations that existed between Abu Dhabi's Sheikh Zayed and the Iranian officials, particularly the Daryabegi, were in breach of the 1892 bilateral agreement between Great Britain and Abu Dhabi, Article 1 of which prevented the sheikh from "entering any agreement or correspondence with any party other than the British government."[41] The Sheikh of Abu Dhabi was cautioned and he ceased his correspondence with the Daryabegi.

ORIENTAL COURTESY

In the aftermath of admonishing the Sheikh of Abu Dhabi, the British representatives in the region began to encourage the Qasimi Sheikh of Sharjah to try and salvage as much territory formerly administered by their tribal cousins as possible. In this connection, a series of letters authored by various Qasimi Sheikhs has often been cited as proof that the Tonbs and Abu Musa belonged to the Qasimi Sheikhs of Sharjah and Ras al-Khaimah. These documents contained a great deal of inconsistencies and contradictions with an amazing scale of fanciful claims on various localities up and down the region, so much so that the Sheikh of Dubai, for one, found these letters unworthy of reply. The most important of these letters is the one written by Sheikh Yusuf, the Qasimi governor of Lingeh, to the Sheikh of Ras al-Khaimah. In part, it read: "Haji Abul Kasim, the Residency Agent, came to me and informed me about your complaint about the island of Tamb. In reality, the island belongs to you the Jawasemis of Oman, and I have kept my hand over it, considering that you are agreeable to my doing so, and that our relations with you are intimate and friendly. But now when you do not wish my planting date offsets there, and the going across of the Busmaithis to cut grass there, God willing, I shall prohibit them, and our mutual relations are friendly."[42]

Considered in isolation, the letter is misleading. Examination of this document in the proper context of the circumstances in which it was written will clarify the true nature of the correspondence. When disputes erupted in 1873 between the Qasimi Sheikhs of Lingeh and Ras al-Khaimah over the issue of grazing of local livestock on Great Tonb, arbitration of British political agents was sought.[43] Sheikh Humaid of Ras al-Khaimah complained on February 10, 1873, to the British political agent in Lingeh, Haji Abu al-Qasim, that the Al Bu Samait tribesmen of the Iranian ports of Aslaviyeh, Charak, and Lingeh, encouraged by Sheikh Khalifah of Lingeh, had prevented his subjects from entering Tonb for grazing their domestic animals. Haji Abu al-Qasim ruled that Tonb belonged to Lingeh (Iran) and the Al Bu Samait had traditional rights to graze there.

As further enquiries into the dispute became necessary, the British political resident, Edward C. Ross, empowered the political agent in Sharjah, Haji Abd al-Rahman, to carry out more extensive enquiries. Having visited the island and interviewed the Sheikhs of Ras al-Khaimah and Lingeh, Haji Abd al-Rahman concluded his report by asserting that Tonb belonged to the Iranian Ayalat of Fars and was administered by the governorship of Lingeh. Based on this report, Ross wrote to the Sheikh of Ras al-Khaimah on April 19, 1873, stating that Tonb belonged to Lingeh and the inhabitants of Ras al-Khaimah should refrain from annoying the Iranian livestock breeders there and should take their horses out of Tonb.[44]

In 1883, when relations had normalized between the Sheikhs of Lingeh and their Qasimi kinsmen in the lower Persian Gulf, Sheikh Yusuf of Lingeh penned the aforementioned letter. The phrase "the island belongs to you" leaves little doubt about the standard use of oriental courtesy and the complimentary nature of the correspondence, which was conditional to maintaining friendly relations.

Reports from the Qasimi Deputy Governorship of Lingeh for the years 1881-1889, addressed to the governor of Lingeh, clearly acknowledged the undisputed Iranian ownership of the Tonbs and Abu Musa. This is also demonstrated in the letters written in 1885-1886 by Sheikh Yusuf, the deputy governor of Lingeh, to Saed al-Molk, the governor of Lingeh and Bandar Abbas, on various aspects of administration of Lingeh and its dependent ports and islands.[45]

ANGLO-RUSSIAN RIVALRY: ISLAND GRABBING

The British fear of Russian encroachment in the Persian Gulf intensified at the turn of the twentieth century. In a letter to the foreign office in November 1900, the British India Office indicated: "In the early part of this year a report was received to the effect that the Russians might land men or hoist their flag at Bandar Abbas. As the outcome of my letter to you, dated the 13th February 1899, authority was given on 14th February. . . . under certain conditions, for hoisting British flag on Hormuz, or Henjam, or Kishm, or whatever island might be considered by the Naval authorities to offer the best advantages for a naval base in that neighbourhood."[46]

The foreign office wrote back suggesting that "[t]he islands of Henjam, Kishm and Hormuz" were found most suitable for the said purpose.[47]

Early in 1902, at a secret meeting at the British Foreign Office, it was decided that in anticipation of a Russian aggression in the Persian Gulf, the strategic islands at or near the Strait of Hormuz should be occupied. This decision was made known to the British political administrators in India and in the Persian Gulf in the form of a memorandum dated July 14, 1902.[48]

In October of 1902, the news of a would-be Russo-Iranian agreement revived the concern over Russian intentions in the Persian Gulf. Based on the reports received from the British minister in Tehran, Sir A. Hardinge, the British War Office in part concluded: "If Persia is broken up, we must at least, secure Seistan, and keep Russia out of the Persian Gulf. . . . It would be dangerous for us to risk war with Russia and France. . . ."[49]

An intriguing aspect of these moves was the fact that the islands of Henjam and Qishm had been partially under British occupation for some years. The fact that the British had their flag flying on Henjam and Qishm Islands during the time of these debates leaves little doubt that the true aim of their strategic deliberations was to occupy additional Iranian islands such as the Tonbs and Abu Musa in the vicinity of the Strait of Hormuz. This ultimate aim manifested itself about a year later, in 1903, when the government of India ordered the occupation of Great Tonb and Abu Musa by and in the name of the Sheikh of Sharjah.[50]

The British Foreign Office documents suggest that occupation of these islands took place in late June and early July 1903 in the form of instructions from the government of India to the Sheikh of Sharjah to hoist his flag on Great Tonb and Abu Musa.[51] Ironically, Lord Curzon, viceroy and governor-general of India at the time, himself had produced a map in 1892 showing clearly the Tonbs and Abu Musa as belonging to Iran.[52] That the sheikh had to be ordered to occupy the islands, which the British government previously had maintained consistently as belonging to Iran, contradicts and defeats the subsequent British attempts at revising history in order to rationalize and justify the sheikh's actions. The following is an example of such an endeavor: "In the second half of the XVIIIth century the Arabs of the pirate (later called the Trucial) Coast of Arabia occupied the islands of Tanb (also called Tunb, Tamb and Tomb) [and] its dependency Nabiyu Tanb, Abu Musa and Sirri; it seems probable that they did so in the very confused period subsequent to the death of Nadir Shah."[53]

The dubious nature of attempts to create historical title for the Sheikh of Sharjah retrospectively, however, was not lost on all. When Iran hauled down the sheikh's flag in 1904 and touched off a diplomatic incident with Great Britain,[54] the British minister in Tehran reported the following to the foreign office: "The Government of India's telegram of 18th June 1903, does not appear to have been received here with reference to Tamb and Abu Musa, but invalidity of Persian claims to these islands is, I presume, established by it. However, they are coloured Persian in India Survey Map of 1897 and Viceroy's unofficial Map of 1892 . . . It is clear on this presumption, that rights acquired by Sheikh of Shargah must be supported: but before Persian flag is hauled down it would be courteous to give Persian Government chance themselves removing it. We could say, if they refused, that we had shown more consideration than they had for Sheikh of Shargah, and could carry out proposal of Government of India. M. Naus might be induced to remove quietly his flag and guards, and Arab flag then could be re-hoisted after a convenient interval without ostentation. A suggestion that we are acting in a high handed way or to give rise to any violent incident I think is to be avoided."[55]

This policy outlined by the British minister was put into action and the Iranian government, including the Belgian director of Iranian Customs Department, Mr. Naus, was forced to lower the Iranian flags on Great Tonb and Abu Musa.[56]

When the Sheikh of Sharjah hoisted and rehoisted his flag on Great Tonb in 1903 and 1904, the island of Little Tonb escaped his and British attention. In 1907, Great Britain and Russia partitioned Iran into two zones of influence, Russia in the north and Great Britain in the south. This secret agreement now made it all the more easier for Great Britain to collar yet an additional Iranian island, this time Little Tonb, which had some significant promise since it contained red oxide.[57]

In 1908, in consequence of the firm of Frank C. Strick seeking to obtain red-oxide concessions on Farur, Sirri, and Little Tonb, the British government found it necessary to claim Little Tonb also. Even though in its initial inquiries the company had reported the Iranian flag flying on the island for many years, in October 1908, the British political resident in the Persian Gulf, Major Percy Cox, suggested that since Little Tonb was of the same name as Great Tonb, its status therefore be automatically the same as that of the larger island. This formulation was adopted by the British Foreign Office and the company was advised to contact the Sheikh of Sharjah for a concession.[58] In 1908, the Sheikh of Sharjah's flag was raised on Little Tonb.

Related to the obtainment of red-oxide concessions by Strick was also the situation regarding the exploitation of red oxide on Abu Musa by the German firm Wönckhaus. When it was discovered that Wönckhaus had begun work on Abu Musa under British naval supervision, the Sheikh of Sharjah's men stopped the work on the island, forcibly removed the workers to Lingeh, and the company was directed by the British to negotiate a new concession with the Sheikh of Sharjah.[59]

FAILURE OF NEGOTIATIONS: 1904-1961

From the very beginning of the Tonbs and Abu Musa controversy with Great Britain, Iran sought to effect the return of the islands by means of negotiations. The withdrawal of the Iranian flag from the islands in 1904 was effected in part by the promise of the British government to negotiate the controversy while no action be taken to prejudice Iran's sovereignty over the islands.

In June 1904, the British Minister in Tehran reported to London that Iranian prime minister Ain ad-Dawleh "[views] our insistence upon the removal of the Persian flag from Tamb and Abumusa as a discouraging indication that we, on our side, were not as considerate to Persia as he could wish, or to her interests in the Gulf."[60]

Meanwhile, the British government had lowered the Iranian flag on Henjam Island and raised the Union Jack in its stead. This now made for added anxiety, because while the British government had acknowledged openly Iran's sovereignty over Henjam, it now had begun to murmur that Henjam belonged to the Sheikh of Dubai.[61] The Iranian government's concerns were reflected in yet another dispatch from the British Minister in

Tehran following a conversation with the Iranian Deputy Foreign Minister, Mohtashem al-Saltaneh Esfandiari. It read in part: "The Persian Government wished for explanation as to these proceedings, which they evidently regarded, to judge by his remarks, as indicating a disposition on our part to question the Shah's sovereignty rights over the island, and as having, in connection with the recent incident respecting Tanb and Abumusa, some possible political significance."[62] Following a series of diplomatic exchanges, on May 24, 1904, the British minister in Tehran reported back to the Foreign Office that "[w]hile reserving their rights to discuss, with His Majesty's Government, our respective claims to the Islands of Tanb and Abu-Musa, the Persian Government have telegraphed orders to Bushire to remove the Persian guards and flag from them."[63]

Subsequently, in 1905, the Shah Muzaffar al-Din Qajar instructed the Iranian prime minister to continue to impress on the British government the matter of the importance of the lowering of the Iranian flag on Tonb and Abu Musa: "Please instruct the Foreign Minister to tell the British Embassy that we had negotiated on this matter last year. The British government pleaded with us to remove our flag from these two islands until the matter is investigated and negotiated, whereas we ourselves do know that these two islands are undisputed territories of the Government of Iran. Hence, how could the British Government expect, in the atmosphere of friendship [with us], that we transfer our undisputed territories to the Sheikh and he hoist his flag there. You should again negotiate and we will under no circumstances neglect our rights."[64]

Recovered from the constitutional revolution, Iran found it too late and herself too weak to influence a reversal of the British decision to usurp these islands for the Qawasim of Musandam. The Iranian concern about these usurpations remained undiminished, however. The subsequent increase in illegal trade landing on the Iranian coast by way of these islands heightened Iran's anxiety all the more to seek the return of the islands to Iranian possession. In the period of 1904-1927, Iran protested against the islands' status several times. In July 1927, the Iranian Customs Department made representations to the British government demanding action against the illegal trade by establishing observation posts on the three islands.[65] A small fleet of the newly-founded Iranian navy was sent to recover Abu Musa and the two Tonbs and to put an end to the problem there, but to no avail.

In the summer of 1928, the Iranian Customs Department began operating a motorboat service from Great Tonb. This was the outcome of a series of secret contacts with the Sheikh of Ras al-Khaimah who was prepared to return the Tonbs to Iran. In August of that year, the motorboat seized a sailing boat from Dubai at anchor in Tonb waters.[66] When the British protested against the action, the Iranian Foreign Ministry asserted that Tonb was under Iranian sovereignty and thus the action was in keeping with international regulations.[67] In connection therewith, the British government based its standing to complain about the seizure on its 1892 treaties with the Trucial sheikhs, to which the Iranian government replied that "the Persian government could not recognize as valid any agreement with the Trucial chiefs which injured or limited the rights and interests of Persia."[68] The two sides, however, agreed that the status of the Tonbs and Abu Musa should be the subject of negotiations in the winter of that year.

The Anglo-Iranian negotiations on the aforementioned captured Dubai boat and other matters of interest began in January 1929, in which the British minister in Tehran, Sir Robert Clive, represented Great Britain, and the Shah Reza Pahlavi's powerful court minister, Teymourtache, represented Iran. Meanwhile, the British had also made a formal claim for compensation amounting to 5,000 rupees for the damage claimed to have occurred as a result of the seizure. In consequence of the Iranian government's refusal to consider the matter, the British government concluded that "owing to the effect produced on the Arab coast by the failure to obtain compensation, His Majesty's Government should pay the sum at once in anticipation of a settlement of the claim."[69]

In February 1930, the Iranian Ministry of War informed the foreign ministry about a communication received by the former from the commander in chief of the Iranian forces in the south, reporting in part that: "A number of flags have been hoisted by the British in the two islands of Tunb and Abu Musa which belong to Iran. Agents were also posted there. This has come as real surprise to the inhabitants. I beg you to pass on this message to His Imperial Majesty."[70] Having received the report, the Iranian Foreign Ministry wrote to the British minister in Tehran protesting against the actions of the British government on the islands, emphasizing that said actions violated the 1904 status quo agreement that had been reached between the two countries as the condition precedent for the withdrawal of the Iranian flag and guards from Tonb and Abu Musa.[71] Attached to the letter of protest was a copy of the June 14, 1904, correspondence between then Iranian foreign minister, Mosheer al-Dawleh, and the British minister in Tehran, containing an outline of the circumstances resulting in the cessation of the Iranian Customs Department's activities on Tonb and Abu Musa and the withdrawal of the Iranian flag and guards from the islands.[72]

In 1929, the British Foreign Office prepared a draft article for inclusion in the proposed Anglo-Iranian treaty that would have provided for the recognition of Qasimi sovereignty over the Tonbs and Abu Musa in return for recognition of Iranian sovereignty over Sirri. Iran rejected the proposal and, following the Anglo-Iranian oil crisis of 1932, the draft of the intended treaty was abandoned by 1934.[73] Two themes dominated the negotiations: (i) a package deal to settle all outstanding territorial disputes between Iran and Great Britain (on her own account as well as the Trucial sheikhs), and (ii) third-party settlement of the dispute over Bahrain, the Tonbs, and Abu Musa.

On the whole, the British objective during the 1928-1934 negotiations was to change Iran's stance regarding the Anglo-Qasimi occupation of the Tonbs, and Abu Musa, resulting ultimately in a settlement in favor of the Sheikhs of Ras al-Khaimah and Sharjah, respectively. To this end, the British draft of the proposed Anglo-Iranian treaty provided for the withdrawal of claims by Iran to Bahrain, the Tonbs, and Abu Musa, in return for which Great Britain would recognize Iran's sovereignty over Sirri, relinquish her position at Bassidu (on Qishm Island) and transfer to Iran the telegraph stations at Lingeh, Bushehr, and Henjam Island.[74] In July 1932, the Iranian negotiator, Teymourtache, told the British minister in Tehran that Iran would renounce her claims to Bahrain in return for the British recognition of Iran's sovereignty over the Tonbs and Abu Musa.[75] This proposal was rejected by the British.

The negotiations having proved fruitless in many regards, in 1929, Iran offered to refer the parties' irreconcilable differences over the issue of the islands to international arbitration. The British government turned down the offer.[76] The negotiations continued until mid-spring 1929 without much progress. The Conservative government of Stanley Baldwin was replaced in May of that year by the Labor government, and Arthur Henderson replaced Austen Chamberlain as the British foreign secretary. Henderson's protectionist policy with respect to Great Britain's colonial role in the Persian Gulf ultimately brought the Anglo-Iranian negotiations to an abrupt end, but only to be resumed later.

In the 1930s, the Iranian government nevertheless continued with its assertive policy toward the Tonbs and Abu Musa. In 1930, Iran once again objected to the hoisting of the British flag on Great Tonb and Abu Musa. The British denied the allegation of such an occurrence. In June 1931, the Iranian Ministry of Imperial Court wrote to the Ministry of Foreign Affairs informing them of reports from Bushehr that the British had leased Great Tonb from the Sheikh of Ras al-Khaimah for a period of fifty years.[77] Again, it was reported in June 1931 that the British had hoisted their flag on the Tonbs and Abu Musa, but the headman of Henjam Island reported that the Sheikh of Ras al-Khaimah had prevented the hoisting of the British (or his own) flag on Great Tonb.[78]

In 1933, an Iranian warship visited Great Tonb and landed a party that inspected the lighthouse. A similar visit occurred again on the eve of the Sheikh of Ras al-Khaimah's decision in 1934 to return the Tonbs to Iranian possession. The British minister in Tehran, Sir R. Hoare, conferred with the Iranian prime minister over the issue and notified the Iranian prime minister of the impending visit by a British warship to Tonb, Abu Musa, and Sirri, requesting that the Iranian government notify its officials on Sirri to that effect.[79]

In December 1934, an Iranian warship seized a Trucial coast *dhow* in waters off Great Tonb and on two occasions Iranian warships visited the island, landing a party of Iranians there. In addition, in the same year, the Governor of Bandar Abbas and other Iranian officials visited Great Tonb in a *dhow* and secret negotiations between Iranian officials and the Sheikh of Ras al-Khaimah led the sheikh to remove his flagstaff from Tonb Island. When these activities attracted the attention of the British authorities in the Persian Gulf, the British government protested against the proceedings.[80]

In seeking the reversal of the Sheikh of Ras al-Khaimah's restoration of Great Tonb to Iran, the British government explained the sheikh's actions as having been intended "to draw attention to the fact that no rent was received from the British for the use of the lighthouse on Tonb."[81] This justification is not comprehensible: Never before or since this incident has a ruler given up part of his territory to a third country because of financial differences between the colony and the colonial power. The only acceptable explanation of this move can be that the Sheikh of Ras al-Khaimah, aware of the unauthorized occupation of these islands, returned the Tonbs to their rightful owners as a result of a disagreement with the colonial power and as a result of secret arrangements with Iran. Furthermore, whatever the explanation, the undisputed fact is that Ras al-Khaimah returned the Tonbs to Iran when Iran was vigorously campaigning for the recovery of these islands. The Sheikh did not give up these islands to Saudi Arabia, Oman, Sharjah, Abu Dhabi, or any other neighboring emirate or entity; he gave them back to Iran.

In March 1936, the Iranian Ministry of Finance wrote to the Iranian Ministry of Foreign Affairs complaining that the British were engaged in mining red oxide on Abu Musa.[82] Henjam Island was evacuated by the British and returned to Iran in 1935. At the end of 1948, the Iranian government expressed the wish to establish administrative offices on Great Tonb and Abu Musa, which the British ignored. In 1949, there were rumors first that Iran was preparing to refer her case regarding the islands to the United Nations and later that she intended to occupy the islands by force. The Iranian government subsequently received a note from the British embassy in Tehran expressing the British government's "clear attitude" in that respect.[83] Later in August, the Iranian government erected a flagstaff on Little Tonb, which was promptly removed by the British Royal Navy.

Early in 1953, during Iranian prime minister Mohammed Mosaddeq's second term, reports were received by the British government that Iran was contemplating the dispatch of troops to occupy the Tonbs and Abu Musa, and so for several weeks reconnaissance was carried out over these islands by the British Royal Air Force.[84] In the same year, following press reports of a pending visit to Abu Musa by an Iranian commission, an Iranian warship landed a party on the island that made enquiries of the inhabitants. The British government notified the Iranian government that it regarded the island as belonging to the Sheikh of Sharjah.

On May 18, 1961, during Ali Amini's tenure as prime minister, an Iranian helicopter landed on Great Tonb. As this move was not protested to by the British authorities, a second landing on the island took place by an Iranian launch on August 9. On the first occasion, the helicopter had flown in an Iranian and two United States citizens who photographed the lighthouse and adjacent buildings. They talked to the lighthouse keeper, but entered no building and accepted no hospitality.[85] On the second occasion, according to a report by British naval officers, the Iranian launch approached from the east, landed a party on the eastern coast of the island, but soon withdrew and went around to the south of the island, where it landed a party at the village. Two of the visitors were described by the locals as Americans and the landing was thought to have been connected with the first and in the nature of an oil survey.[86] The British suspected the helicopter that had ferried the visitors to the island to have been American, only to find out that the helicopter was British-owned and hired by the Iranians. [87]

Confused by these incidents, the British government first decided to protest against the Iranian action.[88] Then they decided to limit their reaction to making it clear to the Iranian government that they knew about the incidents and would like an explanation.[89] On September 5, 1961, the British embassy in Tehran handed a note to the Iranian Ministry of Foreign Affairs a note protesting against the landings on Tonb.[90] On September 21, the Iranian government rejected the British protest, restating its claim of sovereignty over Tonb.[91] The British Foreign Office repeated the protest in the hope that "the Iranians will get tired of this sort of exchange before we do."[92] The British embassy therefore again wrote to the foreign ministry on January 13, 1962, reserving the rights of the ruler of Ras al-Khaimah in regard to Tonb.[93] The foreign ministry in turn restated the contents of its note of September 21, reserving once again their rights to Tonb.[94]

Overshadowing the persistent Anglo-Iranian exchanges over the Tonbs and Abu Musa, beginning in early 1960s, the Iranian government began a policy of expanding friendly relations with various emirates of the Arab coast of the Persian Gulf.[95] This policy entered into a very active phase in 1962 and was in full swing at the time of the 1968 announcement by Great Britain to terminate her treaty obligations in the Persian Gulf by the end of 1971.

NEGOTIATED SETTLEMENT

Determined to prevent the Arab emirates from inheriting the dispute over the ownership of the Tonbs and Abu Musa, which otherwise potentially could spoil and undermine friendship and cooperation between Iran and her Arab neighbors in the Persian Gulf, in as early as 1970, the Iranian government resumed their demand for the return of the islands to Iran. After the settlement of the Bahrain issue that year, rumors began to circulate that Iran had withdrawn its historical claims to Bahrain principally because it had believed, at the time, that her greater interest centered on the strategic Strait of Hormuz and the islands at the mouth of the Persian Gulf, and that Iran had been reassured by the British and some Arab governments that it would get the Tonbs and Abu Musa back in return for Bahrain.

According to the Shah Mohammad Reza Pahlavi's court minister and closest adviser, Amir Assadollah Alam, Iran had been endeavoring to connect the two issues of sovereignty over Bahrain and the three islands in as early as 1969. An entry from his diary for Sunday, March 23, 1969, read in part: "The British Ambassador called. I told him we can reach no settlement in respect to Bahrain until we know the fate of Tunb and Abu Musa. In that case, he declared we have all been wasting our time. "So be it," I said."[96] Similarly, the recollection of then-British Ambassador to Tehran Sir Denis Wright was that "[a]t one point I had to reject an Iranian proposal that agreement on Bahrain must be subject to agreement on the islands. . . ."[97]

A flurry of diplomatic activity in the Persian Gulf seemed to fuel speculation to that effect even though the linkage itself in actuality may have been far from being the case. A month after the signing of the Iran –Saudi Arabia continental-shelf delimitation agreement in November 1968, the Shah of Iran had visited Saudi Arabia, thereby triggering a rapid improvement of bilateral relations in all aspects. Friendship and cooperation became so close and productive that some began to suspect that the two sides had made a secret deal on the issue of Bahrain.[98] The simultaneous holding of parallel negotiations between Iran and Great Britain on the Anglo-Iranian territorial disputes in the Persian Gulf continued to fuel speculation about a deal, which, as endorsed by some Arab governments, including Saudi Arabia, provided for a trade-off that would give Abu Musa to Iran in return for the withdrawal of her claim to Bahrain.[99] According to the Iranian chief negotiator at the time, Amir Khosro Afshar, "[t]here was no trade off deal with the British during our negotiations on the separate issues of Bahrain and the three islands of the Strait of Hormuz."[100]

Nevertheless, it appears that a top-level understanding was reached between the Iranian and British leaders on the two separate issues of Bahrain and the three islands, which loosely linked the two. According to the entry in the diary of the court minister, Amir Assadollah Alam, for Sunday, March 23, 1969: "The Ambassador [Denis Wright] seemed more inclined than he was the other day to link any solution of Bahrain to proposals over the islands. He hinted that if Iran were to back the creation of an Arab Federation in the Emirates then we might be called upon to occupy the islands on the Federation behalf, without any fear of a backlash from the Arabs."[101]

The proposal envisaging Iran regaining possession of the islands at the invitation of the Arab Federation sounded vague and the linkage that Iran had preferred seemed not to be as strong as the Shah had wished. The entry in the court minister's diary for Wednesday, April 30, 1969, read in part: "I reported the comments of the British Ambassador, who tells that the delay in negotiations with Bahrain springs from the Sheikh's reluctance to allow the UN Secretary General U. Tant [sic] to send a fact-finding mission to the island at the invitation of Britain and Iran. This has come as a real surprise. According to [His Imperial Majesty], 'we shall accept no compromise on Bahrain until the status of Abu Musa and Tunbs has been clarified.' I told him that I had already made this point clear to the Ambassador, but HIM instructed me to make it doubly clear."[102]

The proposed Arab Federation was then to include Qatar, Bahrain, and the seven other Trucial sheikhdoms which eventually formed into the United Arab Emirates. The announcement by Iran to withhold recognition from any federation that included territories claimed by Iran—namely Bahrain, the Tonbs, and Abu Musa—further complicated the negotiations. Similarly, Saudi Arabia had declared that she would not recognize the federation because of her territorial disputes with Abu Dhabi in the Buraimi and Liwa regions and also with Qatar. Iraq had also pronounced its opposition to the federation on the basis of its ideological reasons. The British therefore concluded that the creation of the union of the small emirates without the goodwill of the regional powers would put this powerless union in a risky position. Recognition of this fact was the main driving force behind the British decision to reach some kind of compromise with Iran, recognizing, albeit perhaps reluctantly, Iran's rights to the Tonbs and Abu Musa. According to the entry in the court minister's diary for Monday, February 18, 1970: "The British Ambassador . . . told me very confidentially that the case of Tunb Island is practically settled and will definitely be given to Iran, for we have told the Sheikh of Ras al-Kheimeh that if you don't come to some sort of arrangement with Iran—as these islands are situated above the median line [of the Persian Gulf]—Iran will lawfully, and if that was not possible, will forcefully take these islands, and the Sheikh agreed to make a deal over them. I said: what about Abu Musa? He said: this island is situated below the median line. I said: and our power is sufficient enough to put a step below the line . . . He said: [if you resort to force] your relations with the Arabs will be harmed. I said: to hell with it."[103]

As the Iranian officialdom sought to advance the Iranian case, threats to use force began to punctuate the arguments put forth as justification for the return of the Tonbs and Abu Musa to Iran. In February 1971, the Shah stated that "[t]hese islands belong to the nation, and we have British Admiralty maps and other documents which prove this. We will—if necessary—regain them by force, because I don't want to witness my country to be put up to auction."[104] In a second interview, on June 24, 1971, the Shah declared that the islands had belonged to Iran when they were "grabbed some eighty years earlier" by the British, at a time when Iran virtually had "no central government." He further stated that when his father had sent gunboats to recover them, the British assured Iran that no flag of sovereignty would be hoisted until the question was settled. The Shah then added: "I hope this happens now. Otherwise, we have no alternative but to take the islands by force."[105] Similarly, while addressing the people of Bandar Abbas, on June 27, 1971, the Iranian prime minister, Amir Abbas Hoveida, said: "Iran was by no means indifferent to the future of the Persian Gulf, because it constituted its vital access route. Iran needed these islands for its security and prosperity, a goal for the attainment of which Iran would fight with all its might should it fail to settle this problem by peaceful means."[106]

Meanwhile, the Iranian negotiator, Amir Khosro Afshar, and the British negotiator, Sir William Luce, continued to work behind the scenes. Amir Khosro Afshar's recollection of the negotiations is instructive of the dynamics of the talks: "Sir William Luce and I used to negotiate in London. Having reached certain points of understanding, we would go to Tehran and discuss them before the Shah. Having heard the Shah's views, Sir William Luce would go to the emirates discussing the points with rulers of Sharjah and Ras al-Khaimah, from there going to London to brief his Government. We then resumed the talks in London, repeating the same procedure."[107] With respect to the Tonbs, in the later stages of negotiations, the contacts between the Iranian negotiator and the Sheikh of Ras al-Khaimah were, on occasion, direct.[108] Generally speaking, from time to time the negotiating parties would apprise the Saudi and Egyptian governments about the talks.[109]

On November 30, 1971, the Iranian troops landed on the Tonbs and took possession of the islands and overcame a token resistance put up by a detachment of Ras al-Khaimah police on the island. On Abu Musa, a representative of the Sheikh of Sharjah greeted the Iranian troops arriving on the island pursuant to the day-old Memorandum of Understanding.

The financial agreement referred to in the memorandum concerned payments by Iran to Sharjah of one and a half million pounds sterling annually for a period of nine years. This was to cease should Sharjah's oil revenue reach £3 million per annum. Within the federal framework of the United Arab Emirates, Sharjah gained its independence on December 1, 1971. To secure Sharjah's compliance with the terms of the memorandum, the Iranian foreign minister, Abbas-Ali Khalatbari, wrote to the British foreign secretary, Sir Alec Douglas-Home, stating that the Iranian government reserved the right to implement its full sovereignty over the whole of Abu Musa should Iran at any time feel that activities in the Sharjah-controlled area of the island threaten Iran's interests, sovereignty, and security in the island. Replying to this letter, the British Foreign Office informed Iran that the contents of the above letter were communicated to the Sheikh of Sharjah.[110]

The 1971 memorandum, however, left the overall ownership of Abu Musa undefined. In an interview with the *Al-Ahram* correspondent in Sharjah on December 7, 1971, the then-ruler of the Emirate of Sharjah stated that "Sharjah did not believe that its agreement with Iran adversely affected its sovereignty over the island," and that "the agreement was temporary and was an instrument for overcoming crisis and preventing bloodshed."[111] In contrast, the statement of Iranian prime minister Hoveida to the Majlis on November 30, 1971, painted a different picture: "The Iranian flag was unfurled on Mount Halva, the highest peak on the island of Abu Musa. I deem it necessary to declare on this occasion that the government of H.I.M. has in no conceivable way relinquished or will relinquish its sovereign rights and incontestable jurisdiction over the whole island of Abu Musa, and hence, the presence of local agents [Sharjah officials] in a segment of the island of Abu-Musa should in no way be viewed or interpreted as contradictory to this declared policy."[112]

INTERNATIONAL RESPONSE

The Arab reaction to the landing of Iranian troops on the islands was mixed. While radical Arab governments reacted vociferously at home and at the

United Nations, the moderate Arab governments preferred prudence. The Arab League was urged by the radicals to lodge a collective Arab complaint with the United Nations Security Council; however, the proposal was squashed by the majority of the member states. Instead, they agreed to condemn Iran's action individually by issuing statements in their own capitals. All Arab governments did so, except Jordan.

The radical Arab states—namely, Algeria, Iraq, Libya and former South Yemen—took their complaint to the United Nations Security Council. The Council met on December 9, 1971 to examine the case. Representatives of these four countries were joined by representatives for Kuwait and the United Arab Emirates, the latter becoming a member of the United Nations on the same day.[113]

In his account of the event, the Iraqi representative alleged that "Iran had claimed the whole [Persian] Gulf, but 'such ludicrous blanket claims' had been reduced to claims on Bahrain and later to the Tonbs and Abu Musa."[114] He asserted that his government had received a cable from the Sheikh of Ras al-Khaimah claiming that the two Tonbs had belonged to Ras al-Khaimah since ancient times.[115]

The UAE representative made a very mild and conciliatory statement.[116] The Kuwaiti representative claimed that the Tonbs had belonged to Ras al-Khaimah "for centuries."[117] The Algerian representative's view of the historical record was closer to the reality. "There had been conflicting claims to those islands over the years," he stated, "but it was undeniable that during the whole period of British control the islands had been part of the territory that had become the United Arab Emirates."[118] The Algerian's statement, albeit more rational than those made by the Kuwaiti, Iraqi, and Libyan representatives, was not in complete harmony with the historical facts, as the British control of the lower Persian Gulf territories began in 1820, while the Tonbs and Abu Musa were seized from Iran by Britain and given to the Qasimi tribal entity of Sharjah in 1903-1904.

The Iranian representative's statement was relatively short. He rejected the charges against Iran as baseless and said the question was essentially an internal matter for his country.[119] On the motion of the representative of Somalia, whose country was also a member of the Arab League, the council adjourned consideration of the complaint, allowing third-party efforts at mediation to take place.

RECENT CONTROVERSY

While the 1971 Memorandum had left the ownership of the island undefined, its terms were clear as to two sets of rights extended therein: (a) rights of the nationals of Sharjah and (b) exclusive Iranian sovereignty with respect to specified matters. In April 1992, reports alleged that Iran had prevented entry onto Abu Musa by a group of nonnational employees of Sharjah consisting of Pakistani, Indian, and Filipino laborers and technicians and Egyptian teachers. While Iran denied the reports of expulsion of UAE nationals, Iran's permanent representative at the United Nations, Kamal Kharrazi, stated that "those [varying nationals] who have not lived on the island . . . have no right to stay there. . . ."[120] This statement was interpreted by some in the West as implying that only Sharjah nationals with proven connections to the island would be allowed to reside there in the future.[121] Iran's minister of foreign affairs, Ali-Akbar Velayati, stated that the 1971 Memorandum gave the right only to Sharjah nationals to reside on (the Sharjah side of) the island.[122]

A representative of the UAE visited Tehran and suggested that a joint commission of representatives from Iran and UAE be formed to study the issue, but Iranian authorities rejected the suggestion on the grounds that the issue was in essence a matter for Iran and Sharjah.[123] Subsequently, on May 12, 1992, the High Council of the UAE met to discuss the issue of Abu Musa. It was reportedly agreed at the end of the meeting that commitments of each member of the union were to be treated as commitments of the union as a whole.[124]

In August 1992, the BBC reported that Iranian authorities had refused entry to Abu Musa to a party of over one hundred different nationalities (mainly Egyptian).[125] Having proved they were teachers and their families were going to Abu Musa to complete school examinations, they were allowed by Iran to enter the island in November 1992. Reporting the August incident, the *Times* of London stated that "[Iran] planned to use the island in the shipping lane which carries half the world's oil as a base for three submarines that it is now purchasing from Russia." The newspaper also repeated the allegation made in Abu Dhabi and Cairo that Iran had asserted her full sovereignty over the whole of Abu Musa, thereby reneging on the terms of the memorandum.[126] The incidents, however, were welcomed by the UAE, Kuwait, and other Arab states, especially Egypt, as opportunities for anti-Iranian propaganda. Tehran denied all these charges while sending representatives to Abu Dhabi to find a peaceful end to the problem. However, the talks ended abruptly when the UAE demanded the ceding of the Tonbs along with Abu Musa.

The president of the UAE, Sheikh Zayed bin Sultan al-Nahyan, was reported to have noted in London in September 1992 that his government "was taking the dispute to international arbitration."[127] In October, the UAE distributed a position paper to the representatives at the United Nations setting forth the alleged historical facts about these islands. Meanwhile, the Iranian sources reasoned that their actions on Abu Musa was due to their detection in recent months of "suspicious activities" in the Arab part of the island.[128] The suspicious activities complained about by Iran had involved the presence on the Sharjah-controlled side of the island of third-country nationals, including Westerners, who appeared to be engaged in the design and construction of a military installation and possibly housing for an anticipated group of nonresidents due to arrive on the island.[129] The Iranian president, Hashemi-Rafsanjani, announced at the Friday prayer on September 18, 1992 that Iranian authorities had arrested a number of "armed third-party nationals" who were trying to enter Abu Musa illegally, among whom was a Dutch national who had been arrested and put in prison in Tehran. "Iran's policy in the Persian Gulf is not to create enemies and conflicts," he stated, "but to defend her territorial integrity and we will act seriously to ensure this."[130] The UAE, on the other hand, without denying the breach of security, accused Iran of preventing UAE nationals from entering Abu Musa by demanding visas from them. The UAE also accused Iran of gradual encroachment on Abu Musa by building roads and an airstrip there, and of intending to expand its military presence on the island.[131]

There were unconfirmed reports that Iran and Sharjah were prepared to reaffirm the 1971 Memorandum in its entirety but the leaders of the UAE had scuttled the talks by deciding, in October 1992, to tie any agreement on Abu Musa to a demand for the surrender of the Tonbs to UAE sovereignty.[132] In November 1992, Iran attributed the August incident to the misjudgment of "junior Iranian officials."[133]

In October 1992 Qatar and Saudi Arabia fell out over an old border dispute. In early November, President Bush, a staunch supporter of the UAE position, lost the elections to Bill Clinton. The time was therefore opportune for a gathering on November 18, 1992, of academicians in London to help ease tensions between UAE and Iran over the islands. However, in December 1992, even though Iran had by now admitted the visitors to Abu Musa, the closing statements at the thirteenth summit of the Gulf Cooperation Council (GCC) in Abu Dhabi called on Iran to "terminate its occupation of Greater and Lesser Tunb islands, which belong to the United Arab Emirates."[134] On December 25, 1992, the Iranian president, Hashemi-Rafsanjani, warned the GCC that "to reach these islands one has to cross a sea of blood."[135]

CONCLUSION

The foregoing chapter provided an anthology of the major themes encountered in the prolonged and still-continuing territorial history of the Tonbs and Abu Musa. The flare up of the recent controversy between the UAE and Iran regarding the status of these islands is all the more reason for a deeper appreciation of the effects that wholly independent historical trends and larger strategic necessities have had on the issue of control of these islands. As changes in circumstances occur, the expectation is that a legally cogent argument will be fashioned to cover up the real geostrategic justification to usurp the islands from one sovereignty and to place them in the hands of another. Yet, in order to fashion a new legal theory, the party claiming the islands, UAE, would almost by necessity have to fabricate facts capable of sustaining the legal results that it now wishes to flow from the application of the law. The recent argument by the UAE questioning the entire validity of the 1971 Memorandum is one such effort.

The UAE argument asserts that the 1971 Memorandum over Abu Musa was accepted by Sharjah under duress and only as a de facto arrangement at that. The argument fails to recognize that in 1971 Iran was negotiating with Great Britain, who spoke for Sharjah by virtue of the 1864 and 1892 agreements which that Sheikhdom had with Great Britain. The Iranian troops arriving on Abu Musa on November 30, 1971, were greeted personally by His Highness Sheikh Sultan bin Muhammad Al-Qasimi, the present ruler of Sharjah, who at the time was Sharjah's heir apparent and represented his brother, H. H. Sheikh Khalifah bin Muhammad al-Qasimi, then the ruler of Sharjah. This level of cordiality further erodes the conjuration of duress. The financial and economic assistance provisions of the memorandum all the more point to a bargain, an exchange of quid pro quo or consideration, all of which the Sheikh of Sharjah announced with satisfaction a day or so prior to the arrival of the Iranian troops on the island. Moreover, the UAE position paper distributed at the United Nations in October 1992 called on Iran to remain committed to and bound by the 1971 Memorandum, a request which dilutes further any argument as to the invalidity of the memorandum, including the claim of duress.[136]

By the same token, Iran could well argue that the 1971 Memorandum was indeed thrust by Great Britain upon her under duress as well and that the terms thereof favoring Sharjah are therefore null and void. Certainly, notwithstanding the preamble of the memorandum, three of its articles may sustain an Iranian claim to the island by virtue of the memorandum itself. Article 1 of the memorandum provides for the stationing of Iranian troops in the northern section of the island. The legally relevant implication of this provision is that the provision contemplated Iranian sovereignty over the island because only in one's own territory one may establish military presence with full sovereignty. In Article 2, while Iran is recognized to have "full sovereignty" over a specified area, Sharjah is recognized to merely have full "jurisdiction" over the remaining area. Similarly, Article 3 of the memorandum requires the extension of the island's territorial sea to 12 nautical miles, a limit conforming to the breadth of Iran's territorial sea, in contrast to Sharjah's, which at that time was 3 nautical miles (Sharjah, nevertheless, had announced a 12-mile territorial sea in 1969).[137]

The UAE also seeks to undermine the 1971 Memorandum by asserting that the agreement reached in 1971 was a "temporary administrative arrangement." The memorandum contains no term of duration, making it all the more difficult to attribute a temporary character to the arrangements therein contained. If there is any claim at all to the temporary nature of the memorandum it would seem to favor Iran instead.

The revival of an issue that had been settled in 1971 through negotiations between Iran and Great Britain cannot but harm all prospects of cooperation in the Persian Gulf. All the more intriguing is the point of view that seeks to equate the retention of the islands in Iranian hands to a threat to the security of the Persian Gulf and the sea lanes of communication. Since December, 1971, the Persian Gulf has had its share of convulsions: the fall of the monarchy and the establishment of a new regime in Iran in February 1979 was followed in September 1980 by the start of an eight-year war waged against Iran by Iraq, whose effort received the assistance of such Western powers as the United States and France and the financial assistance of Kuwait, UAE, and Saudi Arabia, whose oil continued to be exported from the Persian Gulf all the same, while, in consequence of the detention of diplomatic and consular staff at the United States embassy in Tehran, Iran was placed in dire economic straits as the result of seizures of assets, boycotts, and embargoes instituted by the Western countries. Finally, in recent memory, the Iraqi invasion of Kuwait in August 1990 culminated in the Kuwait Crisis in January 1991, during which contest Iran declared and observed strict neutrality. And, yet, not once during any of these events did Iran use any of the Tonbs or Abu Musa to make a political point or jeopardize the safety and security of passage through the Strait of Hormuz. If anything, the preoccupation with the adverse role of the islands in any regional or international conflict involving Iran seems to be only on the part of Western powers and their allies in the Persian Gulf.

Considering the location of the Tonbs and Abu Musa at the strategically sensitive Strait of Hormuz and considering that both the regional countries of the Persian Gulf and the oil consuming countries of the industrial world depend heavily on peace and security of the Strait of Hormuz, it is important to note that supporting any one of the two sides in this controversy can easily lead to a conflict. Therefore, one would expect that the two sides of the controversy should be encouraged to settle their differences peacefully.

NOTES

1. Lorimer, J. G., *Gazetteer of the Persian Gulf, Oman, and Central Arabia,* Vol. II, *Geographical and Statistical* (Calcutta, 1908)(reprinted from an original in the India Office Library) (Farnborough: Gregg International/Irish University Press, 1970), p. 1276.

2. For a detailed geographical description of the island of Abu Musa, *see* Mojtahed-Zadeh, Pirouz, Mohajer, Shah-Husseini, and Malekpour, "Special Report on Abu Musa," in *San'at-e Haml-o Naghl* (Transport Industry Monthly),1474 (Tehran: November, 1992).

3. *See generally* Mojtahed-Zadeh, Pirouz, "Evolution of Eastern Iranian Boundaries" (Ph.D. diss., London University, 1993), p.23.

4. *See generally* Mojtahed-Zadeh, Pirouz, *The Changing World Order and the Geopolitical Regions of Caspian-Central Asia and the Persian Gulf* (London: Urosevic Foundation, 1992).

5. Ibn Jarir Tabari, Mohammad, *Tarikh Tabari,* Vol. II (Persian translation by Abol-Qasem Payandeh) (Tehran: Bongah-e Tarjomeh va Nashr-e Ketab, 1973), p.462.

6. Wilson, Arnold T., *The Persian Gulf* (London: George Allen S. Unwin, 1928), p. 55.

7. Wilkinson, John C., "The Julanda of Oman," in *Journal of Oman Studies* 1 (1975), pp. 97-108.

8. *See* generally Wilkinson, John C., "Arab Settlement in Oman"(Ph.D. diss., Oxford University, 1969).

9. Wilkinson, "Julanda," ibid.

10. *See generally* Mojtahed-Zadeh, Pirouz, *Countries and Boundaries in the Geopolitical Region of the Persian Gulf* (Tehran: IPIS Publications, 1993).

11. *See generally* Mojtahed-Zadeh, Pirouz, *Evolution of Eastern Iranian Boundaries.*

12. *See generally* Mojtahed-Zadeh, Pirouz, *Sheikh Neshinhay-e Khalij-e Fars* (The Sheikdoms of the Persian Gulf) (Tehran: Ataei Publications, 1970), pp. 35-36.

13. Abul Qasim ibn Hawqal, *Surat al-Ardh* (written in A.H. 367) (London, 1938) 2nd ed. (London, 1988), p.244. *See generally* Mojtahed-Zadeh, Pirouz, *Joghrafiay-e Tarikhi-e Khalij-e Fars* (Historical Geography of the Persian Gulf) (Tehran: Tehran University Press, 1975).

14. Al-Maqdisi, *Ahsan at-Taqasim Fi Marefat al-Aqalim,* 2nd ed. (Liden, 1906), p.18.

15. Hamdallah Mustawfi, *Nezhat al-Qulub* (ca. A.H. 730), published in A.H. 1307 (1928).

16. Rohroborn, Klaus-Michael, *Provinzen und Zentralgewalt Persiens* (Persian edition), Kaykavous Jahandari, trans. (Tehran: B.T.N.K, no. 339 1978), pp. 13-14.

17. Ibid., pp. 2-3.

18. Mirza Mohammad Taqi Lissan al-Molk, *Nasekh at-Tavarikh,* Vol. I (reports of events of early nineteenth century in and around Iran) (Tehran: Mohammad Baqer Behbudi, 1974),p. 206.

19. The original lease document is reproduced in Mohammad-Ali Karim-Zadeh Tabrizi, ed., *Asnad va Faramin-e Montasher Nashodeh-e Qajari* (Unpublished Qajari Documents and Decrees) (London, 1989), at p. 161. (Hereinafter cited as "Qajari Documents.")

20. Article 3 of General Treaty for the Cessation of Plunder and Piracy by Land and Sea, dated 5th February 1820, reprinted in Hawley, Donald, *The Trucial States* (London: George Allen & Unwin, 1970), p. 314.

21. Kelly, J.B., *Eastern Arabian Frontiers* (London: Faber & Faber, 1964), p. 18.

22. Lorimer, J.G., *Gazetteer of the Persian Gulf, Oman, and Central Arabia,* Vol. I, *Historical* (Calcutta, 1915) (reprinted from an original in the India Office Library), (Farnborough: Gregg International/Irish University Press, 1970) p. 625.

23. Hay, Rupert, *The Persian Gulf States* (Washington, D.C.: The Middle East Institute, 1959), pp. 3-6. The personal nature of tribal politics and the geographical peculiarities of the terrain in part explain how a tribe could exercise loyalty to two different claimants of sovereignty seasonally. This seems to have been especially pronounced with respect to the tribes inhabiting the Musandam promontory in the lower gulf: "From local enquiries . . . it seemed certain that Kumzar and Khasab on the western coast, together with the villages between them, actually acknowledged the sovereignty of the Sultanate of Oman; but some doubts remain as to the status of the inhabitants of Film, Shabus and Shisah on the eastern side of the promontory, whom were said to be virtually independent while at home and to become subjects of the Sheikh of Sharjah in the date season . . . ." Lorimer, *Gazetteer of the Persian Gulf,* Vol. I, p. 625.

24. *Qajari Documents.*

25. *See generally* Mojtahed-Zadeh, *Sheikh-Neshinhay-e Khalij-e Fars.* 26. The process is best described by J.C. Wilkinson in the following passage: "This ludicrous partitioning of territory is of recent origin and stems in large measure from the imposing of European notions of territorialism on a society to

which they were foreign. The ad hoc process by which this happened started a century and a half ago when Britain initiated a series of treaties with the Sultan of Muscat and the coastal sheikhs of northern Oman, with the purpose of limiting their maritime activities and foreign relationships. Subsequently, as Britain sought to develop an exclusive influence in the Gulf and, later still, to favor the claims of particular companies to act as concessionaires for oil exploration, she was forced first into defending the protege coastal rulers from attack from the hinterland and then of proclaiming their authority over the population and resources of 'Greater Oman,' by dividing it into a number of territories subject to them. This is not to say that the embryonic states she helped create were entirely artificial. Rather it is to imply that from the start the terms of reference by which they came into existence more or less disregarded important aspects of traditional organization within the region." Wilkinson, J.C., *Water and Tribal Settlement in South-East Arabia* (Oxford Research Studies in Geography) (Oxford: Clarendon Press, 1977), p.6.

27. Hay, *The Persian Gulf State,* p. 148.

28. Bavand, Davoud H., "Bar-rasi-e Mabani-e Tarikhi va Hoquqi-e Jazayer-e Irani-e Tonb va Abu Musa," in *Jame-eh Salem* II (7) (Tehran: December 1992–January 1993), pp. 6-19.

29. Wilson, *The Persian Gulf,* pp. 256-257.

30. Nateq, Homa, *Iran dar Rah-yabi-e Farhangi, 1834-1848* (London: Payam Publications, 1988), pp. 89-90.

31. When, by virtue of concluding the 1861 treaty with the Al-Khalifah Sheikh of Bahrain, the British government claimed the principality of Bahrain as independent of Iran, Iran failed to prove the opposite in spite of the fact that it had received letters of renewed submission and loyalty from Sheikh Mohammad al-Khalifah of Bahrain only a year earlier. The sheikh stated that he, his brother, and the other Al Khalifah and the inhabitants of Bahrain were subjects of Iran. *See* Letter from Sheikh Muhammad bin Khalifah al-Khalifah to Nasir al-Din Shah, dated Ramazan 20, 1276 (April 12, 1860), reprinted in *A Collection of Iranian government Documents* (Tehran), No. 6044, p. 339.

32. On November 21, 1914, the British political resident in the Persian Gulf, Sir Percy Cox, gave the following written assurances to Sheikh Khazal in clear and direct contravention of Iran's independence and territorial integrity: "I am now authorized to assure your excellency . . . that whatever change may take place in the form of the Government of Persia . . . . His Majesty's Government will be prepared to afford you the support necessary for obtaining a solution satisfactory both to yourself and to us in the event of any encroachment by the Persian Government on your jurisdiction and recognized rights or on your property in Persia. . . . These assurances . . . shall hold good as long as you . . . continue to be guided by the advice of His Majesty's Government vis-à-vis the Persian government we shall do our best to maintain your excellency in your present state of local authority." F.O. 416/112: Annual Confidential Report of British Legation in Tehran for the year 1926, par. 74, p. 29.

33. Qishm was the first Iranian island in the Persian Gulf to be used by the British. In 1819, having crushed the power of Arab pirates of the southern gulf, the British General Grant Keir transferred his forces, originally 1,200 men strong, to Qishm Island. This move was strongly protested by the Iranians who called upon the British to evacuate the island. This appears to have been ignored and the British established in 1823 a naval supply depot at Bassidu on the north-western tip of the island. Qishm Island was recovered by the Iranians at a later date. Wright, Denis, *The English Amongst the Persians* (London: Heinemann, 1977), p. 66. It was rumored in 1905 that Iran had ceded, sold, or leased Qishm to the Russians, but the rumor proved to be unfounded. F.O. 371/106: Foreign Office Confidential Report (1961).

34. When the British decided to establish the Indo-European telegraph line that had to pass near or through the coasts and islands of the Persian Gulf, they negotiated in 1868 with the Iranian authorities for a cable station on Henjam. For reasons of their own, they closed the station in 1880, but 24 years later (coinciding with the usurpation of Abu Musa and Great Tonb in 1903-1904), they reoccupied the old site, removed the Iranian flag from the island, and hoisted the Union Jack in its place. Wright, *The English Amongst the Pesians,* p. 67.

35. The history of Sirri Island is no different from that of the Tonbs and Abu Musa. Like the latter three islands, Sirri was assumed by the British in 1887 as being Iranian territory. "A War Office map, presented by the British minister (in Tehran) to the Shah in 1888, showed all the islands (the two Tonbs, Abu Musa and Sirri) in the Persian colour: the Persian case was further strengthened with the publication in 1892 of Curzon's two-volume *Persia and the Persian Question* in which the map, prepared by the Royal Geographical Society under Curzon's own supervision also showed the islands as Persian territory." Wright, *The English Amongst the Persians,* p.68. On the occasion of the scramble among the various Iranian, British, and German parties interested in the exploitation of red oxide in the islands off the Iranian coast, the British embassy in Tehran drafted a memorandum which explained the reason why the British government would oppose attempts by any Iranian to mine for red oxide on Sirri Island: "The discovery of red oxide on the Island of Sirri is comparatively recent, and it was until the spring of 1908 that Messrs. Haji Ali Akbar, of Manchester, intimated to His Majesty's Government their desire to obtain a concession for its exploitation from the Persian Government. It was not possible for His Majesty's Government to give Messrs. Haji Ali Akbar their entire support in their plan, as the territorial ownership of Sirri is disputed, the island being claimed by Persia and by the Jowasim Sheikh of Shargah, who is under British protection. In 1888 it was occupied by the Persian Government. His Majesty's Government protested at the time, and, although they refrained from taking forcible action on behalf of the Sheikh of Shargah, they have never admitted the pretention of the Persian Government. Had His Majesty's Government supported Messrs. Haji Ali Akbar in seeking a concession from the Persian Government, such action would have been tantamount to a recognition of Persian sovereignty over the island. It was

accordingly decided, while not supporting the British company, to inform it that His Majesty's Government would not oppose it, and to address a note to the Persian Government stating that if a concession were granted to any applicant not approved by His Majesty's Government the question of the territorial status of Sirri would forthwith be reopened. A note in this sense was presented to the Persian Government in December, as it was understood that the firm had put in their application for a concession. This proposal was carried out, and in March 1909 Mr. Brown of the Imperial Bank of Persia, was appointed their agent, and it is he who is now conducting the negotiations with the Persian Government for the Hormuz concession in the event of the Moin's rights being cancelled." F.O.416/111: Annual Confidential Report of British Legation in Tehran for the year 1909, pp. 21-30.

36. *See* discussion below. The Iranian ownership of the Tonbs and Abu Musa were already an established fact in as late as the mid-eighteenth century. The French Foreign Ministry's *Carte du Golphe Persique* (1764), the British *Map of the Empire of Persia* (D'Anville, 1770), and the British *Map of the Empire of Persia* (D'Anville, 1794), and 20 other official and semi-official British maps of the nineteenth and twentieth centuries, which this author has identified, showed these islands as belonging to Iran.

37. *See* discussion below.

38. According to Hawley, *The Trucial States,* p. 114: "To prevent any misunderstanding on the part of the Persian government of the object of the British expedition—particularly operations against the Sheikhs of Lingeh and Charak—a special emissary, Dr Dukes, was despatched in advance with reassuring letters from the governor of Bombay for the governor-general of Fars and the Persian governor of Bushire. Another letter was sent to the British charge d'affaires in Tehran, to enable him to inform the Shah. The Shah, however, was not appeased and the Prince of Shiraz wrote to Keir requesting him to refrain from interference at any of his ports, especially Lingeh. Keir therefore thought it inadvisable to land any troops on the Persian soil."

39. [I.O.] Bombay Selection XXIV.

40. Vadiei, K., *Joghrafiya-ye Ensani-e Iran* (*Human Geography of Iran*) (Tehran: Tehran University Press, 1974), pp. 192-193.

41. Lorimer, *Gazetteer of the Persian Gulf,* Vol. I, pp. 737-739.

42. F.O. 371/13721 (1929), Arabia E982/52/91: Letter No. 160-N/28, F.S. to I. O., dated New Delhi, January 29, 1929, enclosure 3: Translated purport of a letter from the Residency Agent at Shargah to the Political Resident, No. 3, January 18, 1888 and enclosure thereto: Extract from translation of a letter from Sheikh Yusuf, Chief of Lingeh, to Sheikh Humaid-Bin-Abdullah, Chief of Rasel-Khyma, dated 1 Jamad 1301/29 March, 1884. *See,* Hassan H. Al-Alkim's presentation to the *Round Table Discussion on the Disputed Gulf Islands,* Arab Research Center, London, November 18, 1992, printed in the

proceedings of the Round Table by the Arab Research Center, London, January 1993, p. 35. (Hereinafter cited as "Round Table.")

43. Bavand, "Bar-rasi-e Mabani-e Tarikhi va Hoquqi-e Jazayer-e Irani-e Tonb va Abu Musa," p. 15.

44. F.O. 60/451: Persia and Arab States, Order in Council, Jurisdiction 1857 to 1882, Part II: Further correspondence respecting consular jurisdiction in Persia 1874-1876: Mr. Reilly's correspondence and memoranda, p.19.

45. Muhammad Morsy Abdullah, *The United Arab Emirates* (London: Croom Helm, 1978), pp. 234-235.

46. F.O. 60/733: Confidential from India Office to Foreign Office, dated 1st November, 1900, enclosure no. 2.

47. F.O. 60/733: From George Hamilton to the Governor-General of India in Council, secret no. 30, dated 23rd November 1900.

48. F.O. 416/10: Confidential Memorandum by Sir T. Sanderson, July 14, 1902.

49. F.O. 60/733: Most Secret: Persia, War Office Memorandum on Sir A. Hardinge's letter of October 14, 1902, by Alton A.Q.M.G.

50. F.O. 416/17: From Government of India to Brodrick, enclosure in no. 130, April 16, 1904, no. 154, p. 191.

51. F.O. 416/17: From Horace Walpole [I.O.] to Foreign Office, dated April 16, 1904, no. 154, p. 191.

52. Curzon, George N., *Persia and the Persian Question,* Vol. I (1892) (London: Frank Cass & Co., 1966), map enclosure.

53. F.0. 371/45507: Extract from the Confidential Document (17188) of H.B.M. Government, "Persian Frontiers," January 31, 1947, par. 72. Similarly, the British political resident in the Persian Gulf from 1958 to 1961, Donald Hawley, sought title for the Sheikh of Sharjah over Abu Musa in historical ambiguity: "Abu Musa. This island is in the effective control of ruler of Sharjah, and has been occupied by the Qawasim for several generations . . . ." Hawley, *The Trucial States,* p. 287.

54. Iran's Ministry of Customs and Posts wrote on 24 Rabi al-Avval 1322 to Prime Minister Ain al-Dawleh informing him that M. Damberian, director of southern customs, had reported in early June 1904 that the Sheikh of Sharjah claimed ownership of the Tonbs and Abu Musa and had hoisted his flag in those islands. From the Ministry of Customs and Posts to the prime minister, dated 24 Rabi al-Avval, reprinted in *A Selection of Persian Gulf Documents* (Tehran: Ministry of Foreign Affairs of the Islamic Republic of Iran's Institute of Political and International Studies, 1989) (Publication no. 91), Document no. 169, p. 265. (Hereinafter cited as "Persian Gulf Documents.") He lowered that flag and ordered the Iranian flag to be hoisted on those islands. He also commissioned two Iranian *tofangchi* (riflemen) at Great Tonb and

Abu Musa. F.O. 416/17: Government of India to Brodrick, dated April 13, 1904, enclosure no. 130, p. 142. The British resident in the Persian Gulf dispatched the Royal India Marine Steamer *Lawrence* to visit Great Tonb. Ibid. Having confirmed the news of the action by M. Damberian, the resident suggested to the British India officials that the Iranian flag should be hauled down in those islands by use of gunboats and replaced by the flag of Sharjah. He saw in such an action a double blessing as not only would such an action teach the Iranians whom they were dealing with, but also "[t]his unwarranted infringement by Persia of rights of a chief under British protection may prove useful, should the removal of flag-staff—which stood on Plinth of old Henjam telegraph-station—give rise to a remonstrance on the part of the Persian Government." Ibid.

55. F.O. 416/17: Sir A. Hardinge (Tehran) to the Marquess of Lansdowne, telegram no. 49, dated April 20, 1904, enclosure no. 165, p. 197.

56. F.O. 416/18: A. Hardinge to Foreign Office, telegram, dated May 1904, p. 160. "I accordingly called to-day at the [Iranian] Foreign Office to be informed of His Majesty's decision. M. Naus was present at our interview, and showed me a telegram which he was just sending to Bushire informing M. Damberian that the question of sovereignty over Tamb and Abu Musa was a disputed one, and ordering him with the least possible delay to remove the Persian flag from those islands."

57. F.O. 416/111: Annual Confidential Report of British Legation in Tehran for the year 1909, p. 21.

58. F.O. 371/506 Persia E 34/42315: From India Office to Foreign Office, dated 2 December 1908; to Viscount Morely of India Office, dated 24 November 1908; in reply to the inquiry of India Office of 20 October 1908, enclose to no. 1: G.I.

59. From First Agency of the Ports of the Persian Gulf and Coasts of Baluchistan to the Ministry of Foreign Affairs, no.64, dated 14 Shavval 1328 (1910), reprinted in *A Selection of Persian Gulf Documents,* Document No. 64, p. 280.

60. F.O. 60/733: From the British Minister in Tehran to the Marquess of Lansdowne, no. III, dated June 20, 1904, p. 2.

61. F.O. 60/734: From Sir. A. Hardinge to Mushire ed-Doleh, Iranian Foreign Minister, dated July 2, 1904.

62. F.O. 60/734: From Sir. A. Hardinge (Gulhak) to the Marquess of Lansdowne, no. 123, dated July 2, 1904.

63. F.O. 416/18: From the India Office to Foreign Office, May 4, 1904, no. 61, p. 92.

64. From the Shah to the Prime Minister, dated 1323 (1905), reprinted in *Persian Gulf Documents,* doc. no. 89, p. 278.

65. From the Customs Office of Ministry of Finance to the Ministry of Foreign Affairs, no. 11469, dated Mordad 5, 1306.

66. F.O. 416/113: Annual Confidential Report of British Legation in Tehran for the year 1928, par. 17, p. 23 of 49.

67. Ibid., p. 24.

68. Ibid., pars. 150-154.

69. F.O. 416/113: Annual Confidential Report of British Legation in Tehran for the year 1929, par. 156, p.23 of 91.

70. Confidential dispatch from the Ministry of War to the Ministry of Foreign Affairs, dated 5 Esfand 1308, enclosure, reprinted in *Persian Gulf Documents*, p. 351.

71. The protest note read in part: "Here I would like to inform your excellency that according to information received here the British flag has been hoisted in the islands of Tunb and Abu Musa. The Government of Iran considers these islands as belonging to them and find themselves with no alternative but to protest against this action. As far as the Ministry of Foreign Affairs is informed, the Government of His Britannic Majesty had no claim to the ownership of these islands and hoisting of the flag, which is the manifestation of claim of ownership, has no precedence, your excellency is expected to act for the restoration of the status quo." Confidential despatch from the Ministry of War to the Ministry of Foreign Affairs, dated 5 Esfand 1308 (24 February 1930), enclosure, reprinted in *Persian Gulf Documents*, p. 355.

72. "For the information of your excellency I would like to state regarding the islands of Tunb and Abu Musa which, the Government of Iran consider them to belong to them, the action of the Customs agents in these islands were to enforce [this sovereignty]. The outcome of the negotiations of a few days ago between myself and your excellency was reported to His Imperial Majesty and Royal instructions were given that for the time being the Customs agents should halt their actions there and no flag should be hoisted by either party until arrangements are made in respect of them." Confidential despatch from the Ministry of War to the Ministry of Foreign Affairs, dated 5 Esfand 1308, enclosure: Mosheer al-Dawleh to Sir A. Hardinge, dated 26 Rabi al-Avval 1322, reprinted in *Persian Gulf Documents*, p. 357.

73. F.O. 371/157031: Foreign Office Confidential Report (1961).

74. *See* F.O. 371/13776: Persia E/284/19/34: Sir Robert Clive to A. Chamberlain, no. 10., dated 16 February 1929.

75. F.O. 371/16070: Despatch from R.H. Hoare (Gholhak) to Sir Lancelot Oliphant (F.O.), dated 15 July 1932.

76. Reporting on his talks with Teymourtache, Sir Robert Clive, wrote: "Then we talked about the islands of Tunb and Abu Musa and I asked the Court Minister what benefit did the government of Iran deem to have in taking these islands other than claiming that smugglers in the Persian Gulf are using them as their base for storing goods and smuggling them into Iran. Teimurtache answered that the government of Iran did not see this matter in the same way we do, but

their main point is that these islands are the indivisible parts of Iran and were occupied by others by force. I answered Teimurtache in accordance with the guideline that you had sent me. The Court Minister said in that case there is no other way but to refer the matter to an international arbitration. Replying to His Excellency I expressed hopes that the two sides could settle the differences without having to refer the case to international arbitration." Sir Robert Clive to Sir A. Chamberlain, dated January 8, 1929, reprinted in Javad Sheikh al-Eslami, *Qatl-e Atabak* (Tehran: Kayhan Publications, 1988), p. 213 (Collection of British Political Documents, no. 420).

77. Minister of Imperial Court (Teymourtache) to Ministry of Foreign Affairs, dated 29 Khordad 1310, reprinted in *Persian Gulf Documents,* Document no. 113, p. 269.

78. Report no. 182 from Headman of Henjam Island, cited in Ministry of Foreign Affairs to War Ministry, dated 26 Khordad 1310, reprinted in *Persian Gulf Documents,* p. 363.

79. F.O. 371/157031: Foreign Office Confidential Report (1961): "Tunb and Bu Musa were precisely the same footing as Sirri Island that when HMS Ormonde visited the Gulf for surveying purposes Her Majesty's government—requested the Iranian government to notify their officials on Sirri Island that the vessel would also pay a visit there. A sentence was added to that communication that this did not imply a recognition of Iran's *de Jure* title to the island. It was thought that the Iranians might refer the case to the Council of the League of Nations but they did not."

80. F.O. 371/157031: Foreign Office Confidential Report (1961). Reporting these events to London, the British minister in Tehran wrote: "Some mysterious happening took place at Tamb in the early part of the year following on the action of the Sheikh of Ras al-Khaimah at the end of 1934 in having his flag-staff removed. There being grounds for suspicion that the Sheikh had been intriguing with the Iranians, the senior naval officer landed a small guard and, though this was later withdrawn, for some weeks a sloop visited the island at frequent intervals." F.O. 371/18980 Persia E1147/1147/34: Knatchbull-Hugessen (Tehran) to Eden, Confidential Annual Report, 1935, dated January 28, 1935. *See also* the same to Foreign Office, dated 9 April 1935.

81. *See* for example, the statement made by Richard Schofield and Hassan al-Alkim at the *Round Table.* (*See* note 42.)

82. Ministry of Finance to Ministry of Foreign Affairs, dated 18 Esfand 1315, reprinted in *Persian Gulf Documents,* p. 379.

83. F.O. 371/157031: Confidential Report on Visit of H.M.S. the *Loch Insh* to Tunb Island on August 24, 1961, by Captain R.M. Owen, p. 1.

84. Ibid.

85. Ibid.

86. Ibid., p. 2.

87. F.O. 371/157031: British Embassy, Tehran, to the Foreign Office, no. BT 1083/10-1084/61, dated November 20, 1961.

88. F.O. 371/157031: From Foreign Office to British Political Resident, Bahrain, no. 227 saving, dated August 24, 1961.

89. F.O. 371/157031: Political Resident in the Persian Gulf, Bahrain, to Foreign Office, no. 1085/1, dated August 25, 1961.

90. F.O. 371/157031: British Embassy, Tehran, to Iranian Foreign Ministry, Note no. 487-1084/61, dated September 5, 1961.

91. The Iranian reply read in part: "As the Embassy are aware, the Imperial Iranian government have never accepted the claim that the island of Tunb is a part of the Sheikhdom of Ras Al Khaimeh or that any other state has a right over it. As has been officially declared to the Embassy on many occasions the Imperial Government of Iran consider the island of Tunb to be part of their own territory over which they have sovereignty. The Imperial Government's sovereignty over the island of Tunb is based on the rules and principles of International Law, and they have never given up their right to it. In the above circumstances the Imperial Ministry of Foreign Affairs do not consider the Embassy's protest as contained in the note under reference to be justified." F.O. 371/157031: Foreign Ministry (Sixth Political Department) to British Embassy (Tehran), Note 3052, dated September 21, 1961.

92. F.O. 371/150731: Foreign Office (SW1) to G.E. Millard, Tehran, no. BT 1083/7, dated November 2, 1961.

93. F.O. 371/163032: Confidential from G.E. Millard, British Embassy, Tehran, to E.F. Geven (F.O.) Arabian Department, dated January 23, 1962.

94. F.O. 371/163032: Foreign Ministry (First Political Department) to H.M. Embassy in Tehran, no. 5724, dated January 20, 1962.

95. "Persia Seeks New Links," in *The Scotsman,* 7 September 1962.

96. Alikhani, Alinaghi, ed., *The Shah and I: Confidential Diary of the Royal Court of Iran by Amir Assadollah Alam* (London: I.B. Tauris, 1991).

97. Denis Wright, "Ten Years in Iran: Some Highlights," in *Asian Affairs* XXII (III) October 1991, p. 269.

98. According to one source, "[b]ecause the chemicals [sic] during that meeting were right, with the Shah in good mood, King Faisal gave him two billion barrels of oil reserves in the disputed [continental shelf] area. In return, the Shah gave up his claim to Bahrain. . . . " Pierre Shammas, "Border Disputes in the Greater Middle East," a paper presented to the Royal Institute of International Affairs, Chatham House, on February 17, 1993, p. 1.

99. *Al-Ahram* (Cairo), November 10, 1968.

100. Interview with Amir Khosro Afshar by the author in London on Wednesday, January 2, 1991. Afshar had been the Iranian chief negotiator with regard to Bahrain, the Tonbs, and Abu Musa. He also represented Iran at the United Nations Security Council meeting in December 1971, which was convened to consider the restoration of the Tonbs and Abu Musa to Iran. Having also served as the Iranian Ambassador to Britain, in 1975, he served as the chief negotiator with regard to the resolution of the Shatt al-Arab dispute between Iran and Iraq, culminating in his appointment as Minister of Foreign Affairs in 1978. (Hereinafter cited as "Afshar Interview (1991).")

101. Alikhani, *The Shah and I,* p. 45.

102. Ibid., p. 58.

103. Alikhani, Alinaghi, ed., *Confidential Diary of Alam,* Vol. I: 1347-1348 (Persian edition, 1969-1970) (1992), p. 130.

104. Interview with Mohammad Reza Shah by the Associated Press, reported in *Kayhan* (Tehran): no. 8278, February 20, 1971.

105. Interview with Mohammad Reza Shah by *Blitz* (New Delhi) reported in *Kayhan* (Tehran): no. 8381, June 25, 1971.

106. "Amir Abbas Hoveida in Bandar Abbas," *Ettelaat* (Tehran), June 27, 1971.

107. Interview with Amir Khosro Afshar by the author in London, April 10, 1994.

108. Mr. Afshar states that he met Sheikh Saqar of Ras al-Khaimah and his heir apparent separately in London to discuss the issue of the Tonbs. According to Mr. Afshar, after the Iranian repossession of the Tonbs, the Saudis intervened, asking him to meet Sheikh Saqr and to see to his financial needs, in connection with which he comments: "I met Sheikh Saqar in the Iranian Embassy in London and told him that we were prepared to extend financial assistance to Ras al-Khaimah provided that he officially renounced his opposition to the reassertion of Iranian sovereignty on the two Tonbs. He said he saw no sense in not doing so, but such an official declaration would put his life in jeopardy with the fanatics." Ibid. The Sheikh may have been alluding to the fate of the Sheikh of Sharjah who was slain by a nephew shortly after the arrival of the Iranian troops on Abu Musa.

109. According to the Iranian negotiator: "I met and discussed our intention of repossessing the three islands once with King Faisal, and three times in London with Prince Fahad [later King Fahad] in London. I had also discussed the matter with Mahmud Riyadh, the Egyptian foreign minister, during a meeting at the United Nations. Several times, I discussed the matter with Sheikh Zayed of Abu Dhabi who was to become the President of the emerging UAE. My last talks on the subject with him took place at the Iranian Embassy in London in the summer of 1971. Sheikh Zayed's suggestions included prosecution of this Iranian intention after the formation of the UAE was officially announced. I explained that Iran wanted cooperation with the emerging UAE and other neighbors in the Persian Gulf in the wake of Brit-

ish withdrawal from the region. This issue constituted longstanding disputes between Iran and the British and had to be settled with them before they left the region. Should we allow this matter to remain unsettled after the departure of the British, the UAE inheritance of the dispute will prevent regional cooperation. He had nothing to say to this argument. Moreover, six hours before landing troops on the three islands, on the instruction of the Shah, I informed King Faisal, through Saudi ambassador in Tehran, of our imminent move to repossess the three islands." Ibid.

110. See Appendix 1 for text of Memorandum and ancillary arrangements. *See also*, Mojtahed-Zadeh, Pirouz, *Political Geography of the Strait of Hormuz* (Joint Geography Department & Middle East Center Publication of the School of Oriental and Asian Studies) (London: London University, 1990), p. 12.

111. *Al-Ahram* (Cairo), December 8, 1971.

112. *Ettelaat* (Tehran), November 30, 1971; *Kayhan* (Tehran) November 30, 1971.

113. *UN Monthly Chronicle* IX(1)(January 1972): Record of the Month of December 1971, p. 46.

114. Ibid.

115. Ibid.

116. Ibid., p. 50.

117. Ibid., p. 47. A similar statement was made by the UAE Foreign Minister at the United Nations General Assembly on September 30, 1992, alleging that the Tonbs and Abu Musa belonged to the emirates "since the beginning of history." *Kayhan* (London), Thursday, October 8, 1992, quoting international news agencies. Such pronouncements are not based on any fact in evidence and they are all the more suspect when one considers that the tribal entity of Sharjah did not come into being until 1864, Ras al-Khaimah until 1921, and the United Arab Emirates until 1971.

118. *UN Monthly Chronicle*, January 1972, p. 48.

119. Mr. Afshar remarked in part: "The area concerned is the Persian Gulf, not the Arabian Gulf, a term used by certain states to distort historical reality and to give the area an Arab character. The riparian states of the Persian Gulf should work together without outside interference. Iran has no territorial ambition. . . . trying to settle disputes peacefully, as shown by its actions in the case of Bahrain, for which she had been praised here. . . . Iraq had created a tense situation in the area in 1961 by its hostile acts against Kuwait, and had carried on a provocative campaign. . . . Iraq had laid claim to Kuwait and had brought the matter to the United Nations. In this case, too, Iraq is taking up the Council's time for baseless claims. . . . The islands (in question) are Iranian territory. Iran's title to them are long-standing, and they are shown in maps hundreds of years old as Iranian. The islands are part of a group forming a virtual archipelago that have always been Iranian. One of the islands is only 17 miles offshore; another is 22 miles offshore. The

nearest Arab land is much further and Libyan Arab Republic, for instance, is thousands of miles away. . . . I mentioned the Libyan Arab Republic because it is reported to have threatened to send troops to the area. Iraq has also said it might send troops. . . . Iran would not allow its sovereignty, or a single inch of its territory, to be violated. Ibid. Elsewhere in his remarks, the Iranian representative stated: "For more than a century, beginning in 1870 British maps marked the Tunb islands as being Persian. In addition, a highly authoritative encyclopedia published as recently as 1967 to cover the events of the last fifty years, by another major power, identified the Tunbs as Iranian territory. It is important to remember that both, the British map and encyclopedia, were published at the time of British control over the islands. The maps show the islands having the same colour as the mainland and in addition they are expressly marked as being Iranian. This was particularly true of the maps published by the Soviet Union and some other countries who had not only used the Iranian colours but also mentioned the Iranian names of the islands." *Iran Almanac* (Tehran, 1972), p. 265.

120. *Foreign Broadcast Information Service,* FBIS-NES-92-076, 20 April 1992.

121. *See,* for example, Schofield, R.N., ed., *Territorial Foundation of the Gulf States* (London: UCL Press, 1994), at pp. 71-72.

122. Ibid.

123. *Echo of Iran* (London): XXXX (5), May 13, 1992, p. 9., quoting the daily *Abrar* (Tehran), May 13, 1992.

124. *Echo of Iran* (London): XXXX (5), May 13, 1992, p. 9.

125. BBC Radio, *Persian Service News Bulletin,* Tuesday, 25 August 1992.

126. *Times* (London), September 22, 1992, p. 11.

127. Ibid.

128. *Echo of Iran* (London): XXXX (8-9, 55-56) (August/September, 1992), p. 3.

129. Ibid. p. 4: "Observers believe Iranian guards and agents were watching the comings and goings of foreigners in the island for some time. Reports from military sources in Tehran say that without the permission of the Iranian government, the United Arab Emirates was building new establishments in the non-military part of the island. It seems that with the agreement of certain Arab countries, a number of non-native Arabs are to become residents on the island. . . . Iran's worst fears were realized when the [Gulf Cooperation Council] foreign ministers at the end of their Jeddah meeting declared that they will support the UAE in regaining sovereignty over the three islands belonging to Iran (September 10, 1992)."

130. Ibid.

131. Hassan al-Alkim's remarks at the *Round Table,* p. 32. (*See* note 42.)

132. *Press Release,* Embassy of the United Arab Emirates, London, October, 1992.

133. *Iran Focus,* November, 1992.

134. *BBC Summary of World Broadcasts*: The Middle East ME/1573/A/7, 29 December 1992. (*See also,* note 42.)

135. *Middle East Economic Survey* (London), 11 January 1993, C3.

136. Dabiri, Mohammad Reza, "Abu Musa Island; A Binding Understanding or Misunderstanding," in *Iranian Journal of International Affairs* V(3/4) (Fall/ Winter, 1993/94), p. 581: "According to law, any contract or agreement signed under duress by either party is invalid and considered null and void. . . . [A]t times the Emirates government has considered this agreement imposed upon and signed under duress; yet at the same time it has called on Iranian government to execute precisely parts of the document."

137. The United Arab Emirates extended its territorial sea limit to 12 miles in 1993.

3

The Legal Basis of Iran's Sovereignty over Abu Musa Island

Davoud H. Bavand

This chapter examines the legal basis of Iran's sovereignty over Abu Musa Island.[1] Traditionally, the status of this island is discussed and analyzed in conjunction with the other Iranian islands of Great Tonb, Little Tonb, and, to a lesser extent, Sirri.[2] For reasons of focus and space, however, this chapter will concentrate primarily on Abu Musa. The term *Anglo-Sharjah* herein used refers to positions taken and activities undertaken or encouraged by Great Britain or done on behalf of the Sheikh of Sharjah with respect to Abu Musa in the period from 1903 through 1971. The term connotes no legally significant fact regarding the status of Sharjah, which until the end of November 1971 was a British protectorate with no independent international legal personality of its own. Therefore, the actions taken by Great Britain in regard to Abu Musa in the name of the Sheikh of Sharjah were acts attributable to Great Britain proper, and, similarly, acts undertaken by the Sheikh of Sharjah with respect to the island, regardless of encouragement by Great Britain, must be imputed legally to Great Britain as well.

Organizationally, this chapter is divided into five parts. Part one will discuss the basis and the evidence in support of Iran's historical title to Abu

Musa beginning in 1903. In part two, the discussion will examine the illegal Anglo-Sharjah usurpation of Abu Musa from Iran in 1903-1904. The breach of the 1904 Anglo-Iranian status quo agreement whereby Great Britain fraudulently induced Iran to remove her flag from Abu Musa will be discussed in part three. The various aspects of the Anglo-Sharjah presence and activities on Abu Musa and their insufficiency to defeat Iran's sovereignty is treated in part four. Part five will conclude this chapter by examining the background to the settlement of the dispute by virtue of the 1971 Anglo-Iranian Memorandum of Understanding, which, while it ended the controversy, in its terms and conditions granted to Sharjah a limited consensual basis for exercise of limited jurisdiction on Abu Musa, within specified quarters and relative to specified matters.

HISTORICAL TITLE

In the Iranian consciousness, Abu Musa Island has belonged to Iran by virtue of her longstanding and substantial historical title to it.[3] Understandably, a country as ancient as Iran whose core territorial character was formed more than two thousand five hundred years ago cannot be expected to produce a certificate of title, bill of sale, or a grant document for every inch of its present-day territory. By the same token, one can hardly expect that a territorial sovereign be made to account for a part of its territory by means of producing documentation to show uninterrupted and continuous chain of custody or title. Yet there can be no doubt that Qom, Tehran, or Shiraz forms as much a part of Iran, for example, as Delhi forms a part of India or Beijing a part of China. Such an appurtenance is based on the historical situation of an area within a territorial sovereignty at the exclusion or absence of any other territorial sovereign and the recognition of this inclusion by others. While the first condition is determined by the historical facts in evidence, the second condition is a matter of law. Together, the aforementioned considerations form the foundation of proof of sovereignty based on historical title.

Abu Musa: A Part of Iranian Territory

The first step in this inquiry is therefore to ascertain the extent to which Abu Musa may have been included in the territorial limits of Iran. A more rigorous research notwithstanding, there appears to be no explicit mention in the pre-eighteenth-century annals of the Persian Gulf about the appurtenance of Abu Musa to a particular territorial sovereignty. A barren island devoid of potable water and far flung from the major shipping lanes, it hardly would have merited any early description by local historians and geographers[4] or, later, by European surveyors.[5]

The absence of an explicit mention however cannot be tantamount to the denial of its existence. Much like in the hard sciences, in which the existence of a phenomenon or element is proved without direct reliance on the human sensory faculties, in this endeavor, too, recourse to the other methods of detection is necessary to determine the territorial status of Abu Musa in the period prior to 1788, when the first-ever explicit reference to the island's territorial status surfaces—placing it squarely within Iran's territorial sovereignty.

The examination of the political circumstance of the Persian Gulf in successive historical periods leads to the conclusion that the island, barring the production of evidence to the contrary, would have been in all likelihood a part of Iranian territory. This conclusion is based upon two interrelated considerations: (i) the territorial extent of the Iranian state in the Persian Gulf which, for the most part, also included coastal sites on the Arabian Peninsula bordering the Persian Gulf and the Sea of Oman, and (ii) the Iranian political, commercial, and military domination in the Persian Gulf.[6]

According to the Arab encyclopedist Yakut al-Rumi's thirteenth-century description of Kish Island, itself a dependency of Iran, "the Island of Qays . . . is the residence of the ruler of this Sea, to whom also belongs Oman and one-third of the revenues of Bahrain. . . . His features are Persian and he dresses similarly to the Dylam. Diving for pearls is carried out here and on the *neighboring islands,* which are many in number, and *all these* belong to the ruler of Qays"(emphasis added).[7] The presumed geographical situation of Abu Musa—it being in the middle of the waters bound by Kish and Oman—argues rather persuasively in favor of inclusion of the island among those under the authority of Kish.[8]

A similar conclusion may be drawn from the territorial and political situation in the Persian Gulf at the time of the arrival of the Portuguese to the area in 1507. At the time, the principality of Hormuz, itself a dependency of Iran, included the territories of Old Hormuz (near Minab) and Moghestan on the Iranian coast, Qalhat, Quryat, Mascat, Sohar, and Khor Fakkan on the northeastern seaboard of Oman, and the islands of Hormuz, Larak, Qishm, Kish, Shuaib, Hendorabi, and Bahrain.[9] A decade later, a more detailed roster compiled by a Portuguese navigator identified the Hormuzi territories as including (i) the tract from Lingeh to Minab on the Iranian coast, (ii) the coast from Julfar (modern Ras al-Khaimah) to Kassab in the lower eastern Persian Gulf, and (iii) the islands in the Persian Gulf, including the Tonbs.[10] Even though Abu Musa is not mentioned explicitly, the presumed geographical situation of Abu Musa—it being in the waters surrounded by Lingeh, Qishm, Tonbs, Farurs, Ras al-Khaimah, and Kassab—

argues rather persuasively in favor of inclusion of the island in the roster of Hormuzi territories.[11]

Beginning in 1601, the Iranian government of the Shah Abbas Safavi mounted a military challenge against the Portuguese colonial power in the Persian Gulf. In a struggle that lasted two decades, the Iranian government reestablished its authority on Bahrain and on the Iranian coast opposite Hormuz Island. Further, the Iranian forces recaptured Ras al-Khaimah on the opposite coast and, finally, with the assistance of the British East India Company, in 1622, the Iranians expelled the Portuguese and restored Iranian sovereignty over Qishm and Hormuz Islands.[12] This and other reversals experienced by the Portuguese resulted in the 1625 treaty of peace between the Shah of Iran and the Portuguese, whereby the Portuguese "restored to him all his coastal possessions, retaining only the pearl banks of Bahrain, and a moiety of the customs of Kong."[13] Considering the reestablishment of Iranian sovereignty over territories previously administered by Hormuzi rulers, it must be concluded that Iran therefore regained also her sovereignty over Abu Musa. Furthermore, the presence of Iranian sovereignty at Bahrain, Lingeh, Qishm and Ras al-Khaimah by 1622 makes it all the more likely that the island located amid this strategic configuration also passed under Iranian sovereignty. A similar conclusion may be reached with respect to the status of Abu Musa in the post-Safavid period from 1737 through 1747, when in the reign of the Shah Nadir Afshar (1737-1747) the Iranian mastery of the Persian Gulf was reinstated in full, inclusive of Ras al-Khaimah on the opposite shore.[14]

In the period from 1747 to 1788, the dominant local authority in the northeastern sector of the Persian Gulf first was Mulla Ali Shah, the former admiral of the Iranian fleet in the Persian Gulf, the governor of Bandar Abbas and administrator of Julfar. In 1754-1755 he took possession of Hormuz and Qishm Islands. Among his allies at the time was counted Rashid ibn Mattar, the sheikh of the Qasimi family holding sway over Ras al-Khaimah. Politically, the relationship between the two was one of servitude by the Qawasim to the Persian governor of Bandar Abbas, who had them in his pay and subsidy.

Succeeding Mulla Ali Shah as the prominent local authority in the eastern Persian Gulf was Sheikh Muhammad Khan Bastaki, on whom the Iranian government conferred in 1763 the governorship of the Iranian coast and islands. Subject to the governor-general of Fars, this latter's domain included the Jahangireh District in south Persia, which included the tract from Gavbandi to Bandar Abbas, including Lingeh. Soon after his investiture, the sheikh proceeded to pacify the several tribal factions warring on the Iranian coast and elsewhere in the eastern Persian Gulf.[15] From this time until the end of the nineteenth century, the port of Lingeh and its corresponding coastal archipelagic islands, namely, the Farurs, Tonbs, Sirri, and Abu Musa continued to be ruled by the governors of Lingeh, itself a port of the Province of Fars.

Next, Muhammad Khan Bastaki was succeeded by his son, Hadi Khan Bastaki, who governed the Iranian coast from 1787 to 1803. On the occasion of a visit to Lingeh in 1788-1789, he is known to have resolved the dispute that had arisen among the Qawasim and Maraziq of Lingeh over pasturage on the (Great) Farur, Sirri, and Abu Musa Islands.[16] Later, he delegated the local administration of Lingeh to a Qasimi Sheikh.[17]

This earliest of notices regarding the connection among Lingeh and the nearby Farurs, Abu Musa, and Sirri Islands signifies more than the territorial link of the islands to Lingeh or the extent of the Jahangireh District in general. The notice reveals also the extent to which these islands, in addition to the Tonbs, together have formed an archipelagic entity within the geopolitical and economic gravitational field of the Iranian mainland, particularly the port of Lingeh.

The beginning of the nineteenth century marked the rise in piratical activities of the maritime tribes of the lower Persian Gulf, notably the Qawasim of Ras al-Khaimah. The acts of depredation committed by these tribes against English shipping in particular resulted in Great Britain mounting several expeditions which ultimately ended in the submission of the tribes in the lower Persian Gulf to British rule. The history of British suppression of piracy in the Persian Gulf (1800-1820), maintenance of maritime peace (1823-1834) and the emergence of the *Trucial* system (1835-1853), consisting of the *pacificated* sheikhs from Ras al-Khaimah to Bahrain is detailed elsewhere.[18] However, three aspects of the situation deserve mention here, as each is legally significant with regard to the status of Abu Musa. First, the British realized that the Qawasim inhabiting the Iranian coast had been historically a political entity separate from the Qasimi Sheikhs residing in the lower Persian Gulf.[19] Second, the British learned also that the tribes dwelling on the Iranian coast, including the ethnic Qawasim inhabiting Lingeh, were distinguishable from the tribes in the lower Persian Gulf in that they hardly participated in acts of depredation, plunder, or piracy.[20] Third, the British realized that only the institution of a restrictive line could curtail the acts of piracy committed by the tribes of the lower Persian Gulf, whereby the Qawasim of the lower Persian Gulf were prevented access to points beyond their immediate coastal waters.[21]

The distinct political character of the Qawasim of Lingeh is legally significant in that it provides the basis for the refutation of an Anglo-Sharjah claim to Abu Musa in 1903 based on a theory that assumed (i) the Qawasim

tribe to be a monolithic whole; (ii) Abu Musa to be a common tribal property[22]; and (iii) the Qawasim of Lingeh who were in charge of the island to
be lieutenants for the Qawasim of the lower Gulf.[23] It must be noted here
that the British government prior to 1903 already had a history of concocting
elaborate theories designed to contradict and undermine Iran's sovereignty over
islands in the Persian Gulf in favor of entities whom they could control.[24]

The self-serving assumptions and then interpretation attached by the
British government to the facts in evidence about the status of the Qawasim
of Lingeh were both intellectually dishonest and theoretically flawed. As
Sir E. Beckett, the legal expert at the foreign office (1932) and a future
member of the International Court of Justice, explained: "My conclusion is
that unless further evidence is forthcoming indicating that it can be proved
that during the period 1880-1887 the [Qasimi] Sheikh at Lingeh ruled the
islands under some title different from that under which he ruled the mainland (Lingeh) (I doubt if it will be easy to show this), the Persians did possess sovereignty over Tamb and Abu Musa during these years."[25] Similarly,
the issue was not lost to the head of the Eastern department at the foreign
office (1934): "It seems to me that the fact that the islands were administered for some time by the Jowasimi Sheikhs, who were not only resident in
Persia, but were Persian subjects and officials, might easily prove very damaging. It is quite true that these Sheikhs administered these particular islands not in their capacity of Persian officials, but in their capacity of
representatives of the Trucial rulers to whom the islands belonged. But this
might easily be represented as a matter of subtle distinction, and the circumstance that the islands were, in actual fact, administered by Persian officials from the Persian mainland might well, it seems to me, be quoted
against us with rather an unfortunate effect."[26]

The other aforementioned significant product of the British involvement in the Persian Gulf in the early part of the nineteenth century was the
institution of the Restrictive Line, also known as the Hennell Line. While
the 1820 General Treaty with the Arab tribes of the lower Persian Gulf had
provided for the cessation of acts of piracy and plunder,[27] there were no
provisions for restricting legitimate warfare and hostilies among these tribes
whose conflicts invariably spilled onto the sea. The need for a maritime
peace regime became even more urgent in April 1835 when a squadron of
boats belonging to the Bani Yas, having a captured Iranian boat in tow,
engaged a British naval vessel off Great Tonb Island. In May 1835, the
acting British political resident in the Persian Gulf, Samuel Hennell, engi-
neered a maritime truce agreement among the various sheikhs of the lower
Persian Gulf and obtained their pledge to confine their hostilities at sea to
the south of a line drawn between the islands of Abu Musa and Sirri. Once

it was pointed out by the officers of the British Persian Gulf Squadron that Abu Musa and Sirri were notorious pirate lairs, the new resident, James Morison, modified the Hennell Line to run from Sham to a point ten miles south of Abu Musa Island and continuing on to Sir Abu Nuair Island.[28] Upon learning about the modification of the Hennell Line that now was to run to the south of Abu Musa, the Sheikh of Sharjah (and Ras al-Khaimah), Sultan ibn Saqar, protested that the line prevented him from sending his boats past the Musandam Peninsula into the Gulf of Oman to defend his possessions around Khor Fakkan. Morison rejected the protest.[29]

The legal significance of the Restrictive Line and its acceptance by Sheikh Sultan ibn Saqar vis-à-vis Abu Musa is threefold. First, that neither access to, nor the defense of, Abu Musa or the Tonbs seems to have been of concern to the sheikh argues persuasively that, in 1835-1836, none of these islands belonged to the Qawasim of the lower Persian Gulf or were part of the territories of Sharjah or Ras al-Khaimah. That Abu Musa and the Tonbs were excluded from the domains of the Qawasim or any other tribal or territorial entity based in the lower Persian Gulf is all the more evident from descriptions of the possessions of the Qawasim of the lower Persian Gulf. In 1844, the assistant resident, Arnold Burrowes Kemball, listed the "territories owned by the Sultan bin Suggar, Chief of the Jowasimee" in which roster the only island mentioned was Hamra.[30] Similarly, no island other than Hamra was mentioned in a later list compiled by the resident in 1854.[31]

The second legally significant aspect of the Hennell Line is that the British government did not deem it necessary, nor apparently thought of obtaining the sheikh's consent ahead of time before establishing a line which presumably could otherwise alienate a portion of his territory. This implies that the British government at the time did not deem any of these islands as belonging to the Qasimi Sheikh or as being a part of the territory ruled by him.

Third, arguably, the Hennell Line may be deemed also to mark Iran's southward limits in the Persian Gulf.[32] That Abu Musa was located on the northern side of the Hennell Line conformed with the understanding that the island was Iranian territory. While any description of the emirates in the lower Persian Gulf made no mention of Abu Musa (or any other island located to the north of the Hennell Line), the literature of the day indeed had identified the island as Iranian. For example, a 1786 survey of navigation in the Persian Gulf divided the islands and the ports of the Persian Gulf into five sections; the fourth section dealt with Iranian islands among which the survey listed the Tonbs and Abu Musa.[33] Similarly, in the writings of the political counsellor accompanying the embassy of John Malcolm on behalf of the British East India Company to the Persian Court in 1800, the Tonbs and Abu Musa were identified as Persian islands.[34]

British Recognition of Abu Musa as Iranian

The foregoing review of the historical evidence with respect to the territorial status of Abu Musa leads to the twin conclusion that (i) Abu Musa was Iranian territory and (ii) it did not belong to the Qawasim of the lower Persian Gulf nor to any territorial entity ruled by them in the Persian Gulf. The second part of this inquiry regarding the basis for Iran's historical title to Abu Musa will discuss the British recognition of the appurtenance of Abu Musa to Iran.

The evidence of the knowledge on the part of the British officialdom about the extent of Iran's sovereignty over the islands lying off the Iranian coast dates to as far back as when they were advised of the same in the period between 1800[35] and the 1820s.[36] The aforementioned 1786 survey of the Persian Gulf and the findings of the Malcolm mission in 1800 evidenced the unanimity of views shared by the Iranian and British governments regarding the status of Abu Musa and of the other islands off Lingeh. What is more, as the circumstance concerning the Hennell Line further demonstrates, neither the Qasimi nor any other sheikh in the lower Persian Gulf held a position contradicting the common Anglo-Iranian view.

In the early phase of maintaining the maritime peace in the Persian Gulf (1823-1834), in the years 1823-1825, Lieutenant George Barnes Brucks of the Bombay Marine completed a survey of the Arabian coast up to the Shatt al-Arab and in early 1826 he began a survey of the Iranian coast. As this latter task proved lengthier than expected, in 1828, Brucks crossed over to the Musandam promontory to begin the survey of the coast of Oman. The charting of the Iranian coast and the islands between Qishm and Cape Jask was finished in 1829.[37] The survey identified the Tonbs, Abu Musa [Bumausa], and Sirri [Surdy] as islands under the administration of the Province of Fars and the map accompanying it, which was also compiled by Brucks, depicted the Tonbs and Abu Musa in the same color as Iran.[38] The enduring accuracy of the survey, a remarkable achievement and a tribute to the skill of the surveyors,[39] was no doubt the result of Brucks's own extensive itinerary in the Persian Gulf and the participation of a number of officers of the Marine in the process. The survey contained very few mistakes or omissions, and those were almost all related to surveying techniques and calculation.[40] "In particular, the comprehensive information it yielded on the tribes, towns, and resources of the Arabian shore was of particular value to the Bombay authorities in their dealings with the maritime tribes in the next few years."[41] Similarly, in 1836, another British official in the Persian Gulf, Lieutenant-Colonel Robert Taylor, compiled a chart of the Persian Gulf, wherein he identified and underlined the Tonbs, Abu Musa [Bomosa], and Sirri [Surry] as "Persian islands."[42]

In the second half of the nineteenth century, Lingeh assumed a height-ened commercial and financial status. In 1854, the resident, Arnold Burrowes Kemball, reported that the Iranian coast from Bushehr to Bandar Abbas was under the sovereign jurisdiction of the Iranian state and the residents of the coast were loyal subjects of the Shah of Iran, making annual contribu-tions to the government treasury. Furthermore, Kemball reported that Lingeh, a port governed by the Qasimi Sheikh Khalif ibn Qadhib under the admin-istrative division and jurisdiction of the Province of Fars, was the more important of the ports on the Fars coast because of harborage and a promi-nent commercial position, which it had achieved in the past 15 years in part because of attracting wealthy merchants, particularly from Bahrain, and in part because of becoming a center of transit for the pearl trade as well as other commercial activities to and from the Persian Gulf area.[43]

Lingeh's commercial position continued into the next decade. Accord-ing to the first edition of *The Persian Gulf Pilot* (1864) published by the order of the Lord Commissioners of the British Admiralty, Lingeh was send-ing 50 boats to the pearl banks as well as being the best place in the Persian Gulf to get any iron-work made or repairs executed.[44] Further, according to the *Pilot,* the governor of Lingeh exercised jurisdiction over all the places on the coast between Birkeh Sifleh and Bostaneh and the islands of Sirri [Surry], Little Farur [Nabiya-Furar], Great Tonb [Tumb], Little Tonb [Nabiya-Tumb], and Abu Musa [Bumusa].[45]

Because of their association with the ports on the Iranian coast, the islands lying off Lingeh, too, came to play a role in the commercial life of the northern littoral of the Persian Gulf. For example, remarking that the geographical loca-tion of Bandar Abbas in a narrow inlet required an alternative but nearby facil-ity for ships to call on, in 1864, the resident, Lewis Pelly, reported on the suggestion by some that the commercial situation at Bandar Abbas could im-prove if an entrepot be established, either on the island of Hormuz, Henjam, Great Tonb, or Sirri, or in the inlet off Bassidu on Qishm Island.[46] While stating that Bassidu was under British flag for the time being, Pelly remarked that the selection of a site for the entrepot should be left in the first instance to the shipping companies who suffered the most immediate inconvenience.[47]

Even though Pelly's report did not mention Abu Musa Island, there were nevertheless two implicit admissions on the part of Pelly. First, the reference to Tonb in connection with the other four Iranian islands inti-mated that there existed a connection between them and the Iranian port of Bandar Abbas. Second, perhaps recalling the difficulty experienced by Brit-ain in obtaining the right to station troops on Bassidu, Pelly did not endorse the suggestion that the entrepot be established on any of the other islands for fear of protest by Iran. Indeed, if Tonb or, for that matter, Sirri had belonged to the Qasimi in the lower Persian Gulf, then the British would have had the freedom to use the island.

In 1864, the Sheikh of Sharjah, Sultan ibn Saqar, wrote to the resident, Lewis Pelly, complaining that the people from Dubai were apparently crossing over to Abu Musa, which the Sheikh now claimed to be his along with Great Tonb.[48] The letter did not disclose the nature of the sheikh's grievance. It would, however, appear that the difficulties may have been with regard to regulation of rights of pasture on the island, since various tribes of both the lower Persian Gulf and the Iranian coast were competing for pasturage in the nearby islands.[49] At the time, in light of the long-established view of the British government—including the residency which held the island to be Iranian territory—the resident ignored the sheikh's claim and no action was taken.

In the period between 1871 and 1879, the residency remained adamant as to the inadmissibility of the sheikh's claim over Abu Musa. In December 1871, the sheikh apparently stated to the residency agent in Sharjah that he intended to prevent anyone from using the island. In reporting this to the resident, the residency agent, Abd al-Rahman advised that the sheikh should not be allowed to carry through with the threat.[50] In 1875, an armed group from the Shihuh tribe (who incidentally were not subject to the maritime truce regime established earlier by Hennell and Morison) fired on boats from Dubai and Lingeh. In June 1875, the new resident, Edward C. Ross, asked the residency agent at Sharjah, Abd al-Rahman, about the ownership of Abu Musa. On December 17, 1875, Abd al-Rahman replied that the Qasimi chiefs claimed the island and therefore the Sheikhs of Sharjah and Ras al-Khaimah can place their men there.[51] Given the amount of self-interest that may have been involved in the statement of the residency agent stationed in Sharjah about a matter affecting the Sheikh of Sharjah, the resident asked Abd al-Rahman to await further comments from him.[52] Apparently, in 1879, the political resident asked another residency agent at Sharjah, Haji Abu al-Qasim, to draw up a list of the dependencies of the Trucial chiefs, in which regard the latter is claimed to have reported Abu Musa as belonging to Sharjah.[53] The indication of Iranian sovereignty over Abu Musa at the time is all the more persuasive when one considers also the failure of the British government to protest to the Iranian government—or the relevant provincial authorities on the Iranian coast, including the Lingeh government—about the alleged interferences by the people from the Iranian coasts and islands crossing over to Abu Musa.

In spite of the sheikh's claims to the contrary, in the period from 1870 to 1903, the British government, including the British India government and the various officials and agents of the British government in the Persian

Gulf, continued to view Abu Musa as an Iranian island. Published in 1870, *The Persian Gulf Pilot* (2nd edition) referred to the Tonbs, Sirri, and Abu Musa islands by name and identified them as belonging to the Iranian port of Lingeh in the Province of Fars.[54]

In February 1873, the Sheikh of Ras al-Khaimah complained to the resident about his subjects being unable to graze their herds on Great Tonb because of the Al Bu Samait tribesmen from Lingeh also crossing over to the island. The residency ordered the residency agents stationed on the Iranian and Arabian coasts to investigate the matter. In consequence of their finding that the island belonged to Lingeh, in March and April of 1873, under orders from the residency agent in Sharjah, the sheikh removed his horses from the island.[55] This, as well as the episode with the Sheikh of Sharjah in 1864 and 1875, in fact tested the accuracy of the information previously contained in the various aforementioned British maps and documents, including the *Pilot.* The British reaction to the episodes, including their inaction, validated or affirmed in effect the Iranian sovereignty over the Tonbs, Abu Musa, and Sirri Islands.

Challenged by events, the supposedly abstract information regarding the appurtenance of these islands to Iran was affirmed in reality and continued to be disclosed in British documentation regarding the Persian Gulf. For example, while referring to the Iranian port of Lingeh as a dependency of the Iranian province of Fars and under the administration of Ali ibn Khalifah, the residency's Persian Gulf Administrative Report for 1875-1876 identified the island dependencies of the Iranian port of Lingeh as Farur [Fareur], Little Farur [Nebi-Fareur], Great Tonb [Tunb], Little Tonb [Nebi-Tunb], Sirri, and Abu Musa.[56] In a map of the Persian Gulf published in 1876 under the auspices of the India government, the Tonbs and Abu Musa were depicted in the same color as the Iranian mainland.[57]

In 1880-1881, the British government opposed the attempts on the part of the Ottoman Empire to grant to a British subject the marine lighting concession for parts of the Red Sea and Persian Gulf, which the Ottoman Empire presumed as Ottoman territory on the theory that the rulers of the shores in question, such as the Trucial coast, were tributaries to the governor of Nejd in Arabia, who was, in turn, an Ottoman subject. The letter of concession included also Abu Musa Island. The English Chamber of Commerce apprised the Foreign Office of the matter and urged the latter to oppose the inclusion of the island as an Ottoman island on the theory that the island was not at all related to the Trucial coast. In consequence of a prolonged exchange of notes between Great Britain and the Ottoman Empire, the name of Abu Musa was removed from the concession letter.[58]

The events of 1887-1888 tested the probative value of the longstanding British documentation evidencing the Iranian ownership of the Tonbs, Abu Musa, and Sirri Islands. Not unexpectedly, the course of policy taken by Great Britain and Iran conformed with the facts already in evidence for centuries. Because of a series of administrative changes in the governorship of Iran's ports and islands in the Persian Gulf, including Lingeh, and also due to fear that the recent disputes between the governor of Lingeh and the Sheikhs of Sharjah and Ras al-Khaimah would produce an adverse consequence for Iranian sovereignty over the islands lying off Lingeh, in September 1887, the Iranian government terminated the Qasimi governorship of Lingeh, and an Iranian force from Qishm Island established a garrison on Sirri Island.[59]

In the early months of 1888, the Iranian agent in the Persian Gulf, Haji Ahmad Khan, reported to the Iranian prime minister on the state of Iranian territories in the Persian Gulf, among which he referred to the Tonbs, Abu Musa, and Sirri.[60] Having obtained surreptitiously a copy of the report, the resident, Edward C. Ross, communicated it to the British minister in Tehran.[61] This appears to be the first known instance whereby the British government was put on notice by a document originating with the Iranian government in which Abu Musa was referred to as Iranian. In connection with Great Britain's representations to Tehran regarding Iran's actions on Sirri, the Iranian government previously had turned over to the British authorities Iranian documentation supporting the appurtenance of Sirri and the Tonbs to Iran.[62]

Fearing Iran's intentions in the Persian Gulf, and concerned about the Sheikh of Sharjah's worries caused by the presence of an Iranian garrison on Sirri and the prospects of a future one on Great Tonb, the British government protested the Iranian action at Sirri; but by September 1888, the British government had accepted Iran's military presence on the Island and did not object to Iran's affirmative declaration that Sirri and the Tonbs were Iranian territory.[63]

In the course of the British protests in Tehran in July 1888, the British minister presented to the Shah of Iran a copy of the *Map of Persia,* which had been published recently by the intelligence branch of the British War Office in 1886. The map depicted the Tonbs, Abu Musa, and Sirri, as Iranian territory.[64] In reporting back to the foreign office on the course of the protest over Sirri, in September 1888, the British minister stated that the Shah had quoted the map "as a bar to any argument on our part in favour of the [Trucial Sheikhs]."[65] It goes without saying, by analogy, the same conclusion would have held true in the case of the depiction of Abu Musa as an Iranian island. The *Map of Persia* (1886), which had been presented to the

Shah in 1888, was reissued in 1891 without any change in its depiction of the Tonbs, Abu Musa, and Sirri as Iranian islands. Similarly, the islands were depicted as Iranian on the *Map of Persia* compiled under the supervision of Lord Curzon in 1892 and conformably on another *Map of Persia* published by the India government in 1897.[66]

Conclusion: Iran's Historical Title to Abu Musa

The historical origins of Iran's territorial sovereignty over Abu Musa are thus clear and unambiguous. While the Iranian government considered Abu Musa as Iranian on the basis of historical documentation, consciousness, and intuition, the British government recognized and accepted the same view by virtue of observation, survey, and deliberate consideration of the facts as they found them. Furthermore, as exemplified by the aforementioned case of the Ottoman concessionaire, the British government, when dealing with other parties, even acted on their belief that Abu Musa belonged to Iran. The British government also did not react adversely to the discovery that Abu Musa had been mentioned as an Iranian island in an Iranian government document (1888), which demonstrates that the discovery was in conformity with the established, longstanding, and uncontradicted view that Abu Musa was politically and territorially an Iranian island.

ILLEGALITY OF THE ANGLO-SHARJAH OCCUPATION

In view of the foregoing evidence, Abu Musa was therefore unmistakably a part of Iran. Map after map and document after document, particularly of British origin, said so. Yet in 1903, the British government encouraged the Sheikh of Sharjah to raise his flag on the island and later justified this action on the basis of the argument that the island had not been formally occupied by anyone and therefore could be occupied.[67]

The evolution of the British government's position from its recognition of Abu Musa as Iranian to disputing Iran's sovereignty to the island, within the short period from 1887 to 1903, was owed primarily to four interrelated aspects of the British position in the Persian Gulf area: (i) resurgence of Iranian political interest in the Persian Gulf; (ii) threat to the British position posed by the European powers, particularly Russia; (iii) reorganization of the Iranian customs administration, particularly in reference to Iran's coast and islands, and (iv) mollification of the desires of the Trucial sheikhs. These aspects are discussed elsewhere.[68] Suffice it to say, in the period from 1885 to 1888, there had been enough comings and goings by the various Iranian missions to the Trucial coast, on the one hand, and a continuous stream of visits by Russian, French, and German navies, on the other, that already by 1888 the British were prepared to conclude that Iran's renewed interest in the Persian Gulf and the garrisoning of Sirri Island in 1887 were being inspired by the Russians,[69] who were locked at the time in a fierce competition with Great Britain for exclusive influence in Iran.

The specter of Russia looming over Iran, the Persian Gulf, and eventually India must have revived interest in Lord Curzon's admonition (1892): "Every claim that can be advanced by Russia for the exclusive control of the Caspian Sea could be urged with tenfold greater force by Great Britain for a similar monopoly of the Persian Gulf."[70] While he fretted about Russia ever gaining a presence in the Persian Gulf,[71] in Curzon's view "no hostile political influence shall introduce its discordant features upon the scene."[72]

Curzon became the Viceroy of India in January 1899. In the midst of rumors that a Russian mission was proceeding to Bandar Abbas to examine the prospects of acquiring an island off the Iranian coast for the purposes of establishing a coaling depot,[73] by early 1900, the British government determined to set aside considerations of Iranian sovereignty in order to confront Russia. The British secretary of state for India instructed the viceroy to counter the hoisting of any Russian flag at Bandar Abbas with the raising of the British flag on the Iranian islands of Hormuz, Henjam, Qishm, or any other island in the neighborhood that the naval authorities considered as offering the best advantage for a naval base.[74] More dangerous to the British position in the Persian Gulf than the mere Russian presence at Bandar Abbas was the possibility of Russian establishments on the nearby Hormuz, Larak, Henjam, and Qishm Islands,[75] all dependencies of Bandar Abbas.[76]

In conjunction with the slowly emerging policy to stave off any Russian advance in the Persian Gulf, the British government instructed the naval authorities to survey the islands lying in the vicinity of the entrance to the Persian Gulf and contact their local chiefs, if there be any, so as to enter into relations with them. The British agents reported back that there were no independent local chiefs in any of these islands and that, with the exception of the tract at Bassidu on Qishm Island that was already under British control, the islands were under Iranian authority.[77]

Due to the establishment of customs posts by the Imperial Iranian Customs Department on the Iranian coast, by 1902 the Lingeh trade had begun to decline in favor of the ports in the lower Persian Gulf, notably Dubai.[78] No doubt steeped in the tradition of laissez-faire and free trade, a contingent of Lingeh merchants suggested to the Bombay & Persia Navigation Company to make Abu Musa its port of call instead.[79] Little did the Lingeh merchants know that the customs department's plan was to establish posts in all Iranian ports and islands. The posts on Qishm and Kish Islands were opened in 1901 and 1902, respectively, while additional posts were being contemplated to be established shortly on Henjam, Shuaib, Abu Musa, Great Tonb, and Sirri Islands as well.[80]

In January 1903, the resident, Colonel C. A. Kemball, visited Dubai and witnessed firsthand the promise of Dubai's impending rise to commercial prominence. He noted that due to the decline in the Lingeh trade caused by the policies of the Iranian Customs Department, the steamers of the British India Navigation Company and Bombay & Persia Navigation Company were making Dubai a port of call.[81] To secure even further the advantages of trade for Dubai and other ports in the lower Persian Gulf, any notion on the part of the Lingeh merchants to create an entrepot on Abu Musa had to be suppressed. Kemball therefore opposed the idea of Abu Musa as a port of call. In so doing, he drew attention to the fact that the Bombay & Persia Navigation Company steamers were calling on Abu Musa and as such might be viewed by Iranian customs as evading Lingeh customs. This would encourage the Iranians to set up a post on the island, which, in turn, would probably lead to disturbances.[82] Fueling this supposition on the part of Kemball were two factors: (i) the resistance and hostility of the local inhabitants who had greeted earlier the arrival of Iranian customs officers at the Iranian port cities of Mohammareh and Bushehr in 1902;[83] and (ii) the news that the customs department had acquired six patrol ships[84] that could be used to project Iranian presence on the islands. The threat of an Iranian naval presence on an island in the middle of the Persian Gulf presently qualified Iran as a possible subject of the following admonition delivered in May 1903 by the British foreign secretary, Lord Lansdowne, before the House of Lords: "[W]e should regard the establishment of a naval base or of a fortified port in the Persian Gulf by *any* other power as a very grave menace to British interests, and we should certainly resist it with all the means at our disposal"(emphasis added).[85]

In reporting on his visit to Dubai to the British India government, Kemball laid out the argument for a policy to prevent the arrival of Iranian customs on Abu Musa; that said policy was to be best realized by the British government taking the view that this island belonged to the Qasimi Sheikh of Sharjah on the Trucial coast. To help devise the theory which could unravel nearly one hundred years of official British recognition of the Tonbs, Abu Musa, and Sirri as Iranian islands, Kemball now informed the British India government that (i) the Sheikh of Sharjah was in possession of documentary evidence in the shape of letters from two former Arab chiefs of Lingeh admitting the claim of the Qasimi of the lower Persian Gulf to Abu Musa, and (ii) so far as the residency was aware, sovereignty over the island had never been asserted by Iran.[86] Dusting off the records of the residency, among the "letters" alluded to by Kemball was the aforementioned 1864 letter from the Sheikh of Sharjah to the resident, which letter, as noted earlier, had failed to sway the resident to the sheikh's point of view.[87] Consequently, in April 1903, the Sheikh of Sharjah was instructed by the British India government to hoist his flag on Abu Musa and also on Great Tonb "as a sign of ownership."[88]

Per their aforementioned intention to install customs posts on Iran's islands, in March 1904, the Iranian customs officials arrived on Abu Musa and Great Tonb only to find the sheikh's Trucial flag flying there. The sheikh's flag was removed, the Iranian flag was raised in its stead, and two armed men were stationed at each island to guard the flag.[89] The British government concluded that the "high-handed proceedings" at Abu Musa and Great Tonb, "though carried out by a Customs officer, had been initiated by the Mushir-ud-Dauleh, Persian Minister for Foreign Affairs, most probably under Russian advice."[90]

In international law, *occupation* is an original mode of acquisition by a state of title to territory belonging to no state *(terra nullius),* through its real, permanent and effective presence and control upon a territory to which it lays claim. In other words, occupation is the act of appropriation by a state by which it intentionally acquires sovereignty over territory that is at the time not under the sovereignty of another state. In this connection, two conditions are deemed essential to title thus acquired. The first and foremost condition is that the occupied territory must have been *terra nullius.* And second, the occupation must have been real and effective.[91] It logically follows that without the fulfillment of the first requirement, namely, that the territory must be *terra nullius,* by definition the label occupation cannot apply.

Two considerations reduce the British position in this regard to a mere legal absurdity. First, in international law, occupation is permitted in cases where the territory in question is *terra nullius,* meaning it belongs to no state (a territorial sovereign recognized as such to be a subject of international law).[92] The history and geography of Abu Musa contradict the existence of the prerequisite facts necessary for Abu Musa to be considered *terra nullius.* By all evidence, Abu Musa had been under the administration of the District of Lingeh, itself a part of the Province of Fars. The evidence of Great Britain's own view of the island as Iranian, Iran's declaration and display of sovereignty thereon, and even the Sheikh of Sharjah's own covetous claim to and tangible interests in the island defeat the Anglo-Sharjah claim based on the concept of occupation. Sir E. Beckett's legal opinion as to the existence of Iranian sovereignty over the Tonbs, Abu Musa, and Sirri in 1880-1887[93] makes the Anglo-Sharjah claim based on occupation of Abu Musa in 1903 all the more a legal absurdity.

Second, the other factor contributing to the legal absurdity once promoted by Great Britain rests on the legal impossibility of occupation by Great Britain or the Sheikh of Sharjah. At the time, Sharjah was not a state and as such could not acquire territory through occupation under international law.[94] Similarly, the Qawasim tribal entity in the lower Persian Gulf legally was incapable under international law to acquire territory,[95] and, as there was no state of war between Iran and Great Britain at the time, the notion that Great Britain alone, or through the agency of the Sheikh of Sharjah, conquered and took the island from Iran in the years 1903 and 1904 would be equally a legal impossibility.[96] Finally, even if the raising of the sheikh's flag could be deemed as tantamount to an act of conquest on the part of Sharjah and/or Great Britain, the lack of subsequent territorial annexation of the island and observance of other formalities in connection thereto renders the notion of conquest as a source of the claimed Anglo-Sharjah title to Abu Musa all the more absurd and untenable in international law.

BREACH OF THE
ANGLO-IRANIAN STATUS QUO AGREEMENT

The British government now sought to effect the removal of the Iranian flag from Great Tonb and Abu Musa. In this regard, the decision was made to first lodge a protest in Tehran against the actions of the Iranian customs department and, if necessary, to send a gunboat to force down the flags and remove the guards to the Iranian coast. On June 14, 1904, the Iranian government agreed to remove the flags and guards from the islands on the condition that neither Great Britain (including the Sheikh of Sharjah) nor Iran raise her flag on either island until Iran and Great Britain have resolved the dispute. However, once the Iranian flags and guards were removed, the British government promptly ordered the sheikh to raise his flag on Great Tonb and Abu Musa, which was effected on June 17, 1904.[97]

The British government's securing of Iran's consent to the removal of its flag from Great Tonb and Abu Musa was achieved by a combination of threats of naval demonstration[98] and the terms of the so-called status quo agreement, whereby "neither party should hoist flags in them pending settlement of the question."[99] Commenting on the diplomatic negotiations in this regard, on June 11, 1904, while instructing the foreign minister, Mosheer al-Dawleh, to pursue the matter with the British representative in Tehran, the Shah Muzaffar al-Din Qajar wrote: "Although Iran views the islands as belonging to Iran, Britain has pressured to have both flags lowered at those places, so that the issue may be settled by arbitration. We do, therefore, expect that the British would not allow the sheikhs to hoist their flag once ours have been removed."[100] After further discussions with the British representative, Sir A. Hardinge, on June 15, 1904, the Iranian foreign minister noted: "It has been agreed to that no flag be hoisted from either side on the two locations."[101]

On June 20, 1904, the Iranian government objected to the raising of the sheikh's flag as an act of usurpation and in violation of the status quo agreement.[102] The British government replied that the status of the islands was "undetermined" and therefore the hoisting of the Sheikh's flag could not be an act of usurpation and as such could not be disallowed.[103]

The Iranian government's good-faith reliance on the British government's promise had been misplaced. The rapidity by which the British government effected the re-raising of the sheikh's flag betrayed a wicked predisposition on the part of the British government which did not intend to honor their part of the bargain under the status quo agreement that had secured the removal of the Iranian flags from Great Tonb and Abu Musa.

The British government had placed therefore strategic expediency ahead of principle and in the process made a mockery of one of the most fundamental rules of international law—*pacta sunt servanda*—that is, agreements must be performed in good faith. On the other hand, it may be argued at law that Iran's consent to remove her flags from the islands was obtained by means of fraudulent inducement. The rule of law was not going to get in the way of the British government in the Persian Gulf. As far as the British authorities in the Persian Gulf were concerned, the strategic necessity to control the islands at the entrance of the Persian Gulf was a law unto itself.[104] As resident Percy Z. Cox, was to observe: "The possession of any of the islands in this group would so far as I am able to judge be a most useful asset in time of war."[105]

In May 1905, the Iranian government called attention to the illegal occupation of the islands by the British government and demanded that a stop be put to the rumored intention of the Sheikh of Sharjah to erect buildings on Great Tonb.[106] Even though the rumor turned out to be baseless, the incident helped reopen the issue of British government's violation of the status quo agreement, generating a lengthy correspondence among the British officialdom. The resident, Cox, who was subject to the British India government and ultimately the India Office, now sought to undermine the status quo agreement, which the British minister in Tehran, subject to the Foreign Office, had concluded with the Iranian government. Cox wrote: "I hold that the actions now being employed by the Persian Government through . . . , in order to keep open the question of ownership of these islands, are prompted by the Russian Legation in Tehran and the Russian Consul-General at Bushire."[107]

Resident Cox's view fit snugly with his strategic assessment of these islands, which could best be controlled for the benefit of the British position in the Persian Gulf by being made the possessions of the Trucial sheikhs who, in turn, were controlled by Great Britain: "If we do not maintain a vigorous policy in connection with these islands . . . it will not be long before we are confronted with difficulties . . . the preservation of which [for the Trucial Sheikhs] has always been one of the fundamental features of our policy in these waters."[108]

The political developments in Iran, including murmurings of a constitutional revolution, coupled with Russia's coming to terms with the consequences of a humiliating defeat at the hands of Japan, made Great Britain the sole arbiter of power in the Persian Gulf by the end of the first decade of the twentieth century. One symbolic manifestation of this dominance was in the form of the Sheikh of Sharjah's flag flying on the islands, a gesture of little interest to the Sheikh himself. On one occasion, in 1912, the resident wrote to the Sheikh of Sharjah saying, "I have so often warned you of the importance of keeping your flag flying, but you do not give heed. . . ."[109] And, when in December 1934, the Sheikh of Ras al-Khaimah lowered his flag on Great Tonb to call attention to his grievance against the British government,[110] the British government issued an ultimatum to the Sheikh of Ras al-Khaimah to raise his flag or else the Sheikh of Sharjah would be instructed to hoist his there, which ultimatum was complied with forthwith.[111] Both incidents bear testimony to the British policy that the Tonbs and Abu Musa not be left to Iran under any circumstance, even if it meant that Great Britain would have to annex the island for herself[112] or refuse to implement a decision by the World Court or the League of Nations favorable to the Iranian claim to the islands.[113]

With the advent of the Iranian constitutional movement (1905-1906) and the partitioning of Iran in 1907 into two zones of influence—Russia to the north and Great Britain to the south—the British government sought to strip, by whatever artifice or inducement, one additional Iranian island after another. In 1908, the British government advised a prospective English concessionaire, who had set up operations on the Iranian coast, to seek a concession for the Little Tomb from the Sheikh of Sharjah. On another occasion, the British government sought to legitimize their hold on Qishm and Henjam Islands by claiming them for the Sultan of Mascat. Finally, in the period from 1913 to 1922, the British government repeatedly conditioned the extension of loans to Iran on Iran's acceptance of their offers to lease or purchase all of Iran's islands in the Persian Gulf (except Hendorabi, Kish, and Farur), which condition was rejected repeatedly by the Iranian government.[114]

INEFFECTUAL ANGLO-SHARJAH PRESENCE ON ABU MUSA

The legal impossibility that Abu Musa could have possibly been subject to appropriation by Great Britain under the theory of occupation was discussed earlier. The limitations of the capacity and international legal personality of Sharjah as the other usurper of Abu Musa notwithstanding, the very acts which Great Britain and Sharjah committed with respect to Abu Musa from 1903 onward were of no legal significance to the Anglo-Sharjah claim of title based on the theory of occupation.

With the passage of time, the British Foreign Office began to adopt a more sophisticated approach to the formulation of the theory underlying their position with regard to Abu Musa. In 1932, the legal adviser at the British Foreign Office, Sir E. Beckett, wrote: "My conclusion is that . . . the Persians did possess sovereignty over Tomb and Abu Musa during these years [1880-1887]. But that now the Sheikhs of Ras-al-Khaimeh and Shargah respectively have a respective title against Persia at about 30 years [1932] duration and that in fact it is this title and this alone on which we or they must rely against Persia."[115]

The argument proposed in the passage above alludes to the theory where title is derived from ostensibly prolonged and effective presence on a territory that has belonged to another state. The doctrine makes lords from thieves and, in international law, it is referred to as acquisitive prescription. To establish the basis for title, the adverse possession must be uninterrupted, undisturbed, and uncontested over an extended period of time.[116] However, it is important to note that the Anglo-Sharjah presence on the island was in violation of the Anglo-Iranian status quo agreement, thereby raising the intriguing possibility that neither the Anglo-Sharjah presence nor their activities on Abu Musa could be deemed as conferring, in law or equity, any right to Great Britain or Sharjah on the theory that one cannot stand to gain from breach of good faith and contract. In any event, title by prescription must be judged on a case-by-case basis and with regard to the character of the territory in dispute.

The persistent Iranian challenge in the period from 1903 through 1971—which included acts of diplomatic protest, naval and aerial surveillance, displays of sovereignty, and visits to the island by Iranian officials—in effect prevented the operation of the principle of acquisitive prescription in favor of Great Britain/Sharjah, because these challenges denied the latter's presence and activities on the island the requisite degree of peace and quiet required to give rise to title.[117]

In the period between 1907 and 1913 the status of Abu Musa became embroiled in an intense dispute between Germany and Britain, which eventually acquired the appellation "The Wönckhaus Affair" as a euphemistic reminder of the larger Anglo-German rivalry for influence in Iran and the Persian Gulf. Briefly, in 1879, Robert Wönckhaus, a German entrepreneur, established himself in the mother-of-pearl trade at Lingeh and in June 1906, when a German shipping service was about to begin regular runs to the Persian Gulf, Wönckhaus obtained from three Lingeh merchants a concession to mine for red oxide on Abu Musa. Apparently, the Lingeh merchants had obtained the concession covertly; that is, without the knowledge of the British resident, from the uncle of the Sheikh of Sharjah (who was on pilgrimage to Mecca), whose flag now flew over the island.[118] The British government, which previously had forestalled the Russian advances in the Persian Gulf, now encountered the makings of yet another strategic challenge to their supremacy in the Persian Gulf, particularly in view of the rumors that Germany was about to gain a port on the Persian Gulf. The decision having been made to extricate Wönckhaus from the area, the resident instructed the Sheikh of Sharjah to cancel the original concession. That being done, Wönckhaus refused to abandon his activities on the island. In September 1907, the British government, operating from Bandar Abbas on the Iranian coast, forcibly shut down the Wönckhaus operations, removed the personnel to Lingeh on the Iranian coast, and touched off a protracted Anglo-German diplomatic incident,[119] during which the German government stated emphatically that Abu Musa and the Tonbs belonged to Iran.[120]

In 1922, the Iranian government lodged a protest with the British government in connection with the conclusion of a five-year contract between the British consul general in Bushehr and the Sheikh of Sharjah over the exploitation of red oxide on Abu Musa.[121] In 1923, the British minister in Tehran discovered that the Iranian national holding the concession for red oxide on Hormuz Island was urging the Iranian government to refer the British occupation of Abu Musa and the Tonbs to the League of Nations. The British government responded by a threat to counter with naval action as they had contemplated to do in 1903-1904.[122]

In 1925, the Iranian government dispatched a motor launch to Abu Musa and brought back a sack containing red oxide. In response to the British protest, the Iranian government justified their action by making reference to Iran's longstanding sovereignty over the island. In reply, the British government again threatened to dispatch a gunboat to the area.[123]

In 1929, the Iranian customs authorities in Lingeh reported that the British flag had been hoisted on Great Tonb and Abu Musa. The Iranian government protested the matter. The British government responded that the islands did not belong to Great Britain and intimated that perhaps the Sheikhs of Sharjah and Ras al-Khaimah had raised the flag on their own initiative.[124]

In 1934, an English company acquired a concession to extract red oxide on Abu Musa. The Iranian government protested, stating that the grant of the concession was contrary to the 1904 status quo agreement. The British government responded that the status quo agreement referred to political matters, while the exploitation of red oxide was a commercial matter and as such did not come within the terms of the 1904 understanding.[125]

In 1939, a bill was introduced before the Iranian parliament to approve and ratify a contract signed between the Iranian Ministry of Industry and Mines and Algemeine Exploratie Maatschappij, a Dutch company, for exploration and exploitation of mineral resources, among other places, in an area which included Sirri, Abu Musa, and the Tonbs.[126] While knowing of the grant, the British government did not protest.[127]

In 1948, acting on the recommendations of the Ministry of the Treasury, the Iranian government reminded the British government of Iran's longstanding sovereignty over the Tonbs and Abu Musa and asked that Great Britain not interfere with Iran's exercise of said sovereignty.[128]

In May 1953, the Iranian Foreign Ministry informed the prime minister that the planes of the British Royal Air Force were keeping surveillance over the Tonbs and Abu Musa. The Iranian government protested against the overflights and demanded that the British government halt them.[129]

In November 1953, an interdepartmental delegation composed of representatives from the Iranian Foreign Ministry, the Ministry of the Interior, the National Defense Council, and the Customs Department visited the south of Iran. The head of the delegation, Soleiman Khosravi (Interior Ministry) paid a visit to Great Tonb and Abu Musa. In his report, he recommended that a wireless station be set up on the two islands.[130]

In 1954-1955, the Iranian government reorganized the administrative structure of the Iranian coast and islands into a single provincial unit called the governorate-general of the Ports and Islands of the Persian Gulf in which Abu Musa was included as part of the Kish district.[131] The British government made no protest in this regard.

In 1971, the Iranian government protested against the British jets and ships patrolling the waters near the Tonbs and Abu Musa and ordered the Iranian Navy to shoot down any aircraft violating the Iranian airspace. The British government denied the allegation of flights over Iranian ships and islands.[132]

In light of the foregoing retrospective, in the period from 1903 through 1971, the Iranian government consistently and repeatedly challenged and contested the Anglo-Sharjah presence and activities with respect to Abu Musa. These acts of protestation deny the Anglo-Sharjah possession of the island the satisfaction of the primary requisite for acquisition of title by prescription, which is that such possession had to be peaceful, undisturbed, and uncontested.

Analysis of the evidence leads to the incontrovertible conclusion that Iran's sovereignty over Abu Musa is rooted deeply in history, a fact that was neither contested nor challenged until 1903 when the requirements of the British government's policy in the Persian Gulf dictated a view contrary to their longstanding, adamant, and deliberate recognition of Abu Musa as Iranian territory.

CONCLUSION: THE ANGLO-IRANIAN
SETTLEMENT OF THE DISPUTE

The evidence laid out above suggests strongly that the British government themselves were never fully convinced of the legality of the 1903 usurpation of Abu Musa in favor of the Sheikh of Sharjah. The open British opposition to Iran's sovereignty over the islands notwithstanding, the evidence also suggests strongly that the British government had two fall-back arguments for dealing with Abu Musa as they did, each of which justified a particular British position or objective.

First, there were times when the British government's conduct was based on the "avoidance of anything in the nature of a needless challenge to Persia, especially in matters connected with the Persian Gulf."[133] Therefore, when the Iranian government reorganized the aforementioned Governorate-General of the Coast and Islands of the Persian Gulf (1954-1955), which treated Abu Musa as part of the Kish Island district, the British government remained silent. Similarly, in 1939, when the Iranian parliament ratified a concession whose terms included Abu Musa, the British government did not protest. Therefore, it can be concluded that when it came to Iranian actions regarding the island as an internal Iranian matter, the British government displayed an acquiescent attitude toward Iran's sovereignty over the island.

Second, when suited their purpose, the British government would treat the status of the Tonbs and Abu Musa neither as Iranian nor British/Sharjah—the islands would be held up as being of "uncertain" or "disputed" status. In as early as 1904, the Anglo-Iranian status quo agreement had contained, in the minimum, a British promise to discuss with Iran the status of the Tonbs and Abu Musa.[134] The promise to discuss implied at the time the existence of a dispute. Later, in matters which required an appearance of neutrality, particularly with respect to maritime and navigation matters in the Persian Gulf, the British government would paint the status of the islands as "undetermined" or "disputed."

To illustrate: In connection with the placement of lights and buoys in the Persian Gulf, the British admiralty had divided the islands and coastal points overlooking the shipping lanes into three categories: (i) points located in Iranian territory or territorial waters; (ii) points located outside Iranian territory or territorial waters; and (iii) points outside Iranian territorial waters but in territory claimed by Iran or territory of uncertain status. In this last-mentioned category were included Great Tonb, Abu Musa, Bahrain, and Bassidu on Qishm Islands.[135] This depiction in essence achieved two purposes. First, it would give the appearance of an even-handed British approach in a matter about which Germany and Russia had declared a position in favor of Iran. Second, the depiction ensured the British government the appearance of neutrality, which was necessary for the continuation of their role as the self-styled traditional arbiter of matters pertaining to buoyage and lighting in the Persian Gulf.

The British government's multiple stances with respect to the status of Abu Musa ensured them the flexibility necessary for the protection of their interests. This flexibility also enabled the British government to engage in duplicitous conduct. For example, on the occasion of the establishment of the lighthouse on Great Tonb, in 1912, the resident wrote to the Sheikh of Sharjah, ordaining that "this island will be preserved for you by the mere presence of the lighthouse."[136] However, when Iran protested vehemently against the establishment of the lighthouse on an Iranian island without her permission,[137] the British minister in Tehran replied that the lighthouse was needed for navigation and the reason why it was being set up by Great Britain was because Iran "cannot afford the expenses of such an undertaking."[138] The reply implied that the lighthouse did not have a legal significance. Ostensibly, the mere presence of the lighthouse also meant little insofar as the sheikh's position may have been concerned. As discussed earlier, in 1934-1935 the British government indeed considered stripping Great Tonb from the Sheikh of Ras al-Khaimah and allowing the Sheikh of Sharjah to raise his flag there.[139] And, in the context of negotiating a comprehensive Anglo-Iranian treaty, in 1928-1929, the British foreign office was prepared to offer up the Tonbs to Iran in return for Abu Musa.[140] This and other suggestions that this be accomplished by way of a purchase or long-term lease were ruled out by the British Admiralty and India Office, stating "we would not really like the Persians to have Tamb in any circumstances."[141]

In part acquiescent toward Iran's claim of sovereignty and in part motivated more by British interests than the claim of ownership by the Sheikh of Sharjah—the British government's position in essence considered the Anglo-Sharjah usurpation and possession of the island a matter governed by the exigencies of British interests in the region. When Great Britain decided in 1968 that those exigencies would be there no longer by the end of 1971, the fate of the Tonbs and Abu Musa became negotiable. Great Britain and Iran agreed therefore to the possessory restitution of Abu Musa to Iran.

From the very beginning of the controversy in 1903-1904, the Iranian government had held Great Britain as the party responsible for the usurpation of Abu Musa and treated the issue, as did the British government, as a matter between the two states. The involvement of the Sheikh of Sharjah by invoking his name and flag ensured the British government the politically and legally correct cover necessary for the maintenance of their hegemony in the Persian Gulf.

While the Anglo-Sharjah actions in 1903-1904 had challenged Iran's sovereignty over Abu Musa, the sheer presence of Great Britain on this island provided the Sheikh of Sharjah and other inhabitants of Sharjah the opportunity to develop interests on the island, which, although void or voidable as fruits of an illegal occupation or breach of the status quo agreement, nevertheless, needed to be recognized and protected as a political matter. Therefore, in the 1971 Memorandum of Understanding between Great Britain and Iran,[142] which was communicated to the Sheikh of Sharjah as the third party beneficiary thereunder, Iran granted certain administrative, economic, and financial interests to Sharjah.

Under the terms of the memorandum, the territorial sea limits of Abu Musa were increased from 3 to 12 nautical miles,[143] which brought it in line with Iran's territorial sea limits at the time. Iran also agreed to allow an oil company drilling for oil in the waters off Abu Musa to continue operations there and agreed to allow Sharjah to retain one-half of the revenue thereby generated.[144] Further, Iran consented to Sharjah maintaining a police post in a defined area of the island[145] and agreed to grant to Sharjah nationals equal fishing rights in the waters around the island.[146] While the memorandum provided for the arrival of the Iranian armed forces on the island,[147] the annex to the memorandum provided for the Iranian government to assume exclusive responsibility for the defense and security of the island, as to which "it enjoys, complete freedom to take any measures in the Island of Abu Musa which in its opinion would be necessary to safeguard the security of the Island or of the Iranian forces."[148] Moreover, Iran agreed to provide to Sharjah an economic and financial assistance package until the oil revenues of the sheikhdom reached a certain amount.[149]

On November 18, 1971, as the third-party beneficiary, the Sheikh of Sharjah conveyed to the British government his acceptance of the terms and conditions of the Memorandum of Understanding and its enclosures, and on November 29, 1971, he announced that he had reached an agreement with the Iranian government on the dispute over Abu Musa.[150] Meanwhile in London, on November 18, 1971, the *Times* had quoted the British official negotiating with Iran, Sir William Luce, as saying that "Iran and Britain had sorted out their differences over the islands."

In Tehran, on the occasion of the arrival of the Iranian troops on Abu Musa on November 30, 1971, the Iranian premier stated to the parliament that the Iranian government "have in no conceivable way relinquished or will relinquish their sovereign rights and incontestable jurisdiction over the whole island of Abu Musa."[151] In addition, he stated, "the presence of local Sharjah officials on a segment of the island of Abu Musa should in no way be viewed or interpreted as contrary to this declared policy."[152]

In response to the plaintiff inquiry about the whereabouts of the honor of Great Britain with regard to protecting what for decades had been claimed by the British government as the property of the sheikhs, on December 1, 1971, the *Times* of London quoted a British government spokesman as saying: "Her Majesty's Government could hardly be expected to exercise her treaty responsibilities on the final day." This comment regarding the repossession of the islands by Iran all the more highlighted the existence of a direct historical and causal link between the fact of usurpation of Abu Musa by Great Britain in 1903-1904 and the British interests in the Persian Gulf. With the ending of the object which the Anglo-Sharjah possession had served, so also ended the need for the continued Anglo-Sharjah possession of the island. This latter at last permitted Great Britain and Iran to effect an orderly and negotiated return of Abu Musa to Iran's possession.

NOTES

1. This chapter is based on Bavand, Davoud H., *The Historical, Political and Legal Bases of Iran's Sovereignty over the Islands of Tunb and Abu Musa* (New York: Internet Concepts Incorporated, 1994).

2. The reason for this aggregation is three-fold: (i) the human, geographical, and political interconnection of the islands to one another, (ii) the historical, tribal, commercial, and territorial affiliation of these islands with the Iranian mainland, particularly the port of Lingeh, and the Iranian islands of Qishm and Kish, and (iii) the course and content of the Anglo-Iranian controversy over these islands since 1903-1904 when Great Britain sought actively to cause the usurpation of the Tonbs and Abu Musa from Iranian sovereignty in favor of

the Sheikhs of Sharjah and Ras al-Khaimah, on whom, by virtue of an elaborate treaty system, Britain maintained full control. For details, *see,* for example, Bavand, ibid.; Burrell, R.M., "Britain, Iran, and the Persian Gulf," in D. Hopwood, ed., *The Arabian Peninsula* (London: Allen and Unwin, 1972); Morsy Abdullah, Muhammad, The United Arab Emirates (London: Croom Helm, 1978); Jenab, M.A., *Khalij-e Fars: Ashenaii ba Amarat-e An* (Tehran: Padideh, 1970); F.O. 371/13010 (1928), Arabia E4266/421/91: [Confidential India Office Memorandum, I.O. B397, P4512/28], *Status of the Islands of Tamb, Little Tamb, Abu Musa, and Sirri,* J. G. Laithwaite, 24 August 1928. (Hereinafter cited as "Laithwaite Memorandum.")

3. *See,* for example, United Nations Security Council, *Official Records,* 26th year, 1610th meeting, 9 December 1971, par. 211 (remarks of the Iranian representative at the Council's meeting).

4. *See,* for example, Minorsky, V., trans. and ed., *Hudud al-'Alam* (w.982 A.D.)(London: Luzac and Co., 1937), p. 58 (alluding to the existence of numerous islands in the Persian Gulf that merit no mention because they are desolate, unknown, and small). *See also,* Playfair, J., *System of Geography,* Vol. V (Edinburgh: Peter Hill, 1813), pp. 321-322 (islands westward of Qishm "merit no description"); Mustawfi al-Kazwini, Hamdallah, *Nuzhat al-Qulub* (w.1340)(Guy Le Strange edition)(Leyden: E. J. Brill, 1913) pp. 171, 186, 234 (reference is made to the islands of Bahrain, Kharg, Kharku, Tonb, Farur, Larak, Henjam, Qishm, and *others* "which are known, inhabitable, and belong to Iran").

5. *See,* for example, Miles, S.B., *The Countries and Tribes of the Persian Gulf,* Vol II (London: Harrison and Co. 1919), p. 449 ("Previous to this important work [Nautical Survey 1820] the coast and islands of the Persian Gulf were very little known and the navigation had always been found by European seamen to be difficult and hazardous").

6. For a detailed analysis of the history of the Persian Gulf affecting the legal status of the coasts and islands in the eastern Persian Gulf in successive historical periods from the rise of the Achaemenid Empire (546 B.C.) through the middle of the eighteenth century, *see* Mirfendereski, Guive, "The Tamb Islands Controversy, 1887-1971: A Case Study in Claims to Territory in International Law" (Ph.D. diss., The Fletcher School of Law and Diplomacy, Tufts University, Medford, Massachusetts, 1985), pp. 207-309. The author gratefully acknowledges the research and information contained in Dr. Mirfendereski's work, which formed in part the basis for Bavand, *Tunb and Abu Musa.*

7. Yakut al-Rumi, *Mudjam al-Buldan,* (ca. 1224), Vol. IV (Beirut: Dar Sader, 1955), p. 422.

8. In light of the distances involved, this presumptive inclusion of Abu Musa among the territorial dependencies of Kish Island is not an oddity. Already in as early as the tenth century, the Buyid rulers of Iran had entrusted the administration of Iran's possessions in the Persian Gulf to the provincial government in Fars. Among

this latter's jurisdiction were included Bahrain, Qatif, Oman (including Ras al-Khaimah which served as the point of disembarkation of the Buyid transports landing in Oman) and the islands of Kharg, Kish, and Qishm. *See* Mirfendereski, "The Tamb Islands Controversy, 1887-1971," pp. 228-236. In 1954-1955, the Iranian Government organized the Governorate-General of the Ports and Islands of the Persian Gulf, wherein Abu Musa was identified as a subdistrict of Kish Island. In 1958, Abu Musa was incorporated directly into the Kish Island district. *See* Mossaheb, Gholam Hossein, *Da-yarat ol-Ma'aref-e Farsi,* Vol. I (Tehran: Franklin Publications, 1966-67), under "Abu Musa."

9. *See* D'Albuquerque, Braz, *The Commentaries of the Great Afonso D'Albuquerque,* Vol. I, Walter de Gray Birch, ed. and trans.(London: Hakluyt Society, 1872-84), chapters 20-27; Miles, *The Countries and Tribes of the Persian Gulf,* Vol. I, pp. 144-151.

10. *See* Dames, Mansel Longworth, trans. and ed., *The Book of Duarte Barbosa,* Vol. I (An Account of the Countries bordering on the Indian Ocean and their Inhabitants)(written by Duarte Barbosa and completed about the year A.D. 1518)(London: Hakluyt Society, 1918), pp. 68-82, especially pp. 79-81.

11. According to Mansel Longworth Dames, ibid., the roster compiled by Duarte Barbosa was less than complete. Ostensibly missing from the list of islands in the Persian Gulf was Kish Island and some others which were later added to the list. Furthermore, the list contained names written in sixteenth-century Portuguese which the editor could not match with their later nineteenth-century equivalents. Finally, Duarte Barbosa's account shows a primary concern with the main shipping lane of the times, which at the entrance to the Persian Gulf extended in the direction of Farur (Firol) before breaking south toward Bahrain or north toward the Mesopotamia. *See* Dames, *The Book of Duarte Barbosa,* p. 79-80 (fn. 1).

12. For details *see* Mirfendereski, "The Tamb Islands Controversy, 1887-1971," pp. 280-282.

13. George N. Curzon, *Persia and the Persian Question,* Vol. II (1892) (London: Cass and Co., 1966), p. 419.

14. For details, *see* Miles, *The Countries and Tribes of the Persian Gulf,* Vol. I, pp. 253-264; Savory, Roger M., "A.D. 600-1800," in Alvin J. Cottrell, gen. ed., *The Persian Gulf: A General Survey* (Baltimore: John Hopkins University Press, 1980), pp. 29-37.

15. For details, *see* Mirfendereski, "The Tamb Islands Controversy, 1887-1971," pp.312-318.

16. Movahed, Jamil, *Bastak va Khalij-e Fars* (Tehran: 1970), p. 43, relying on Muhammad Azam Bani Abbassian, *Tarikh-e Jahangireh va Bani Abbassian-e Bastak* (a Persian manuscript dating to the early nineteenth century).

17. *See* Eqbal, Abbas, *Motala'ati dar Bab-e Bahrain va Jazayer-o Savahel-e Khalij-e Fars* (Tehran: Chapkhaneh-e Majlis, 1948-49), at p.116, *citing* Hassan al-Fassai, *Farsnameh Nasseri,* Vol. II (ca. 1883) (a Persian manuscript), p. 290.

18. *See* Kelly, J. B., *Britain and the Persian Gulf: 1795-1800* (Oxford: Clarendon Press, 1968), pp. 99-166, 193-259, 355-409; Wilson, Arnold T., *The Persian Gulf* (Oxford: Clarendon Press, 1928), pp. 192-212.

19. *See* Mirfendereski, "The Tamb Islands Controversy, 1887-1971," pp. 325-349 (enumerating the differences between the Qawasim of Lingeh and Ras al-Khaimah). *See also* Kelly, *Britain and the Persian Gulf,* pp. 17-21.

20. On the occasion of the British forces being poised to attack the Qawasim of Lingeh the Iranian governor of Fars wrote to the commander of the expeditionary force: "The port of Linga is one belonging to the Province of Fars, . . . the inhabitants are subjects of the Persian Government and have in no way acted contrary to the subjection they owe as dutiful subjects . . . You will, therefore, as long as you remain in the Gulf, be pleased to order that none of the inhabitants belonging to any of the seaports of Fars, and of Linga in particular, shall in any way be molested. . . ." [Excerpt of] Letter from Husain Ali Mirza to Keir, Shiraz, Rabi'i, 1235 (January 1820), cited in Kelly, *Great Britain and the Persian Gulf,* p.161. Nevertheless, the over-zealous expeditionary force attacked a total of four vessels belonging to the ports of Charak and Lingeh on the Iranian coast, for which the India government ultimately paid reparations. *See* Kelly, *Great Britain and the Persian Gulf,* pp. 161-162; Lorimer, J.G., *Gazetteer of the Persian Gulf, Oman and Central Arabia,* Vol. I, *Historical* (Calcutta 1915)(reprinted from an original in the India Office Library) (Farnborough: Irish University Press/Gregg International, 1970), pp. 669-670.

21. For details, *see* Kelly, *Great Britain and the Persian Gulf,* pp. 354-360.

22. *See,* for example, Laithwaite Memorandum, Part II: History of the Islands Prior to 1887, at par. 7: "[t]he islands were apparently part of the hereditary estate of the Jowasimi Arab Sheikhs, the Sheikhs on the Arab shore having an equal interest with those on the Persian littoral."

23. *See* for example, Laithwaite Memorandum, par. 7: "[The islands'] management, administration, and jurisdiction had, however, for many years prior to 1887 by common consent been vested in the chief Joasimi Sheikh of the Persian coast, viz. the of Sheikh of Lingeh, but in his capacity of Jowasimi Sheikh and not of Persian official."

24. On several occasions, the British foreign office participated in the concoction of theories whereby to weaken and ultimately deny Iran's sovereignty over such islands in the Persian Gulf, which the British government, particularly the India government, wished to control for their own purposes. In 1800, the British emissary to the Court of Persia, John Malcolm, reported to the Governor-General of India, Richard Colley Wellesley, that he foresaw no difficulty in

Britain acquiring possession of Qishm Island from the Shah to be used as a British base. In conjunction therewith he wrote: "Although the King exercises no positive authority over any of [the] Islands of the Gulph, those on the northern shore are all considered as part of the Empire, and an application to him for grants of the Island of Kishm and Anjam would be the first step towards carrying this plan into execution. . . These grants would be easily obtained, as the Islands in their present state are of no advantage whatever to the Government.'" Kelly, *Great Britain and the Persian Gulf,* p. 71, citing [I.O.] Sate Papers, Bombay: East India Company's First Connection with the Persian Gulf: Malcolm to Wellesley, Bushire, 26 February 1800. Two decades later, as the British search for a base in the Persian Gulf recommenced, in 1820, the British chargé d'affaires in Tehran, Captain Henry Willock, raised the possibility of the British troops being stationed on Qishm Island, an Iranian island at the time leased by Iran to Oman. To overcome the Shah's opposition to a British base on Iranian soil, Willock threatened that in view of such an opposition "it was possible that the right and title of the Shah to all the Islands in the Gulph might be questioned. . . ." Kelly, *Great Britain and the Persian Gulf,* p. 169-170, citing [I.O.] Persia and Persian Gulf, Vol. 34, Willock to Keir, 10 March 1820, enclosure in Willock to Sec. Committee, 17 March 1820. In consequence of the Iranian refusal to allow a British base on Qishm, Willock, in apparent frustration, wrote: "'The vanity of the Persians makes them regard their country as the most favoured spot of the universe and the object of envy and desire to all neighboring states.'" Ibid. Consequently, the British Government began to court the ruler of Oman and established a garrison on Qishm Island and, later in the face of Iranian protests, they defended their presence there on the basis of an elaborate theory that denied Iran's title to the island and elaborated in its stead the basis of a convenient but fictitious claim to the island on behalf of the ruler of Oman, which the ruler of Oman himself knew to be false. For details, *see* Kelly, *Great Britain and the Persian Gulf,* pp. 170-171, 181-186. Again, in the early 1820s, when it suited their purposes, the British government essayed to weaken Iran's claim to Bahrain by setting up relative to the island a rival but fictitious claim thereto on the part of the ruler of Oman. For details, *see* Kelly, *Great Britain and the Persian Gulf,* pp.187-191.

25. F.O. 371/18901: Beckett Memorandum, dated March 12, 1935. In support of his opinion, Beckett observed: "In or about 1880 the Jowasimi Sheikh at Lingah (according to our view) became a Persian subject and a Persian vassal and thence forward it would appear that the Persians possessed sovereignty over Lingah and ruled it through this Jowasimi Sheikh as their vassal. It would hardly seem that after this date the Jowasimi Sheikh at Lingah can have continued to rule there as representative of the Jowasimi Sheikhs of the Trucial coast, and there is no evidence before me that during this period there was any distinction to be drawn between his position with regard to the territories on the mainland which he ruled and with regard to the three islands; that is to say there is nothing to show that, though he became a Persian vassal as regards

the territories of the mainland he ruled the three islands in a different capacity, i.e., still as a representative of the head of his family on the other side of the Gulf. I think this point is important; but I do not know whether it is possible to get any further information with regard to it. I think it is very likely that the conclusion to be drawn is that during this period the Sheikh at Lingah ruled all his territories, including the islands as a Persian vassal. Moreover, that at this time, on the other side of the Gulf, Ras al-Khaimeh and Sharjah, formerly part of the same principality under the single head of the Jowasimi family, had become divided between the branches of the family ruling quite independently one from the other (it seems that the first period of separation between Sharjah and Ras al-Khaimeh was from 1869 to 1900), and this separation would not make it any easier to show that the Sheikh at Lingah was continuing in this period to rule the Islands as the representative of his now completely divided family across the Gulf." Ibid.

26. F.O. 371/17827 1934, Arabia E5652/3283/91: G.W. Rendel (F.O.) to J.G. Laithwaite (I.O.), dated 13 October 1934, cited in Mirfendereski, "The Tamb Islands Controversy, 1887-1971," p.390.

27. The text of the Treaty is found in C.U. Aitchinson, *A Collection of Treaties, Engagements and Sunnuds* (Calcutta, 1876), Vol. III, pp. 59-63. Article I provided for "a cessation of plunder and piracy by land and sea on the part of the Arabs, who are parties to this contract, for ever."

28. For details, *see* Kelly, *Great Britain and the Persian Gulf,* pp. 355-359.

29. Kelly, *Great Britain and the Persian Gulf,* p. 359.

30. [I.O.] Selections from the Records of the Bombay Government, New Series no. 24 (compiled and edited by R. Hughes Thomas, Bombay, 1856) (herein cited as "Bombay Selections"): "Observations on the Past Policy of the British Government towards the Arab Tribes of the Persian Gulf," by Lt. A. B. Kemball, dated 18 October 1844. The other territories listed by Kemball were Mumzur, Khan, Leia, Shargah, Fasht, Heera, Himreeah, Zidina, Buddeeya, Rooban, Khore Fukuum, Kaleef Kureeyan, Sikumkun, Fugeera Soor-el-Muknood, Ghulla, and Khore Kalba.

31. Pelly, Lieutenant-Colonel Lewis, "Remarks on the tribes, trade and resources around the shore line of the Persian Gulf," in *Transactions of Bombay Geographical Society* 17 (1863). According to Pelly: "The maritime resources of the Jowasimee are stated to be Ras-el-Kheimeh, Rames, Juzerat-el-Hamra, Himreeah, Shargah, Heyrah, Fasht, Khan. In addition to the places here enumerated as Jowasimee territory, Sheikh Sultan bin Suggar possesses several small places as Commza, Dibah and Khore Facaun. His supremacy over Cassab is merely nominal."

32. For a discussion of the merits of this argument, *see* Bavand, *Tunb and Abu Musa,* pp. 40-41; Jenab, *Khalij-e Fars,* p. 317.

33. John McCluer, *An Account of Navigation between India and the Persian Gulf* (London: publisher not known, 1786). The praises of this survey's

reliability and durability are contained in Wilson, *The Persian Gulf,* pp. 280-281.

34. Kinneir, John Macdonald, *A Geographical Memoir of the Persian Empire* (London: publisher not known, 1813) (British Museum no. 454.F). In the second edition of this book the colorized map of the area depicted the Tonbs and Abu Musa as Iranian territory.

35. *See,* for example, the report on the matter filed by Sir John Malcolm, excerpts of which are cited above in note 24.

36. *See,* for example, the excerpts from remarks of Willock to the commander of the British expeditionary force in the Persian Gulf cited above in note 24.

37. Kelly, *Great Britain and the Persian Gulf,* pp. 194-195.

38. Bombay Selections, pp. 531-643: "Trigonometrical Survey made by order of the Honorable Court Directors of the United East Indian Company," by George Barnes Brucks, Commander H. C. Marine, 1830, later styled as G. B. Brucks, "Memoir Descriptive of the Navigation of the Gulf of Persia" and "Memoir of Manners, Customs, Religions, Commerce and Resources of the People inhabiting Persian Gulf Shores and Islands." The other islands identified with Fars and Kerman included: Deera, Bunah, Karrak, Kargo, Mulgssab, Mongeller, or Monkeel, Mulgarram, Shitwar, Inderabia, Kenn, Polior, Nabi-Freur, Bassidor, Kishm, Larack, Hormuz, Bu-Shoeib, and Angaum. For a map of this period depicting the Tonbs, Abu Musa, and Sirri Islands, *see* Appendix 2, map 2.

39. Kelly, *Great Britain and the Persian Gulf,* p. 195.

40. Ibid.

41. Ibid.

42. [I.O.] [Bombay] Marine Miscellaneous: Letter No. 20 of 1836, section 15: "A List of Names of Positions of the Persian Gulf," by Lt. Col. Robert Taylor, Political Agent in Turkish Arabia, no. 1059, 25 February 1836. The other islands identified as Iranian included Derah, Bunah, Jebreen Monokilah, Kishm, Bussidore, Ormuz, Larak, Angor, Ploir, Nobyfrue, Guase, Inderabia, Shitwar, Sheikh-Shoeib.

43. Bombay Selections, p. 2860: "Statistical and Miscellaneous Information Connected with the Possessions, Revenues, Families of Imam of Muskat, the Ruler of Bahrein, Chiefs of the Maritime Arab States in the Persian Gulf," submitted by Captain A. B. Kemball, 1 July 1854.

44. Constable, Captain C.G., and Stiffe, Lieutenant A.W., *The Persian Gulf Pilot, including the Gulf of Omman* (London: Hydrographic Admiralty, 1864), p. 158. This *Pilot* was compiled on the instruction of the Hydrographic Department of the British admiralty, which commissioned the two officers to make a detailed and authentic study of the ports and islands of the Persian Gulf as well as to survey their legal and political status.

45. Ibid.

46. [I.O.] *Précis on Commerce and Communication in the Persian Gulf, 1801-1905,* by J.A. Saldanha (Simla, 1906): Lewis Pelly, Political Resident in the Persian Gulf, Report No. 41, Bushire, August 23, 1864, to H. L. Anderson, Chief Secretary to the Government, Bombay.

47. Ibid.

48. [I.O.] Records R/15/14/8, Arab Coast, Sultan b. Saqr to Pol. Res., 28 December 1864, cited in Morsy Abdullah, *The United Arab Emirates,* p. 233.

49. For example, in the period from 1872-1884, the Sheikh of Ras al-Khaimah habitually complained about the Al Bu Samait of Lingeh crossing to Great Tonb for pasturage and in each of the four replies, delivered in a language laced with expressions of diplomatic politeness, the governor of Lingeh brushed off the criticism and drew attention to the people from Dubai, Ajman, Umm al-Qaiwain, and Bassidu who also were crossing over to the island. For a discussion of this series of correspondence, *see* Mirfendereski, "The Tamb Islands Controversy, 1887-1971," pp. 350-356, 370-390.

50. Morsy Abdullah, *The United Arab Emirates,* p. 234.

51. Ibid., p. 234.

52. Ibid. Interestingly, in the case of Abu Musa, Morsy Abdullah relies on the opinion of Abd al-Rahman as accurate (p. 234), but he criticizes Abd al-Rahman's opinion about Great Tonb belonging to Lingeh as one motivated by economic self-interest, a desire to avert an Arab-Persian war, and reluctance to appear favoring the Qawasim (p. 235).

53. Ibid., p. 236. Morsy Abdullah does not cite any source. The result of Haji's survey may have well been influenced by his position at Sharjah. Interestingly, he does not appear to have been as emphatic about Great Tonb, which, incidentally, he reported as being a codependency of Ras al-Khaimah and Lingeh, which report the resident revised noting that the islands were "considered Persian." Ibid., p. 236.

54. Constable, Captain C. G. and Stiffe, Lieutenant A.W., *The Persian Gulf Pilot, including the Gulf of Omman,* 2nd ed. (London: Hydrographic Admiralty, 1870), p. 158.

55. For details regarding this episode, *see* Mirfendereski, "The Tamb Islands Controversy, 1887-1971," pp. 371-372, 392-393.

56. [I.O.] Annual Administration Reports of the Persian Gulf Residency and Muscat Political Agency, 1875-1876 (Calcutta): Province of Fars, pp. 60-63.

57. Captain C.B.S. St. John, *The Persian Gulf* (Bombay, 1876).

58. F.O. 78, Turkey: Chamber of Commerce to F.O., Confidential Correspondence Respecting Light-House Red Sea and Persian Gulf, 22 August 1881.

59. For details, *see* Mirfendereski, "The Tamb Islands Controversy, 1887-1971," pp. 350-360.

60. Laithwaite Memorandum, Ibid. note 2, Part III, par. 15.

61. Ibid.

62. For details, *see* Mirfendereski, "The Tamb Islands Controversy, 1887-1971," pp. 378-383, 421-424.

63. Laithwaite Memorandum, Part III, pars. 15-16. For details, *see* Mirfendereski, "The Tamb Islands Controversy, 1887-1971," pp. 423-424, 442-449.

64. F.O. Map Room, no. 2699. F.O. 371/18917 1935 Arabia E2145/653/91.

65. F.O. 371/13009 1928 Arabia E4152/421/91: Parr to Foreign Office, Tel. no. 254, 20 August 1928.

66. For details regarding these maps and the legal weight that they carry, *see* Mirfendereski, "The Tamb Islands Controversy, 1887-1971," at pp. 402-403, 405-419, 434-440.

67. *See* F.O. 371/310 1907, Persia 34/41755, no. 1: Memorandum Respecting the Persian Gulf Islands of Abu Musa, Tamb, and Sirri, by Alwyn Parker, 17 December 1907 (hereinafter cited as the Parker Memorandum), Part I: Sir A. Hardinge (Tehran) to F.O., no. 104, 15 June 1904 ("what [the Sheikh of Sharjah] did was to hoist his own flag upon the islands which were not yet formally occupied by any other Government, and he has the right to fly it as the first occupant, till his lawful possession of these islands is disproved").

68. For details, *see* Lorimer, *Gazetteer of the Persian Gulf,* Vol. I, pp. 288-290, 293-294, 300-302, 306-312, 319-321, 325-348.

69. Ibid., p. 920.

70. Curzon, *Persia and the Persian Question,* Vol. II, p. 464.

71. Ibid., p. 465 (he went as far as to threaten impeachment for treason of any British official who would acquiesce in Russia every gaining concession over a port on the Persian Gulf).

72. Ibid., p. 465.

73. For details, *see generally* Busch, Briton Cooper, *Britain and the Persian Gulf: 1894-1914* (Berkeley: University of California Press, 1967), pp. 120, 128-129.

74. Ibid., pp. 128-129 (citing SSI telegrams to Viceroy, February 13 and 14, 1900, Fl 216/00 and F.O. to I.O., No.35-M, 14 February 1900).

75. Holdich, Col. Sir T. Hungerford, *The Indian Borderland, 1880-1900* (London, 1901), pp. 223-224, cited in Busch, *Britain and the Persian Gulf,* p. 120.

76. Busch, *Britain and the Persian Gulf,* p. 47.

77. Bavand, *Tunb and Abu Musa,* pp. 65-66.

78. Lorimer, *Gazetteer of the Persian Gulf,* Vol. I, p. 745.

79. Parker Memorandum, Part I; Laithwaite Memorandum, Part IV, par. 17; Lorimer, *Gazetteer of the Persian Gulf,* Vol. I, p. 745.

80. *See,* Lorimer, *Gazetteer of the Persian Gulf,* Vol. I, Appendix O, pp. 2597, 2605, 2607.

81. Morsy Abdullah, *The United Emirates,* p. 232 (citing IOR, R/1/14/15, Abu Musa and Tanb, Kemball to SGI, 12 January 1903) and p. 244.

82. *See* Parker Memorandum, Part I; Laithwaite Memorandum, Part IV, par. 17.

83. Lorimer, *Gazetteer of the Persian Gulf,* Vol. I, Appendix O, p. 2597.

84. Morsy Abdullah, *The United Arab Emirates,* p. 231.

85. Parl. Deb., 4th series, 121 (1903), p. 1348, cited in Busch, *Britain and the Persian Gulf,* p. 256.

86. *See,* [I.O.] Records, Abu Musa and Tamb, R/1/14/15: Kemball to Secretary of Government of India, 12 January 1903, cited in Morsy Abdullah, *The United Arab Emirates,* p.232; Parker Memorandum, Part I; Laithwaite Memorandum, Part IV, para. 17.

87. *See* text above corresponding to notes 48 through 53.

88. Parker Memorandum, Part I; Laithwaite Memorandum, *The United Arab Emirates,* Part IV, par. 17.

89. *See* Lorimer, *Gazetteer of the Persian Gulf,* Vol. I, p. 745; Parker Memorandum, Part I: Viceroy to I.O, telegram, 14 April 1904; Laithwaite Memorandum, Part IV, pars. 18-19. Iranian customs mission also visited Little Tonb, on which it did not encounter a Trucial flag. Ibid.

90. Lorimer, *Gazetteer of the Persian Gulf,* Vol. I, pp. 745, 2605.

91. Bledsoe, Robert L., and Boczek, Boleslaw A., *International Law Dictionary* (Santa Barbara, CA: ABC-CLIO, 1987), at p. 149.

92. *See* Lauterpacht, L., ed., *Oppenheim's International Law,* Vol. 1, 8th ed. (New York: David McKay Company, Inc., 1962), pp. 554-566.

93. *See* note 25 and corresponding text.

94. Occupation is the act of appropriation by a *state.* Lauterpacht, *Oppenheim's International Law,* p. 555. In the minimum, the act must be imputed to a state.

95. Conquest or subjugation is another mode of acquiring territory by a *state.* Ibid., pp. 566-567. For example, in consequence of their victories against the Matabele and Zulu tribes between the years 1836-1838, the Dutch farmer emigrants—the "Trekkers"—decided to form an independent state in the area they had come to occupy. The British government rejected the notion on the grounds that at the time when the emigrants took possession of the territories in question they had been the residents of the Cape Colony and as such were deemed by Britain as British subjects and therefore the

land they had occupied automatically came therefore under British sovereignty. *See* M.F. Lindley, *The Acquisition of Territory and Government of Backward Territory in International Law* (London: Longmans Green and Co., 1929), pp. 89-90.

96. *See* Lauterpacht, *Oppenheim's International Law,* pp. 566-575.

97. Parker Memorandum, Part I: I.O. to F.O., 4 May 1904; Hardinge (Teh.) to F.O., no. 61, telegraphic, 24 May 1904; Hardinge (Teh.) to F.O., no. 91, telegraphic, 24 May 1904; Major Percy Z. Cox (P.R.) to I.O., 20 September 1904; Laithwaite Memorandum, Part IV, par. 20: Hardinge (Tehran.) to F.O., 14 June 1904; Lorimer, *Gazetteer of the Persian Gulf,* Vol. I, pp. 745-746.

98. Iranian Ministry of Foreign Affairs, File No.33/150 A, Part II, section 1.

99. Laithwaite Memorandum, Part IV, par. 20: Hardinge (Teh.) to F.O., 14 June 1904 (reporting back to London the statement by the Iranian foreign minister on June 14, 1904).

100. Muzaffar al-Din Shah's letter of instructions to Mosheer al-Dawleh, dated 22 Rabi al-Aval 1323.

101. Ibid., Mosheer al-Dawleh's minutes, dated 26 Rabi al-Aval 1323.

102. Digest of Mosheer al-Dawleh's Note to British Legation (Tehran), dated 1 Rabi al-Sani 1323.

103. Ibid., Digest of British Legation's Reply-Note to Foreign Ministry (Tehran) dated 22 June 1904.

104. *See,* for example, Busch, *Britain and the Persian Gulf,* p. 48: "Their strategic importance at the mouth of the Gulf—and particularly the feasibility of the construction of a naval base there—insured that the status of these islands would fall under review when questions of Gulf strategy were debated."

105. Parker Memorandum, [I.O.] Percy Z. Cox (P.R.) to G.I., no. 350, 31 July 1905.

106. Laithwaite Memorandum, Part IV, par. 22: Arthur Hardinge (Teh.) to Political Resident (Bushire), 20 May 1905.

107. Parker Memorandum, [I.O.] Percy Z. Cox (P.R.) to G.I., No. 350, 31 July 1905.

108. Parker Memorandum, [I.O.] Percy Z. Cox (P.R.) to G.I., No. 350, 31 July 1905. The view that this had *always* been the British policy is not supported by history.

109. F.O. 371/1717 (1913), Persia E34/926: Political Resident to Sheikh Sagar bin Khaled, Chief of Shargah, 28 September 1912 (re. Great Tonb).

110. *See* Mirfendereski, "The Tamb Islands Controversy, 1887-1971," pp. 637-638.

111. F.O. 371/18901 (1935), Arabia E814/4/91: Minutes of the Middle East (Official) Sub-Committee, 8 March 1935, Part II: The Island of Tamb; Arabia E1894/4/91: Pol. res. to Sec. of State for India, telegram 68, 20 March 1935; Arabia E2382/4/91: Pol. Res. to Sec. of State for India, no. 2044, 10 April 1935.

112. F.O. 371/18901 (1935), Arabia E531/4/91: G. W. Rendel's minutes, dated 31 January 1935 (the Sheikh of Ras al-Khaimah "does not care two hoots about Tamb"); Arabia E814/4/91: Note Regarding Tamb, Line of Action suggested by Mr. Baggallay, before the Intradepartmental (F.O. and I.O.) meeting on 6 February 1935 (annexation as a possible option); Arabia E1670/4/91: Minutes of the Middle East (Official) Sub-Committee, 8 March 1935, Part II: The Island of Tamb (annexation rejected as an option).

113. F.O. 371/17894 (1934) Persia E5669/139/34: I.O. to F.O., No.PZ5602/34, 8 September 1934 (decision to reject any judgment rendered by the World Court favoring Iran's claim); F.O.371/11442 (1926), Arabia E419/419/91: P. Loraine (Teh.) to A. Chamberlain (F.O.), 30 December 1925, citing passages from an earlier correspondence by Lord Curzon to P. Loraine, tel. no. 88, 1 May 1923 (danger of submitting the issue to arbitration).

114. Bavand, Tunb and Abu Musa, pp. 79-81.

115. F.O. 371/18901 (1935), p. 116.

116. In the dispute over El Chamizal Tract between the United States of America and Mexico (1910), the International Border Committee, which acted as arbitrator, found that America's occupation of the territory from 1848 to 1895 had not been uninterrupted and undisturbed and, therefore, the principle of prescription could not be deemed to have conferred title to America. *Chamizal Arbitration Award* (United States/Mexico) (1910) (U.N.R.I.A.A. Vol.XI), in *American Journal of International Law* 5 (1911).

117. Lauterpacht, *Oppenheim's International Law,* pp. 576-577 (display of sovereignty in the face of protests and claims cannot be considered undisturbed). This has been upheld in the case law. *See* for example, *Chamizal Arbitration Award,* pp. 782, 803. For an analysis of the application of the principle of acquisitive prescription with historical and geographical relevance to Abu Musa, *see* Mirfendereski, "The Tamb Islands Controversy, 1887-1971," pp. 531-536 (regarding the Tonbs).

118. The act of obtaining the concession from the sheikh and the sheikh granting it to them are manifestations of the resourcefulness of the business community to deal pragmatically and expediently when obtainment of commercial advantage is involved, rather than to base their decisions on the niceties of jurisprudence and international legal technicalities.

119. For details, *see* Busch, *Britain and the Persian Gulf,* pp. 148, 353-357, 369-380.

120. *See generally* F.O. 371/156-157 (1906); F.O. 371/310-311, 311, 347 (1907); F.O. 371/506, 508 (1908); F.O. 371/712-719, 766-781 (1909); F.O. 368/317 (1909); F.O. 371/1707-1709, 1812, 1835, 1845 (1913). The German newspaper accounts of the Abu Musa incident as reported to the British Foreign Office highlighted the German government's position with respect to Abu Musa belonging to Iran. *See,* for example, F.O.371/310 (1907), Persia E34/42499: D. W. Lascelles (Berlin) to Sir Edward Grey (F.O.), 27 December 1907.

121. Bavand, *Tunb and Abu Musa,* p. 95.

122. Laithwaite Memorandum, Part IV, par. 30; F.O. 371/11442 (1926) Arabia.

123. F.O. 371/11447 (1926) Arabia.

124. F.O. 371/13010 (1928) Arabia; F. O.). 371/14478 (1930), Arabia; F.O. 371/14484 (1930) Persia. Iranian Foreign Ministry, Digest of events of 1312 (1933-1934) and 1313 (1934-1935).

125. Iranian Foreign Ministry, Digest of events of 1312 (1933-1934) and 1313 (1934-1935).

126. F.O. 371/23264 (1939), Persia E3026/3026/34.

127. Ibid.

128. Iranian Foreign Ministry, Foreign Minister to Council of HIM's Ambassador (London), 24 Amordad 1328 (15 August 1949), Foreign Ministry to British Embassy (Teh.), 27 Amordad 1328, Foreign Ministry to Council of Ministers, no. 2723, 10 Mehr 1325, Foreign Ministry to War Ministry, no. 3612, 24 Amordad 1328.

129. Ibid., Foreign Ministry to Prime Minister, no. 1035, 21 Ordibehesht 1332, Foreign Ministry to Swiss Embassy, no. 1027, 29 Ordibehesht 1332.

130. Ibid., Interior Ministry to Foreign Ministry, no. 2/13892/12975, 14 Azar 1332.

131. Mossaheb, *Da-yarat ol-Ma' aref-e Farsi,* (under "Abu Musa").

132. *The Middle East Journal,* 25 (1971): Chronology: Iran, May 8-9, 1971.

133. F.O. 371/17827 (1934), Arabia E4042/3283/91: G. W. Rendel (F.O.) to Undersecretary of State for India, 2 July 1934.

134. Lorimer, *Gazetteer of the Persian Gulf,* Vol. I, p. 746.

135. Bavand, *Tunb and Abu Musa,* p. 101.

136. F.O. 371/1717 (1913), Arabia E34/926: Political Resident to Sheikh Sagar bin Khaled, Chief of Shargah, 28 September 1912.

137. Laithwaite Memorandum, Part VI, par. 26: I.O. Records P4778/21, Political Resident to Government of India, 13 October 1912.

138. Iranian Foreign Ministry: Digest of events of 1913, summary of Moazed al-Sultan's conversation with the British Minister (February 1913).

139. *See* above text corresponding to notes 110 and 111.

140. F.O. 371/13777 (1929), Persia E4085/19/34: Rendel's minutes, 10 September 1929.

141. F.O. 371/18901 (1935), Arabia E814/4/91: Baggallay's minutes of the inter-departmental conference of 6 February 1935. The India Office and Admiralty position was later endorsed by the Middle East Sub-Committee of the Cabinet. Ibid., Arabia E1670/4/91: Minutes of the Middle East (Official) Sub-Committee, 8 March 1935, Part II: The Island of Tamb. For a detailed analysis of the Anglo-Iranian negotiations regarding the trading-off, leasing, and purchasing of the Tonbs, *see* Mirfendereski, "The Tamb Islands Controversy, 1887-1971," pp. 615-652.

142. Memorandum of Understanding, signed by the Iranian Minister of Foreign Affairs on behalf of Iran and the Principal Secretary of State for Foreign and Commonwealth Affairs, dated 25 November 1971. *See* Appendix 1 for the text of memorandum and exchange of notes among various parties concerning the terms thereof.

143. Ibid., article 3.

144. Ibid., article 4.

145. Ibid., article 2.

146. Ibid., article 5.

147. Ibid., article 1.

148. Ibid., enclosure no. M/21284, dated November 25, 1971. *See* Appendix 1, p. 4.

149. Ibid., article 6 and enclosure no. M/21284.

150. Albaharna, Husain M., *The Arabian Gulf States* 2nd rev. ed. (Beirut: Librairie du Liban, 1975), pp. 345-346. As a doctoral dissertation, this work was entitled "The Persian Gulf States."

151. Iranian Ministry of Foreign Affairs, *The Imperial Government's Relations with the Countries within the Jurisdiction of the Ninth Political Department* (Tehran, 1976), Annex, No. 4 (text of speech).

152. Ibid.

4

The Ownership of the Tonb Islands: A Legal Analysis

Guive Mirfendereski

This chapter examines the legal arguments advanced in the period from 1887 through 1971 by Britain on behalf of Ras al-Khaimah and Sharjah, on the one hand, and by Iran, on the other, each claiming ownership of the Tonb Islands located at the entrance to the Persian Gulf.[1] The purpose of this discussion is threefold: (i) to state the argument and present the evidence in support thereof; (ii) to evaluate the evidence and weigh each argument in reference to international legal standards, and (iii) to determine the ownership of the islands at the time of Iran's repossession of the islands on November 30, 1971, from which time the islands have been under Iran's full, exclusive, and effective sovereignty.

The burden of proof for each argument is on the party making the claim. The standard of proof for any argument or claim is the preponderance of the evidence. The existence of conflicting or contradictory evidence does not defeat an argument or claim, it merely affects the weight of the contradicted evidence.

The term *Anglo-Arab* herein used refers to a claim, argument, position, or action by Britain on behalf of, in the name of, or in concert with the Sheikh of Ras al-Khaimah and/or Sharjah, or by either of these with respect to the Tonbs. Herein, at least for the sake of argument and based on over seventy years of history, it is presumed that the status of Little Tonb is dependent on Great Tonb.[2]

CLAIMS BASED ON GEOGRAPHY

Great Tonb is located about 17 miles south of the southwestern tip of Qishm Island and about 26 miles south of Lingeh on the Iranian mainland; it is 46 miles from the nearest point at Jazirat al-Hamrah in Ras al-Khaimah. Little Tonb is situated 7 miles to the west of Great Tonb, 20 miles from Qishm Island, 24 miles from Lingeh, and 45 miles from Ras al-Khaimah.

In international law, factors or considerations based on geography or location, such as contiguity, security interest, strategic value, inclusion in, or proximity to areas of national maritime jurisdiction do not confer title to an offshore island. These considerations, however, like proximity, do provide a basis for allotting an island to one state rather than another, either by agreement between the parties, or by a decision not necessarily based on law.[3] To this extent, therefore, claims to the Tonbs based solely on such geographical factors are defeasible at law.[4]

While proximity in itself confers no title, geographical considerations, including proximity, albeit indirectly, are highly relevant to and of paramount importance in the development or adduction of evidence in support of claims of ownership based on political history. Regardless, in 1929, the head of the Eastern department at the British Foreign Office had argued that Britain should consider conceding Great Tonb to Iran because "*it is indeed geographically a Persian island*"(emphasis added).[5] There is no evidence of Iran ever claiming ownership of the Tonbs solely on the basis of the islands' proximity to the Iranian mainland.[6] However, Iran often advanced proximity of the islands as one reason why the islands should be allotted to Iran as part of a political or negotiated settlement of the controversy.[7] Nevertheless, proximity at best may be a relevant factor to consider when dealing with the legal status of islands.[8]

CLAIMS BASED ON ETHNICITY

Claims of sovereignty over the Tonbs based solely on Arab or Iranian/Persian ethnic considerations are inarguable at law. When made by various Arab governments, the Arab claim has rested on the premise that the Tonbs were Arab by virtue of being inhabited by Arabs and therefore they formed a part of an anthropo-geographical environment that is Arab in character.[9] This view ignores the longstanding connection between the inhabitants of Great Tonb and the Iranian coast and islands. Significant among these were the Ibn Hule of the Iranian coast in early 1800s[10] and, thereafter, the Al Bu Samait and other inhabitants of the Iranian ports and islands.[11] The most noted inhabitant of Great Tonb circa 1885 was Ahmad Tonbi, a native of the district of Lar in the Iranian province of Fars.[12] Variously, the Iranian component of the population of Great Tonb has been reported as follows: thirty persons in 1929 (50 percent of the population), four Iranian families in 1931, and nine persons in the mid-1930s.[13]

In international law, ethnographical or anthropo-geographical considerations by themselves do not confer title. The rule regarding the place of nationality or ethnic principle in matters of territorial ownership is as follows: "(T)he territory of a State is totally independent of the racial character of the inhabitants of the State."[14] Therefore, the racial or cultural background of the Tonbs alone cannot be a basis for title.[15] However, because sovereignty is asserted and exercised through the human agency, race or language of the persons inhabiting an island may be an important moral, political, or social factor explaining the affinity of the island with a particular territorial sovereignty.[16]

The most notable ethnic influence in the legal history of the Tonbs may well be in the origin of the name of the islands. The present-day name of the islands, in its many orthographic variations, in all likelihood derives from the Iranian *gunbad* (meaning "dome") as in Gonbad-e Bozorg (Great Dome) and Gonbad-e Kuchek (Little Dome)[17] and Isola Doma (1550)[18] by way of Tomon[19] and other derivations.[20] No claim appears to have been made to the Tonbs on the basis of their name. However, in the history of the Persian Gulf there have been cases in which the names of islands have helped define a particular political outcome. In the 1930s the British government concluded that the name of Farsi Island betrayed an Iranian connection sufficient for Iran to base a grievance against any party seeking to seize it.[21] The proximity of Farsi to the Iranian coast and the frequenting of the island by subjects of the Iranian government, Arab as well as non-Arab, staved off an outright attempt by the British government to claim the island for their wards in the western Persian Gulf.[22]

CLAIMS BASED ON POLITICAL HISTORY

The gist of Iran's claim of sovereignty over the Tonbs on the basis of "incontestable historical precedent"[23] was articulated publicly in 1971 by the Shah Mohammad Reza Pahlavi: "The islands were ours, but some eighty years ago Britain interfered with the exercise of our sovereignty and grabbed them and subsequently claimed them for her wards, Sharjah and Ras al-Khaimah."[24] He later elucidated: "What we are demanding is what has always belonged to our country throughout history. It is perfectly natural and reasonable that, now that imperialism is withdrawing, Iran should regain what has always been its possession historically."[25] The Anglo-Arab refutation of Iran's sovereignty on the basis of historical title rested on the view that (i) there existed no clear evidence of any effective dominion exercised by Iran in the Tonbs prior to 1750; (ii) there existed no clear evidence of any Iranian dominion from 1750 onward[26]; and (iii) at least during the British presence in the Persian Gulf, the Tonbs formed a part of the territory that became the federation of the United Arab Emirates.[27]

The challenge here to a jurist and historian is to examine records covering tens of centuries of Persian Gulf history in order to unearth evidence about the connection of the Tonbs to either claimant. A modest endeavor in this vein has resulted in spotting a few direct pieces of evidence regarding the status of the Tonbs. The bulk of the findings, however, consists of indirect evidence along with all the necessary inference and conjecture which flow from it.[28] The paucity of reference to the Tonbs in pre-nineteenth century material is no doubt owed to the Tonbs being among those islands in the Persian Gulf, which, to paraphrase a tenth century geographer, are numerous but desolate, unknown, and small, and therefore unworthy of mention.[29]

The earliest mention of the Tonbs seems to date to January 325 B.C. when Alexander the Great's fleet after weighing off Qishm Island came upon "another island."[30] The earliest cartographic reference to the Tonbs appears to be Tabiana, referred to by Claudius Ptolemy as one of "the islands adjacent to Persia."[31]

As explained by the Dutch naval commander and jurist, Jan Helenus Ferguson, "(t)he occupation of any *terra firma* is supposed to include the presumption of possession of its adjacent unoccupied islands, on the principle that, when two things are conterminous or in close connection, the more valuable annexes to itself that which is less valuable."[32] In other words, "[i]slands adjacent to the coast of the main land, though not formed from it by alluvium or increment, are considered as appurtenant, unless some other power has obtained title to them by some of the recognized modes of acquisition."[33]

The political and military domination of Iran over the Persian Gulf in successive periods also supports the necessary conclusion that in ancient and medieval times the Tonbs would have had to belong to Iran. The Achaemenid Empire (550-330 B.C.) in the Persian Gulf consisted of the 14th *satrapy* (administrative division), which included "the islands of the (Persian Gulf), where the king sends those whom he banishes."[34] This is the earliest mention of the exercise of criminal or penal jurisdiction in the islands of the Persian Gulf by any sovereignty from either mainland of the Persian Gulf.

The likelihood of the appurtenance of the Tonbs to Iran appears even stronger at the times when the Iranian dominion extended to the lower coast of the eastern Persian Gulf thereby placing the Tonbs at least theoretically in the penumbra of Iranian sovereignty. The political and commercial domination of Iran over the Persian Gulf in the Seleucid (312-150 B.C.), Parthian (238 B.C.–A.D. 224) and Sassanid (A.D. 224-641)[35] periods points to the conclusion that in pre-Islamic times the Tonbs most likely belonged to Iran.[36] Upon the conclusion of the Sassanid period, the control of the Tonbs in all likelihood may have remained with the Ibn Karkar clan of the Bani Salimah section of the Malik ibn Fahm branch of the Azd tribe of Oman, to whom the Sassanid kings of Iran had entrusted the control of the area adjacent to the Strait of Hormuz. The Ibn Karkar maintained control of the Strait of Hormuz well into the middle of the tenth century.[37]

The rise of the Buyid rulers in Iran in the middle of the tenth century marked the return of direct Iranian political control in the Persian Gulf. The Buyids annexed Oman in A.D. 973 and made it a part of the Iranian province of Fars. The position of the Tonbs near the Iranian coast and the bicoastal dominion of the Buyids in the eastern Persian Gulf leads to the inescapable and necessary conclusion that in Buyid times (A.D. 945-1055) the Tonbs in all likelihood belonged to Iran.[38] Just as Oman was annexed to Fars, the Tonbs too in all likelihood belonged to Fars as a matter of the administrative structure of Iran's maritime possessions.

The Iranian dominion in the Persian Gulf during the Seljuq period (A.D. 1055-1194) continued unabated.[39] The Tonbs at this time pertained to Fars and in all likelihood were administered for the Seljuq by the Banu Qaysar rulers of Kish Island.[40] In Ibn al-Balkhi's *Farsnama*[41] (completed in A.D. 1111) reference is made to the islands of Henjam, Kharg, Tonb, and Farur as belonging to the Ghobad *Kureh* (District) in Fars.[42] While the Seljuq power declined, the rulers of Kish Island continued to govern Kish and its vicinity until A.D. 1226.[43] Soon thereafter, the Salghurid rulers of Fars ousted the Banu Qaysar from Kish and incorporated into Fars the territories of Kish and its dependencies (including Hendorabi Island) and of Hormuz and its dependencies (including Jerun, Qishm, and Henjam Islands).[44]

The period A.D. 1260-1330 was marked with occasional feuds among the rulers of Kish, Hormuz, and Fars, in the course of which a number of naval expeditions crisscrossed the eastern Persian Gulf. It is difficult to say what effect these developments would have had on the status of the Tonbs. In A.D. 1329-1330, the rulers of Hormuz took possession of Kish, Hendorabi, Kharg, Darab, and Bahrain Islands, and parts of the Arabian coast, including Hasa and Qatif,[45] in consequence of which it may be surmised that the rulers of Hormuz in all likelihood gained directly or vicariously control over the Tonbs as well.

In *Nuzhat al-Qulub*,[46] written about A.D. 1340, reference is made to the islands of Bahrain, Kharg, Kharku, Tonb, Farur, Larak, Henjam, Qishm, and others "which are known, inhabited and belong to Iran."[47] From this period until the arrival of the Portuguese in the Persian Gulf in the early 1500s, the Iranian dominion in the Persian Gulf qua the local rulers of Hormuz remained unabated. With the exception of an occasional internecine quarrel regarding succession or disagreement with the Iranian central or provincial authority, very little change, if any, seems to have occurred in regard to the control of Hormuz over the coasts and islands of eastern Persian Gulf.[48]

At the time of the arrival of the Portuguese in the Persian Gulf, the territories held by the rulers of Hormuz consisted of Old Hormuz (near Minab) and Moghestan on the Iranian coast, the ports of Qalhat, Quryat, Mascat, Sohar, and Khor Fakkan on the Omani coast, and the islands of Hormuz, Larak, Qishm, Kish, Shuaib, Hendorabi, and Bahrain.[49] It is likely that the Tonbs formed a part of the territories under Hormuzi control and passed along with the rest of Hormuz to Portuguese control in 1507.

According to the Portuguese seafarer and geographer Duarte Barbosa, who wrote circa 1518, the territories belonging to Hormuz included Shamil, Julfar (Ras al-Khaimah), Kassab, and Umm al-Qaiwain opposite the Tonbs in the lower Persian Gulf and the islands of Qishm, Hendorabi, Shuaib, Larak, Farur, Bahrain, and Tonb.[50]

Following the expulsion of the Portuguese from the Iranian littoral in 1622-1625, Iran regained the coastal possessions formerly under Hormuz/Portuguese control, including the garrison in Ras al-Khaimah.[51] Under these conditions, it is likely that the Tonbs too reverted to Iranian possession or control. It is also likely that in the course of the ascendancy of the Al Yaariba rule in Oman the Tonbs may have passed temporarily under their control in 1679-1711.[52]

Due to the concurrent withdrawal, because of internal strife, in 1721-1736 of the central governments in Iran and Oman from the affairs of the Persian Gulf, the Huwalah Arabs, a large grouping of Iranian Arabs living on the Iranian coast from Kangan to Bandar Abbas, began to gain prominence in the eastern Persian Gulf. In 1718-1720, the Qasimi branch of the Huwalah émigrés in Ras al-Khaimah assisted the Omanis in their campaigns against Bahrain and Bandar Abbas before participating in the Omani civil wars in 1721-1736. In 1725, the Qawasim of Ras al-Khaimah established momentarily a depot at Bassidu on the northwestern extremity of Qishm Island. In 1734, however, the Iranian government quelched the Qasimi autonomy on the Iranian coast and Qishm Island. Contemporaneously, Iran reasserted her authority over Ras al-Khaimah and its Qasimi rulers and these remained subject to Iran well into 1750.[53]

The circumstances surrounding the repeated Iranian expeditions sent from southern Iran to Oman and Ras al-Khaimah may have added a greater importance to the Tonbs, as these islands lay on the sea lanes plied at the time by the Iranian navy, which maintained communication between the Iranian ports and Ras al-Khaimah into 1748, carrying men and provisions for the Iranian garrison at Ras al-Khaimah.[54]

In view of the strained relationship between the Iranian government and the Huwalah Arabs, who manned but also occasionally mutinied against the Iranian fleet, coupled with the role of the Qawasim of Ras al-Khaimah in supporting the Huwalah mutineers in 1737-1748,[55] it would appear unlikely for the Iranian government to have permitted control by the Qawasim over strategic islands such as the Tonbs.[56] Islands lying as close to the Iranian coast as the Tonbs "are held to be natural dependencies of the territory of the nation that owns the coast, to which the sovereignty over these islands is of infinitely greater importance than to any other for the sake of its security at sea and on land."[57] While this doctrine alone does not confer title any more than proximity alone would, it is clear that the requirements of security and strategic interests would have provided Iran (as it did Great Britain 150 years later) with sufficient motive to secure the Tonbs for herself or deny them to an adversary.

The political history of the eastern Persian Gulf in the period between 1750 and 1887 is often viewed as the historical origin of the Anglo-Arab claim to the Tonbs. The rise of the Qasimi maritime power and its curtailment by Great Britain, establishment of the British trucial system over the piratical and other tribes in the lower Persian Gulf, including over the Qasimi Sheikhs of Ras al-Khaimah and Sharjah, the relations between the Qawasim residing on the Iranian littoral and the Qawasim in the lower Persian Gulf, and the definition and pursuit of British imperial interests in the Persian Gulf all contributed to a state of affairs with enormous implications for the ownership of the Tonbs.[58] Shaped by the events of this period, the Iranian view holds that the Tonbs formed a territorial part of the Iranian port of Lingeh that successive ethnically Qasimi governors of Lingeh administered in their capacity as Iranian subjects and officials. The Anglo-Arab view holds that the Tonbs belonged to the larger Qawasim tribe and that these governors of Lingeh on the Iranian coast administered the Tonbs as the tribal property of the Qawasim tribe.[59]

The Qawasim who gained the government of Lingeh owed their rise to political prominence to a complex web of associations with the Iranian government, other Arab tribes inhabiting the Iranian coast, political and matrimonial alliances with local governors and rulers on the Iranian coast, and to defining themselves by deed apart and distinct from their kinsmen in the lower Persian Gulf. The rise and fall of the Lingeh Qawasim is told else-where.[60] Suffice it to say: (i) in or about 1780, the Iranian government con-ferred on a Qasimi inhabitant of Lingeh the government of the port; (ii) the successive Qasimi administrators of Lingeh remained subjects and officials of the Iranian government until their divestiture in 1887; and (iii) already a faction of the larger Qawasim tribal group that was often at odds with the Qawasim in the eastern lower Persian Gulf, the Qawasim of Lingeh were subjects of the Iranian government throughout their settlement on the Ira-nian coast.[61] The Tonb islands were included in the administration of Lingeh because of their close proximity to Lingeh.[62]

The exercise of jurisdiction by the Qasimi governor of Lingeh on Tonbs and the Tonbs' relationship to Iran in the period 1869-1887 are subjects of a series of "letters" between the Qasimi governors of Lingeh and the Qasimi sheikhs in the lower Persian Gulf and between the former and their Iranian superiors. The first letter from the Qasimi governor of Lingeh to the Qasimi sheikh of Ras al-Khaimah, dated November 15, 1872, politely sidestepped the latter's complaint about the former's Al Bu Samait followers going to Great Tonb[63] and, instead, politely asked the latter to prohibit people from the lower Persian Gulf from going to Great Tonb for pasturage.[64] The Sheikh of Ras al-Khaimah complained again, and in a second letter dated Novem-ber 22, 1872, while restating his position about the Al Bu Samait and the people from the lower Persian Gulf visiting the island, the governor of Lingeh wrote "(a)s regards the island, it belongs to you just as it was under the authority of your father. We have nothing to interfere with you about it."[65] Yet, the Al Bu Samait continued to cross over. When the Sheikh of Ras al-Khaimah again complained to the British representative at the Iranian port of Bushehr, in February 1873, the governor of Lingeh told the British repre-sentative that the island belonged to him (governor of Lingeh).[66] The ex-cerpted contents of these letters are printed and analyzed elsewhere.[67]

The continuing crossing-over by the Al Bu Samait to Great Tonb for grazing precipitated another round of correspondence between the Qasimi governor of Lingeh and the Sheikh of Ras al-Khaimah. On January 8, 1877, the governor of Lingeh wrote to the Sheikh of Ras al-Khaimah stating, among other things, that he "(was) satisfied that the Island of Tamb is a depen-dency of the Jowasemis of Oman" and that he would prohibit the Al Bu Samait from going to the island.[68] Finally, when the Sheikh of Ras al-Khaimah again complained through the British representative at Lingeh, the governor of Lingeh—in a letter to the Sheikh of Ras al-Khaimah dated March 29, 1884—while promising to prohibit the Al Bu Samait from going to Tonb, stated "(i)n reality the island belongs to you the Jawasemis of Oman, and I have kept my hand over it, considering that you are agreeable to my doing so."[69]

The originals of these letters do not seem to exist. Therefore, any translation thereof, which was undertaken by the British authorities, or by persons in their influence, must be viewed with a certain amount of healthy skepticism. For example, in Persian and Arabic the words *satisfaction, consent,* and *agreeable* are rooted in the word *riza.* If this word or its derivation was indeed used in the correspondence to mean consent, then the intent to be bound by the consent must be ascertained in reference to the remainder of the text and the condition of the times. The use of the plural *you* as in the Qawasim of Oman, referring to a larger and differing entity than Ras al-Khaimah, and the repeated crossing-over of the Al Bu Samait to Great Tonb in spite of complaints by the Sheikh of Ras al-Khaimah, taken together, seem to suggest that the intent of these letters was anything but consent to or recognition of the rights of the Sheikh of Ras al-Khaimah over the island. The platitudes contained in these letters, akin to *mi casa es su casa, your obedient servant,* and *your wish is my command,* cannot be passed on as evidence or proof of territorial ownership or of political vassalage.[70]

These letters at best may constitute evidence of the manner in which the Qasimi governor of Lingeh and the Sheikh of Ras al-Khaimah regulated grazing rights among and between their respective subjects. The letters point to the existence of a claim to an ambiguous usufructuary right or grazing easement on the part of the Sheikh of Ras al-Khaimah. Even so, in the spring of 1873, the residency agent instructed the sheikh to remove his horses from the island and to apologize to the governor of Lingeh for the trespass (See discussion below). None of these letters, however, suggests admission by the Iranian government that the Tonbs belonged to a Qawasim tribal or territorial sovereignty. As far as the outside world was concerned, the governor of Lingeh's aforementioned response to the British representative in February 1873 placed the Tonbs within the Iranian territorial sovereignty qua the governorship of Lingeh.

On September 11, 1887, the Iranian government terminated the tenure of the Qasimi governor of Lingeh and four days later a detachment of Iranian troops led by the governor of Qishm Island proceeded to Sirri Island where he hoisted the Iranian flag and erected a garrison.[71]

In defense of their action, the Iranian government claimed that Sirri and Great Tonb were dependencies of Lingeh and that the government had evidence of them paying taxes for at least the past nine years (i.e., 1878-1887).[72] When the query was put to the Sheikh of Ras al-Khaimah, he replied, among other things, Great Tonb had been uninhabited in that period.[73]

Yet, curiously, there is irrefutable evidence that by 1885, if not earlier, the governor of Lingeh was busy exercising jurisdiction over Great Tonb and reporting on his activities to his superior in the Iranian government (i.e., the governor-general of Bandar Abbas and Lingeh). One of the residents of Tonb at this time was an Iranian, known in the Persian Gulf as Ahmad Tonbi (literally meaning from or of Tonb). A native of Lar in the Iranian province of Fars, he exported tobacco from Lar. In 1885, one of his boats was seized by the governor of Charak while it was loading tobacco at Charak on the Iranian coast on the grounds that some people of Charak had a claim against the merchant.[74] The governor of Lingeh intervened on behalf of the merchant and this exercise of jurisdiction by the governor over a resident of Tonb did not meet with protest on the part of any Qasimi sheikh in the lower Persian Gulf, suggesting therefore that the incident in all territorial and personal jurisdictional respects may have been deemed as an internal Iranian matter.

Shortly thereafter, as a result of an internecine conflict, the governor of the Iranian island of Qishm sought refuge on Great Tonb. Still in 1885, the governor of Lingeh sent an emissary to Tonb asking its people to receive the governor with respect and then proceeded to the island to send the governor off in the company of a special agent back to Qishm in order to effect a reconciliation between the feuding factions.[75] At the same time, the governor of Lingeh suggested to his Iranian governmental superior to send to the Iranian island of Kish an emissary to settle an estate matter; for the task, he recommended a Khamsin-ibn-Musa, whom the governor of Lingeh had sent previously to Tonb "to settle that Tamb business."[76] Although no direct mention of Tonb is made in the British extract of reports submitted by governor of Lingeh to governor-general of Bandar Abbas and Lingeh, it is clear however that in 1885 the Qasimi governor of Lingeh collected revenue on behalf of the Iranian government on Sirri Island,[77] and in all likelihood he did the same on Great Tonb.

In light of the foregoing, Iran's claim of ownership to the Tonbs based on the political history of the eastern Persian Gulf appears to be valid and sufficiently substantiated so to support Iran's historical title to the Tonbs down to 1887.

BRITISH RECOGNITION OF IRANIAN SOVEREIGNTY

The planting of the Iranian flag on Sirri Island in 1887 signaled to Great Britain the necessity of checking and, if possible, rolling back the assertive policies pursued by the Iranian government in the Persian Gulf. Little by little, the British consciousness began to disassociate itself from its deliberate and considered former view that the Tonbs belonged to Iran and began to espouse gradually a view dictated by new political realities. By 1903, the aforementioned intra-Qawasim correspondence, which until then had been ignored, conveniently and fortuitously came to justify and support the change in the British position, thereby ostensibly creating a prima facie case for her wards and placing Iran in the defensive position of having to rebut the presumption of Anglo-Arab sovereignty over the Tonbs. However, in rebuttal of the Iranian response, the Anglo-Arab claim itself would have had first to overcome Britain's well-documented prior actions, positions and statements which, as a matter of historical record, recognized Iran's sovereignty over the Tonbs.

In the period from 1870 through 1896, various officials and agents of the British government in the Persian Gulf and elsewhere held the view that the Tonbs belonged to Iran. In the 1870 edition of the *Persian Gulf Pilot,* a British admiralty publication, the islands of Tonb, Sirri, and Abu Musa were mentioned as islands belonging to Iran.[78]

In February 1873, in consequence of a feud between the governor of Lingeh and the Sheikh of Ras al-Khaimah regarding the Al Bu Samait's grazing on Great Tonb, the British political resident in the Persian Gulf, headquartered in Bushehr on the Iranian coast, instructed the residency agent at Sharjah to inquire about the ownership of the island. However, the residency agent, apparently knowing the answer, instructed the Sheikh of Ras al-Khaimah to keep clear of Great Tonb. The sheikh stated that Great Tonb belonged to the Qawasim of the lower Persian Gulf, while Little Tonb belonged to the Qawasim of Lingeh. Subsequently, in March 1873, the residency agent visited Great Tonb and thereafter instructed the Sheikh of Ras al-Khaimah to either apologize to the Qasimi governor of Lingeh for his horses grazing on the island or to remove the horses. At the same time, the residency agent reported back to the political resident that Great Tonb was a dependency of the Iranian province of Fars and was under the chief of Lingeh. In April 1873, the political resident adopted the residency agent's report and approved the latter's recommendation that the Sheikh of Ras al-Khaimah remove his horses from the island.[79]

In June 1879, in consequence of another round of complaints by the Sheikh of Ras al-Khaimah about grazing by the Al Bu Samait on Great Tonb, the political resident asked the residency agent in Lingeh to prepare a report on the dependencies of the Sheikhs of the lower Persian Gulf. The residency agent seems to have described Great Tonb as property held jointly by the Qasimi Sheikhs of Ras al-Khaimah and Lingeh. Noting in the margin of the report "considered Persian," the political resident corrected the residency agent's impression.[80]

In 1881, the residency agent in Sharjah procured "letters" seemingly written in 1872 and 1877 by the governor of Lingeh to the Sheikh of Ras al-Khaimah about Great Tonb. These letters were sent to the attention of the political resident, who wrote to the residency agent and advised that his previous position regarding the island (that it was considered Iranian) should be held until he could discuss the matter with the Sheikh of Ras al-Khaimah.[81] That discussion did not take place.

In 1886, the intelligence branch of the British War Office published the *Map of Persia* and on this map the Tonbs were depicted in Iran's color.[82] In the context of the Anglo-Iranian negotiations regarding the delimitation of the Iran-Afghanistan border on July 27, 1888, the British minister—on behalf of the British foreign secretary—gave a gift copy of the *Map of Persia* to the Shah Nasir al-Din Qajar, with the wishes that "it would be useful and interesting to His Majesty as His Majesty has on several occasions asked to be supplied with geographical information."[83]

In less than two months, the British minister in Tehran reported to London that the courtesy shown to the Shah in presenting him with the map produced "certain results which I fancy were hardly contemplated . . . with regard to the island of Sirri the Shah has quoted the map in which that island is marked in the Persian colours as a bar to any argument on our part in favour of the (Qasimi chiefs of the lower Persian Gulf) who lay claim to it, a claim which the Resident at Bushire considers we should support."[84] Upon being informed of the matter, Foreign Secretary Marquis of Salisbury commented: "Take note, maps shall never be presents in future."[85] The British government not only did not object to the Shah's interpretation of the contents of the *Map of Persia* (including the depiction of Sirri and Tonbs in Iran's color) but also, in fact, by August 1888, "decided tacitly to acquiesce in the Persian occupation of Sirri."[86]

In October 1887, the Sheikh of Sharjah complained to the political resident about Iran's actions in the previous month on Sirri Island and asked that the British government prevent such actions at Great Tonb. The British government decided however to confine their representations solely to Iran's actions on Sirri Island.[87] In April 1888, the agent of the Iranian government in the Persian Gulf prepared a document for the Iranian prime minister wherein he reported on Iran's ownership of the Tonbs, Abu Musa, and Sirri Islands and cited the aforementioned *Persian Gulf Pilot* as further authority. The British authorities in the Persian Gulf and Iran, having obtained a copy of the report through "private" channels, did not object to the contents of the report. In communicating a copy of the report to the British minister in Tehran, the political resident observed that the report did not contain anything new other than a claim to Abu Musa Island.[88]

Reissued without revision in 1891, the *Map of Persia* later formed the basis for Lord Curzon's *Map of Persia, Afghanistan, and Baluchistan* (1891) and the Government of India's *Map of Persia* (1897). On all these, the Tonbs continued to be depicted as Iranian territory.[89]

The aforementioned official British actions and publications at most amount to evidence of Britain's recognition of Iran's ownership of the Tonbs on the basis of immemorial prescription. In the least, the aforementioned actions and statements may be deemed as evidence of Britain having acquiesced in Iran's claim to the islands regardless of the underlying juridical basis. In either way, on the force of the evidence adduced above, international law precludes the flow of the legal consequences that Britain later would want to effect in order to support the Anglo-Arab claim of sovereignty over the Tonbs.

The Iranian action on Sirri Island in September 1887 and the Sheikh of Sharjah's concern that the same may be repeated on Great Tonb were *followed* by the presentation of the *Map of Persia* to the Shah in July 1888. The presentation of the map was trumpeted as a gesture to satisfy the monarch's request for geographical information. Yet this gesture, made at the time of Anglo-Iranian negotiations about the Iran-Afghanistan boundary, probably was intended to induce the Shah to interpret politically the information about the Iran-Afghanistan border as Britain would have liked the border to be delimited.

The information on the *Map of Persia* about Sirri Island had been consistent with Iran's view that the island had belonged to Iran. Further, the map coming almost a year *after* the Iranian action on Sirri also validated the action in spite of the various protests that Britain was lodging in Tehran. Ultimately, Britain's recognition of Iran's sovereignty over Sirri confirmed the Iranian claim to Sirri, recognized the validity of the Iranian action, and agreed with the Iranian interpretation of the information about the sovereignty of the island as depicted on the *Map of Persia*. Similarly, the inaction or lack of protest on the part of the British government regarding the Sheikh of Ras al-Khaimah's concern about Great Tonb, Iran's statement of claim to the Tonbs, and the depiction of the Tonbs as Iranian territory on the map all were consistent with and necessary consequences of Britain's recognition of or acquiescence to Iran's ownership of the Tonbs.

In a situation such as this, where the views of the parties converged or were in agreement, there existed no contest and therefore acquiescence is hardly a relevant doctrine. For the sake of the argument, however, an analysis of the case from the point of view of acquiescence can bolster only Iran's position. In international law, silence does not necessarily mean consent, but it is axiomatic that the failure to object to a stated claim is capable of giving rise to adverse legal consequences for the silent or non-objecting party. In the words of the International Court of Justice, "(i)t is clear that the circumstances were such as called for some reaction . . . on the part of the . . . authorities . . . They did not do so, either then or for many years, and thereby must be held to have acquiesced."[90] The consequence of this doctrine is called preclusion or estoppel.

In its most basic formulation, estoppel states that a party who makes or concurs in a statement, upon which another party relies and changes its position, is prevented from later asserting a different state of affairs.[91] As a general principle of law recognized by civilized nations,[92] estoppel or preclusion is recognized as part of general international law applied by international tribunals.[93] In *Temple of Preah Vihear* (1962) the World Court stated the principle as follows: "The essential condition of the operation of the rule of preclusion or estoppel, as strictly to be understood, is that the party invoking the rule must have 'relied upon' the statements or conduct of the other party, either to its own detriment or to the other's advantage."[94] The agreement that existed at the time between the Iranian and British views about the status of the Tonbs, as evidenced by official British conduct and statements, obviated the need by the Iranian government to do anything more with respect to the Tonbs in 1887-1888. To that extent, Iran relied upon Britain's conduct and in so doing may have acted in detriment of its interest by not erecting a flag or a garrison on the Tonbs as she had done on Sirri, therefore, leaving that form of display of sovereignty to a later time (1903) when doing so received vociferous and militant opposition by the British due to change in Britain's political attitude.

While the showing of detrimental reliance may result in estoppel or preclusion of the Anglo-Arab claim to the Tonbs, there seems to be at work also a principle of law which may operate to exclude evidence that is contradictory, regardless of detrimental reliance. The maxim *allegans contraria non est audiendus* means "one whose statements contradict each other is not to be heard."[95]

In *Behring Sea Arbitration* (1893),[96] the proceedings "demonstrated that some advantage is to be gained by one State, party to a dispute, by convicting the other State of inconsistency with an attitude previously adopted. This is not estoppel *eo nomino,* but it shows that international jurisprudence has a place for some recognition of the principle that a State cannot blow hot and cold—*allegans contraria non audiendus est.*"[97] The existence of this anti-inconsistency principle in international law is warranted and supported by the implied covenant or principle of good faith underlying dealings among nations.[98] In Iranian legal theory and practice and with respect to the British recantation over the Tonbs, the practice of blowing hot and cold is governed by the prohibition against admission of *post*-confession denials.[99] Accordingly, in 1888, the Shah of Iran pointed to the *Map of Persia* (1886) "as a bar to any argument" against Iranian sovereignty over Sirri.[100] The acquiescence of the British government in the Iranian sovereignty over Sirri, itself, in the minimum, validated the existence and application of the anti-inconsistency rule to the island at that time.

The British government's denials of the legal effects of their earlier statements in 1870 through 1896 regarding the Iranian status of the Tonbs acknowledges the adverse legal consequences that result from blowing hot and cold. In April 1888, the political resident commented to the British minister in Tehran that the Iranian agent's report on the status of the islands in the Persian Gulf was based on the *Persian Gulf Pilot,* which, being a nautical and not a political compilation, could not be considered authoritative.[101] As regards the *Map of Persia* (1886), the Marquis of Salisbury's aforementioned general admonition about presenting maps as gifts also remained within the British circles. At no time during the period from 1870 through 1896 did the British government communicate to the Iranian government a view other than the plain and simple meaning of the depictions and descriptions contained in these two official British government documents consistent with the political resident's considered opinion that the Tonbs were Iranian territory.

Some forty years after the fact, in 1928, the British government stated to the Iranian government that the depiction of the Tonbs in Iranian colors on the *Map of Persia* (1886) had been a "mistake" and that "the error in question is extremely regrettable from the standpoint of His Majesty's government" and that "it cannot be taken as a formal declaration by His Majesty's government of their view of the status of the islands."[102] Internally, the British government was not as dismissive, however. In 1928, the head of the Eastern department at the foreign office observed that "the evidence of the map is in no way conclusive, but it is inconvenient."[103] The Acting Principal Secretary of State for Foreign Affairs stated: "Yes, our case seems pretty good but it is not one in which we can plead 'no evidence to go to the jury.'"[104] In 1934, the assistant head of the Eastern department noted that the depiction of the Tonbs as Iranian on the map was "unfortunate."[105]

Research indicates that the depiction of the Tonbs on the *Map of Persia* (1886) as Iranian was not and could not have been a mistake. The depiction was wholly consistent with the Iranian and longstanding British political views at the time that the Tonbs belonged to Iran. Furthermore, in view of the Shah's open, categorical, and adversarial reliance on the *Map of Persia* (1886) in 1888 and the Marquis of Salisbury's subsequent admonition, it is unlikely that no one in the British Empire at the time would deny, correct, or otherwise rectify the "mistake." Instead, in 1891, the British war office reissued the *Map of Persia* on which the Tonbs, Sirri, and Abu Musa islands still were depicted as Iranian.[106]

In 1892, the Royal Geographical Society of London published the *Map of Persia, Afghanistan, and Baluchistan* (hereinafter referred to as "Curzon's Map") that depicted the Tonbs, Sirri, and Abu Musa in Iran's color (pink).[107] This map was compiled in 1891 by George N. Curzon, the then member of Parliament and the future viceroy of India, and a close friend of the Marquis of Salisbury.[108] According to the explanatory note accompanying it, Curzon's Map was compiled in reference to British, German, and Russian admiralty charts, maps constructed by intelligence departments, and surveys. With respect to Persia and the Persian Gulf, specifically, the map drew directly from a large number of maps and charts, including the 1886 and 1891 editions of *Map of Persia.* "In the case," Curzon noted, "how frequent I should hardly like to confess, where our authorities were disagreed, the pros and cons have not been lightly balanced before a decision was made."[109] There can be little doubt about the deliberate, learned, and considered nature of Curzon's depiction of the Tonbs as Iranian: In his *Persia and the Persian Question* (1892), Curzon mentions the Tonbs by their Iranian nomenclature.[110] In view of the Tonbs' location in the middle of the Persian Gulf, straddling the busy sea lanes of communication extending in all directions, and being sandwiched between the assertive Iranian state to the north and the Trucial sheikhdoms to the south, at least a doubt could have been expressed as to the islands' status and, if so, judging by the subsequent depiction of the map in Iran's color, the doubt, therefore, must be assumed to have been resolved in Iran's favor.

In 1897, two years before Curzon's investiture as viceroy of India, the British India government published its own version of the *Map of Persia* on which the Tonbs, Sirri, and Abu Musa islands were depicted again in Iran's color (green).[111]

The successive cartographic depictions of the Tonbs as Iranian, without any effort to deny their accuracy by Britain at a time when such denial or rectification would have been warranted, was tantamount to the British declaration that 'we in the so and so government view the world in a thus and such manner and in that worldview we see your territory including these islands.' In *Alaskan Boundary Arbitration Award* (1903),[112] the tribunal found that for a period of sixty years official maps published by Russia, Great Britain, Canada, and United States were in agreement with regard to the location of a particular boundary. In virtue thereof, the tribunal noted, "it became a common understanding of mankind" that the territory in question belonged to a particular sovereign.[113] It concluded, "only the clearest case of mistake could warrant a change of construction after so long a period of acquiescence; and no such case of mistake had been made out before the tribunal."[114]

The *Map of Persia* and other similar cartographical evidence depicted a clear and manifest agreement or convergence of views between Iran and Britain regarding the status of the Tonbs, a common understanding unencumbered at the time by contestation. In the words of the British agent in the *Passamaquody Case* (1794), these maps "must to any unprejudiced mind most strongly evince the sense of both nations at that time with regard to the right to these islands."[115]

Ultimately, the British recognition of or acquiescence in Iran's sovereignty over the Tonbs can be deemed as binding also on the sheikhs and sheikhdoms of Ras al-Khaimah and Sharjah as a matter of British imperial law.

LEGAL EFFECT OF CARTOGRAPHICAL EVIDENCE

Notwithstanding the relevance of the British maps to the recognition of or acquiescence in the status of the Tonbs as Iranian, the British maps may be viewed also independently as evidence of Iran's title to the Tonbs. In *Island of Palmas* (1928), the arbitrator Max Huber articulated a set of criteria whereby a map may be admitted as evidence involving recognition or abandonment of rights to territory, offering an indirect proof of the existence, not exercise, of sovereignty in law.[116] The first condition required of maps that are to serve as evidence on points of law is their geographical accuracy. Second, the map should not contradict the existence of legally relevant facts. Third, the map must be based on information carefully collected, preferably by researchers on the spot, for the purpose of indicating political distribution of territories. Fourth, the map must be, preferably, an official or semi-official map asserting the sovereignty of the country whose government has issued it.[117]

In the case of *Map of Persia* (1886) and progeny, the first condition is met in that the information supplied by the intelligence branch of the British War Office must be presumed to have been accurate. Further, the accuracy of the information therein contained is buttressed by the absence of any disagreement at the time between Iran and Britain about the Tonbs being Iranian territory. Second, the depiction of the Tonbs in Iran's color was consistent with the legally relevant facts at the time according to which the Tonbs were deemed by Iran and Britain as belonging to Iran. Unlike in the *Island of Palmas* where the cartographical information submitted by the Netherlands and United States were often contradictory and at variance, in the case of the Tonbs there were no differing views. Further, that view was shared also by the commercial mapmakers of the time.[118] Third, while the *Map of Persia* may have been vague in its origin, the later reissue of the same information regarding the Tonbs in Curzon's Map and the *Map of Persia* by the British India government must be presumed to have verified and ratified the information contained in the earlier map. Finally, the *Map of Persia* and progeny were official and semi-official British maps which, rather than proving the Anglo-Arab claim, admit adversely the Iranian claim instead. According to Huber's scale, therefore, these maps indicate in law the proof of existence of Iranian sovereignty over the Tonbs.

ANGLO-ARAB CLAIM BASED ON OCCUPATION

In the period from 1887 and 1903, Iran and other countries, including Russia and France, began to challenge Britain's position in the Persian Gulf. Consequently, the British government obtained from, among others, the Sheikhs of Ras al-Khaimah and Sharjah certain "preliminary exclusive undertakings" whereby each Sheikh agreed (i) not to enter into agreement with any government save the British government and, (ii) not to permit an agent of any government to reside in his dominions. In 1891-1892, these undertakings were made into permanent exclusive agreements, with the added condition that no sheikh cede, sell, mortgage or otherwise give for occupation any part of his territory to any government other than the British government. Simultaneously, in consequence of the disturbances near Lingeh and the trade policies pursued by the Iranian government, the port of Lingeh declined, customs revenues decreased, and the local merchants began to look into the possibility of making Abu Musa Island a port of call instead.[119]

With the reorganization of the Iranian Customs Department under Belgian administration, in 1901-1902 a number of customs posts were established on the Iranian coast, including at Kung near Lingeh, and on Qishm (1901) and Kish (1902) Islands. Among other islands each marked to receive an Iranian customs post were Sirri, Abu Musa and Great Tonb.[120]

Concerned over Iran's further presence in the Persian Gulf, the British India government asked the political resident to report on the rumor of the impending arrival of Iranian customs on these islands. The political resident reported that the Sheikh of Sharjah possessed letters from two former Qasimi chiefs of Lingeh as to the status of the Tonbs and that as far as the political resident was aware, "sovereignty over (Great Tonb) island had never been asserted by Persia."[121] However, he cautioned that any action by the sheikh on the island would provoke an Iranian reaction. Nevertheless, the British India government ordered the sheikh to hoist his flag on Great Tonb as a sign of ownership and in July 1903 the latter obliged.[122] The British government, in 1903, conveniently turned a blind eye to (i) the Iranian statement of claim in 1887-1888 about Sirri and Great Tonb, (ii) the depiction of the Tonbs as Iranian on the *Map of Persia* (1886) and progeny and the

Persian Gulf Pilot, (iii) the political resident's conclusions regrading the status of Great Tonb as Iranian, and (iv) the existence of Iranian documentary evidence about exercise of jurisdiction on Great Tonb by the Iranian government qua the Governorate-General of Bandar Abbas and Lingeh. This amnesia in effect served Britain (i) to deny its prior longstanding recognition of the Tonbs as Iranian, and (ii) to deny the fact of Iran's prior claim to the Tonbs. Thus the portrayal of the Tonbs in 1903 as "land belonging to nobody and claimed by none" now would make the islands in law susceptible to occupation by the Sheikh of Sharjah.

In March 1904, the director of Iranian customs visited Great Tonb, where he removed the sheikh's flag, and hoisted the Iranian flag and posted an Iranian contingent of riflemen to guard it. The Sheikh of Sharjah complained to the political resident and Britain lodged a diplomatic protest in Tehran in May. On June 14, 1904, the Iranian government lowered the flag, while, as the British minister in Tehran reported, "reserv[ing] their right to discuss with His Majesty's Government the respective claims to the islands."[123]

According to the British documentation, contemporaneous with the lowering of the Iranian flag, the Iranian government handed a note to the British minister stating Iran's claim to Great Tonb and "proposing" that neither party should hoist its flag on it pending settlement of the question.[124] The British reply note stated that the Sheikh of Sharjah should be permitted to rehoist his flag because his flag had pre-dated the Iranian flag on the island. The reply note further stated that the sheikh was flying his flag as the first occupant on an island not yet formally occupied by any government.[125] The reply note concluded that the sheikh's flag refly on the island "until his lawful possession of the island is disproved" and asked the Iranian government to forward to the British India government any proof outweighing the claim of the Sheikh of Sharjah.[126]

According to the Iranian documentation on the matter, the British government secured the lowering of the Iranian flag at Great Tonb by means of threats and pressures.[127] The pressure applied in Tehran was in all likelihood the threat of gunboat diplomacy. Earlier, in April and May of 1904, the British India government had proposed to dispatch a gunboat to the island, with a representative of the Sheikh of Sharjah on board, to haul down the Iranian flag, reinstate the sheikh's flag, and remove the Iranian guards to the Iranian mainland.[128]

At the end of the June 14-15 Anglo-Iranian proceedings over the Tonbs, which the Iranian documentation refers to as negotiations (*mozakerat*), the Iranian foreign minister noted, "(i)t has been agreed to that no flag be hoisted from either side on the two locations."[129] As it relates to Iran's future position with respect to the islands, this entente is referred to as the 1904 status quo agreement, whose existence the British documentation does not seem to explicitly recognize. Regardless, on June 17, 1904, the Sheikh of Sharjah hoisted his flag on Great Tonb. Following an Iranian protest, the British Legation replied that "the Sheikh had the right to fly his flag on an island of undetermined ownership."[130]

In international law, occupation is defined as the intentional appropriation of sovereignty by a State over territory which at the time is not under the sovereignty of another State. In order for occupation to be valid, first, the territory must be *terra nullius,* meaning belonging to no State,[131] and, second, the occupation must be real or effective. To be deemed real or effective, intent to occupy (*animus occupendi*) and actual possession (*corpus occupendi*) must be shown to exist.[132]

The evidence adduced above points to (i) the likelihood of Iranian sovereignty over the Tonbs before 1870, and (ii) the absence of any other territorial sovereignty before 1870. The evidence adduced for the period between 1870 and 1897 points to the Iranian ownership of the Tonbs. Even by the evidence tending to support the Anglo-Arab claim (i.e., the intra-Qawasim correspondence), the Tonbs therefore could not have been in fact *terra nullius* when the Sheikh of Sharjah raised his flag on Great Tonb in 1903.

As formulated and practiced by European powers, under the doctrine of *occupatio,* a particular territory assumed the status of *terra nullius* irrespective of its settlement by the natives since they were considered, regardless of their organization into a political society, to be outside the international legal order.[133] Neither the Qawasim tribe as a whole, spread in and around the eastern Persian Gulf, nor the individual entities under the sway of the Qasimi Sheikhs in the lower Persian Gulf can be viewed as having had the requisite international legal personality and power to acquire territory in international law. Therefore, the hoisting of the Sheikh of Sharjah's flag on Great Tonb in 1903 was legally an insignificant act, unless it be interpreted in terms of conquest of Iranian territory by an agent or a subject of international law (i.e., Great Britain). By the same token, were the Tonbs *terra nullius* in 1903, the hoisting of Iran's flag on Great Tonb in that year may be construed as the first instance of an act of occupation of the island by a subject of international law (i.e., a State) with the legal power to acquire territory in international law.

In view of the foregoing, the legally significant historical facts regarding the Tonbs are such that, as a matter of law, any Anglo-Arab claim to title over the Tonbs by virtue of *occupatio* must be barred for the failure to meet the requirement of showing the Tonbs as *terra nullius* in 1903-1904.

ANGLO-ARAB CLAIM BASED ON PRESCRIPTION

In international law, prescription refers to the "[a]cquisition of sovereignty over a territory through continuous and undisputed exercise of sovereignty over it during such a period as is necessary to create under the influence of historical development the general conviction that the present condition of things is in conformity with international order."[134]

On the basis of the evidence adduced above, it may be held that Iran had title to the Tonbs up to 1903-1904 by virtue of immemorial prescription. However, during these years, the Sheikh of Sharjah challenged Iran's sovereignty over the island. This marked the starting point of the Anglo-Arab claim over the Tonbs by virtue of acquisitive prescription, a concept akin to adverse possession in municipal law, whereby good title is created through possession even though the first act of taking possession may have been wrongful. In municipal law, to acquire title by adverse possession, it is required that possession be open, hostile, notorious, exclusive, and with the intent or color of title.[135] In international law, acquisitive prescription confers title where possession is actual (or real), peaceful (or undisturbed) and continuous (or uninterrupted) for some determinative length of time.[136]

Under instructions from the political resident and apparently in violation of the Anglo-Iranian 1904 status quo agreement, on June 14, 1904 the Sheikh of Sharjah rehoisted his flag on Great Tonb. One British report described the event as such: "Flagstaffs were erected on Tamb and Abu Musa and guards stationed, and the Chiefs and inhabitants of the Pirate Coast were glad, and felt assured that the British government would protect them versus enemies and would maintain their honour, and the people highly praised the British government."[137]

In August 1906, the British inspected the flag on Great Tonb. Following a lengthy correspondence with the foreign office, in 1909 an English firm began prospecting for red oxide on the Tonbs. In 1912-1913, Britain erected a lighthouse on Great Tonb for which purpose the British obtained the assent of the Sheikh of Sharjah. In connection therewith, while assuring the Sheikh that the lighthouse would preserve forever his ownership of the island, Britain admonished the Sheikh for not keeping his flag in good repair and for not flying it regularly for his own good name and the dignity of the Qawasim. In 1921, Ras al-Khaimah separated from Sharjah and Britain determined finally, in as late as 1929, that the Tonbs formed a part of Ras al-Khaimah. In September 1929, it was reported that one of the inhabitants of Great Tonb was the representative of the Sheikh of Ras al-Khaimah. In 1931, reports indicated that the Sheikh of Ras al-Khaimah collected a hauler's share from fishing

boats on Great Tonb. In November 1965, Iranian intelligence reported
that Ras al-Khaimah's flag was flying over Great Tonb, where the Sheikh
intended to build an airport and a naval base and to claim the Tonbs' conti-
nental shelf. According to reports, the sheikh's flag was flying on Great
Tonb in 1967 and 1968. In November 1971, Union Oil of California reported a
modest oil and gas find in the waters off the Tonbs under an oil concession
from the Sheikh of Ras al-Khaimah. In the same month, Ras al-Khaimah
established a police station on Great Tonb.[138]

As for the Iranian activities with respect to the Tonbs, in March 1904,
Iran hauled down the Sheikh of Sharjah's flag. When the Sheikh of Sharjah
rehoisted his flag on Great Tonb in June 1904, Iran protested to Britain. In
May 1905, Iran lodged a protest with the British government about rumors
of the sheikh's intention to build houses on the island (news that was found
to be baseless). In 1912-1913, Iran complained to Britain on several occasions against the erection of the lighthouse on Great Tonb, to which Britain
responded, *inter alia,* that the lighthouse was being put in for the good of
navigation and only because Iran did not have the financial wherewithal to
set up one herself. In conjunction with the furtherance of Iranian commercial interests in the eastern Persian Gulf, in 1923 and again in 1925-1926,
Iran recommunicated to the British government her claim over the Tonbs.[139]

In July 1928, Iranian customs seized near Great Tonb a Dubai boat suspected of smuggling. The controversy produced a protracted series of me-
morials and counter-memorials by Iran and Britain regarding sovereignty
over the Tonbs and the exercise of jurisdiction over the suspected crime,
persons, cargo, and boat involved in the incident. In the end, in April 1930,
Britain paid compensation to the persons claiming damages as the result of
the incident but Iran remained unrepenting. During this incident, in 1928-
1930, Iranian customs vessels paid several visits to Great Tonb and on one
occasion, in October 1930, Iran protested to Britain about the British flag
found flying on the island. In April 1933, the governor of Bandar Abbas,
chief of police, and the collector of customs visited Great Tonb; Britain
decided not to protest the visit. In July 1933, the Iranian navy paid a visit to
Great Tonb causing Britain to lodge a protest with the Iranian government.
In early August 1934, the Iranian navy paid another visit to Great Tonb, but
this time the visit went undetected by Britain. The subsequent visits to
Great Tonb by the Iranian navy, however, in late August and again in
mid-September 1934, drew British protests.[140]

In January 1935, the British senior naval officer in the Persian Gulf
(SNO) reported that the town manager at Bassidu on Qishm Island had
asked a resident of Great Tonb to carry a letter back with him to the island.
At the same time the SNO reported that the director of Bandar Abbas cus-

toms was due to arrive on Great Tonb in February to collect customs dues and hoist the Iranian flag. The visit did not materialize. However, in April 1935, the governor of Bandar Abbas sent a letter to the headman on Great Tonb enclosing therewith for immediate circulation three copies of the *Esteemed Decree of His Imperial Majesty Relating to the Election of the 10th Period of the Majlis.* For a variety of reasons, including the interception of the letter by the British authorities, Britain elected not to protest the matter.[141]

On April 12, 1939, the Iranian parliament passed an enabling act granting to a Dutch company exploration rights regarding, *inter alia,* an area which included the Tonbs. The British government elected not to protest the inclusion of the islands in the concession area.[142]

In December 1940, a native of Ras al-Khaimah and resident of Tonb reportedly collected tolls in the name of the Iranian navy from ships passing by the Tonbs, issuing receipts bearing the Iranian navy's insignia. The activity, which received the Shah Reza Pahlavi's personal endorsement, was neither questioned, challenged, nor protested by the British government or the Sheikh of Ras al-Khaimah. In the period from 1948 through 1950 Iran repeatedly stated her claim to the Tonbs, which the British government refuted as before. While the Iranian War Ministry was urging the Iranian government to take possession of the Tonbs by force and install a garrison there, in April 1953, the Iranian Ministry of Foreign Affairs set up a commission of inquiry to study the various means whereby Iran could resolve her differences with Britain over the Tonbs. The commission considered options ranging from the use of force to international adjudication. Use of force and referral to the United Nations were ruled out, as was third party mediation. The commission's sole recommendation was for the matter to be referred to the International Court of Justice. In the meantime, the commission urged the government not to allow the controversy over the issue to die out. In May 1953, Iran objected to British surveillance flights over the Tonbs. Britain responded that she did not recognize Iran's claim to the islands. Later in the year, in November, an interdepartmental delegation from Tehran visited Great Tonb and upon return recommended that a detachment be sent to occupy the island and set up a telegraph station. Britain did not protest the visit.[143]

In the period from November 22, 1954 through January 1955, Iran consolidated and reorganized her southern coastal districts into a single Governorate-General of the Ports and Islands of the Persian Gulf. Thereunder, Great Tonb was incorporated into the subdistrict of Qishm Island, while Little Tonb was incorporated into the subdistrict of Kish Island.[144] Britain did not protest.

In June 1960, under instructions from the Shah Mohammad Reza Pahlavi, the Iranian government looked into unobtrusive ways to erect on Great Tonb seemingly insignificant installations such as a weather monitoring station.

In September 1961, an Iranian army helicopter ferried a team of surveyors to Great Tonb to demarcate the location of the weather station. Britain protested the visit and Tehran and London undertook the customary exchanges of notes and reply-notes. Following the discovery of the Sheikh of Ras al-Khaimah's intention to build military installations on Great Tonb and after a prolonged interdepartmental debate in Tehran, the Iranian government, on January 7, 1968, finally protested to Britain against the sheikh's intentions. Four days later the Iranian navy began to patrol the Tonb waters and for the next week or so the British airplanes buzzed the Iranian ships prompting a protest by Iran. Britain's response was followed by further aerial harassment of Iranian warships in Iranian and international waters, which, in turn, drew further protests from Iran. Meanwhile, an unmarked Iranian boat landed at Great Tonb and reported back that a British delegation had arrived there a few days earlier to survey the island with a view toward setting up a police station. In May 1971, the Iranian warships returned to patrol in Tonb waters. Britain reacted by overflights. Iran protested the overflights and served notice on Britain that the Iranian ships now were under orders to fire on British planes.[145]

The aforementioned Anglo-Arab activities may be claimed to pass the standards set forth in the case law regarding the quantity and quality of acts which could be viewed as evidence of actual and continuous possession over territory, which, without else, could be deemed sufficient to confer title to Ras al-Khaimah.[146] However, the Anglo-Arab claim based on acquisitive prescription fails to obtain title because Iran's rival acts with respect to the Tonbs and her protests over Anglo-Arab activities there rendered the Anglo-Arab possession neither peaceful nor undisturbed or undisputed. The aforementioned Iranian activities (i) denied the Anglo-Arab claim of title based on acquisitive prescription the essential attribute of peaceful, undisputed, and undisturbed display of sovereignty which is required to confer title, and (ii) evidenced display or assertion of Iranian sovereignty in continuation of and conformity with Iran's pre-1903/1904 recognized sovereignty over the island.

The criterion for peaceful (undisputed and undisturbed) manifestation of sovereignty is the requirement that "the first assertion of sovereignty must not be an usurpation of another's subsisting occupation nor contested from the first by competing acts of sovereignty."[147] In the case of the Tonbs, Iranian sovereignty over the islands predated the hoisting of the sheikh's flag in 1903 and thereafter Iran's continuous protests about the Anglo-Arab activities, coupled with competing sovereign acts of her own, disputed, disturbed and compromised the Anglo-Arab position in the Tonbs. As borne out by the case law on the subject, the display of sovereignty in face of protests and claims cannot be considered undisturbed.[148] The quality and frequency of Iran's actions, claims and protests therefore defeat any Anglo-Arab claim over the Tonbs based on acquisitive prescription.

THE COMMON UNDERSTANDING OF MANKIND

With the exception of two works, the maps and other works published in the period from 1904 and 1971 continued to evince the common under-standing of mankind that the Tonbs belonged to Iran, despite the fact that Iran and Britain bitterly contested the status of the islands since 1904. A Dutch atlas published in 1938 depicted the Tonbs in the same color (pink) as the Trucial coast, while indexing the islands as British territory. How-ever, in the same work, Sirri Island is given in the same color as Iran (green) and again in the same color as the Trucial coast (pink).[149] Similarly con-fused, an American gazetteer published in 1952 described the Tonbs as be-longing to Sharjah,[150] even though since 1930 the Tonbs were being claimed by and for Ras al-Khaimah.

In 1903, the Russian government and, in 1907-1913, the German gov-ernment weighed in on the side of Iran's claim to the Tonbs, although, in view of the politics of the day, these sentiments may be said to have been more anti-British than pro-Iranian.[151] However, the view of the French vice-consul at Bushehr in southern Iran appears to have been untainted by politi-cal considerations. In *Le Golfe Persique* (1920), he referred to Great Tonb as *un port persan* (an Iranian port).[152]

The Soviet Union's view of the status of the Tonbs was expressed in two editions of the *World Atlas* published in 1954 and 1967. Compiled under the supervision of the Council of Ministers of the Soviet Socialist Republics, the earlier one depicted the Tonbs as Iranian territory by both color and explicit designation.[153] The later revised publication, issued on the occasion of the fifti-eth anniversary of the October Revolution, depicted the Tonbs as Iranian terri-tory by color, explicit designation, and reference to the islands by their Iranian name (Tumbi-buzurg and Tumbi-kuchik).[154] This depiction's significance is also in that, at the time, the Soviet Union was the patron of the radical Arab, anti-Iranian governments in Egypt and Iraq, both of which were challenging Iran's position in the Persian Gulf and elsewhere.

The 1909 edition of *Hammond's Atlas* depicted the Tonbs in Iran's color (yellow).[155] In Rand McNally's *Cosmopolitan World Atlas* (1956), Great Tonb was indexed as Iranian territory.[156] Among European works mention can be made of the Swedish *Stora Atlas* (1951), which showed the Tonbs in Iran's color (green),[157] and of the French *Atlas Larousse* (1965), which did the same using the color purple.[158] The depiction of the Tonbs in the Italian work *Atlante Internazionale* (1968) is particularly interesting in that the work took notice of the differences between Iran and her Arab neighbors regarding the nomenclature of the Persian Gulf—on the plate focused on Iran, the gulf is designated as Persian Gulf and the Tonbs are depicted in Iran's color (orange)[159] and on the plate which shows the Arab lands the gulf is referred to as the Arabian Gulf *but* the Tonbs are still in Iran's color (light green).[160]

The views of private or commercial British mapmakers in the period under consideration also was completely in tune with the official view of the Bristish and other governmental authorities regarding the Iranian status of the Tonb Islands. While the map appended to William Jackson's *Persia: Past and Present* (1909) depicted the Tonbs as Iranian territory,[161] similar attributions were made by various other lesser maps of British origin dated 1920 and 1922.[162] More importantly, the *Time Survey Atlas of the World* (1922)—prepared at the Edinburgh Geographical Institute under the direction of H.M.'s cartographer, J. G. Bartholomew, and dedicated to King George V—referred to Great Tonb as an Iranian island.[163] In the midcentury edition of the *Times Atlas of the World* (1959), the Tonbs were designated as Iranian territory.[164] And, the *Times Index-Gazetteer of the World* published in 1965 referred to Great Tonb by its Iranian name (Tamb-e bozorg).[165]

CONCLUSION

In *Island of Palmas* the arbitrator evaluated first the claim of the Netherlands and then determined whether the claim of the United States was "equivalent or stronger."[166] Similarly, in *Eastern Greenland* the tribunal sought to determine which of the two claims was "stronger."[167] In *Minquiers and Ecrehos* the World Court reviewed the evidence submitted by each party and sought then "to appraise the relative strength of the opposing claims."[168] It must therefore be considered as a settled principle of international jurisprudence, particularly with respect to the quieting of claims over territory, that when "both parties put forward claims which, even though if taken separately and in isolation, would perhaps suffice to give each of them a valid title, but, when confronted with each other, the tribunal called upon to determine the issue will have to decide which of the contestants has made out a *better* or *superior* title"(emphasis added).[169]

In light of the facts in evidence as adduced and evaluated above, the genesis of the Anglo-Arab claim to the Tonbs does not predate 1750. Therefore, the Anglo-Arab claim is neither comparable nor competitive with Iran's claim of historical title over the Tonbs prior to 1750. This conclusion based on the pre-1750 political situation in the eastern Persian Gulf is reinforced by the references found in medieval and early modern works identifying the Tonbs exclusively with Iran.

Any claim to the Tonbs based on ethnicity, even if allowable in law, does not favor one side or the other, as Iranians and Arabs, including Arabs from territories other than Ras al-Khaimah and Sharjah, frequented Great Tonb. Any claim to the Tonbs based on proximity can favor only Iran, as the Tonbs are closer to the Iranian coast than they are to the Arabian littoral, a fact that the Iranian and Anglo-Arab views credit as the reason why the Tonbs were being governed or administered from Lingeh on the Iranian coast.

The presumed Iranian sovereignty over the Tonbs in the period 1750 and 1887 appears to have remained unmolested as a matter of international law, even though that sovereignty may be questioned by the intra-Qawasim correspondence about Great Tonb. The intra-Qawasim correspondence, in turn, is impeached on its own terms and challenged even further by the existence of rival Iranian documentation showing exercise of jurisdiction with respect to the Tonbs by the Lingeh government. The British recognition of Iranian sovereignty, as documented in, *inter alia,* nautical and carto-graphical works and in internal deliberations, further substantiates the Iranian ownership of the islands in this period.

Britain's continuing recognition of Iran's sovereignty over the Tonbs and her acquiescence in Iran's claim to the Tonbs in 1887 and onward, including the evidence of the maps, weigh heavily and exclusively on the side of the existence of Iranian sovereignty over the islands.

The years 1903-1904 marked the beginning of the Anglo-Arab claim over the Tonbs by virtue of *occupatio,* even though the islands could not have been *terra nullius* by virtue of prior British position, prior Arab ad-mission and claim, and Iranian evidence and claim. Just as the Anglo-Arab claim based on occupation is untenable as a matter of law, so is the notion that Anglo-Arab actions from 1903 onward created for the actors title in the Tonbs by virtue of adverse possession. In the latter case, the evidence of Iranian activity with respect to the Tonbs, itself considerable and poten-tially title-creating in a reversed situation, denies the Anglo-Arab claim the requirement that adverse possession be peaceful, undisputed, or undisturbed in order for it to create title.

In view of the foregoing, Iran's longstanding sovereignty over the Tonbs appears indefeasible in law and, by the force of the substantial and superior evidence herein adduced, her claim of ownership to the Tonbs appears stronger or better than or superior to any Anglo-Arab claim to the islands, thereby meeting the burden of proof of ownership in a clear and convincing manner.

NOTES

1. This chapter is based on Mirfendereski, Guive, "The Tamb Islands Controversy, 1887-1971: A Case Study in Claims to Territory in International Law" (Ph.D diss., Fletcher School of Law and Diplomacy, Tufts University, Medford, Massachusetts, 1985), i-xxii, 798 pages, bibliography, appendices, maps, and illustrations.

2. For a detailed explanation of the dependent status of Little Tonb, *see* Mirfendereski, ibid., pp. 96-103.

3. *Island of Palmas* (United States/Netherlands)(Permanent Court of Arbitration at The Hague, Award of 4 April 1928), reprinted in J.B. Scott, ed., *The Hague Court Reports* (2nd ser., 1932), p. 111. For a discussion of the use of the proximity principle by Britain to justify the allotment of certain islands in the Persian Gulf to sheikhs and territories controlled by or friendly to Britain, *see* Mirfendereski, *"The Tamb Islands Controversy, 1887-1971,"* pp. 117-128.

4. For details regarding such arguments and their general inapplicability to the case of the Tonbs, ibid., pp. 129-164.

5. F.O. 371/13777 (1929), Persia E4369/19/34: G. W. Rendel's minutes, 10 September 1929.

6. *See,* for example, United Nations Security Council, *Official Records,* 26th year, 1610th meeting, December 9, 1971 (hereinafter "U.N.S.C.O.R."), para. 215 (Iran representative's allusion to the Tonbs' geographical position).

7. In 1928-1930 Iran and Britain were engaged in a tedious round of negotiations aimed at settling their differences in the Persian Gulf region. Iran based her demand and justification for the allotment of the Tonbs on the view that these islands, being closer to Iran, were being used as a regular depot by Arab smugglers. *See* F.O. 371/13777 (1929), Persia E4085/19/34: Robert Clive (Tehran) to A. Henderson (F.O.), No. 426, 10 August 1929; F.O.371/13721 (1929), Arabia E4700/52/91: No. 1: Robert Clive (Tehran) to A. Henderson, confidential No. 454, 31 August 1929.

8. Ibid.

9. *See,* for example, the remarks of the Arab government representatives at the Security Council on December 9, 1971, U.N.S.C.O.R. For a detailed examination of the human geography of the Tonbs and the rejection in international law of claims to ownership on the basis of ethnic considerations, *see* Mirfendereski, *"The Tamb Islands Controversy, 1887-1971,"* pp. 165-203.

10. *See,* for example, *Persien* (1804)[Harvard College Library, No. 2276/8], and *Charte von Persien* (Prague, 1811)[Harvard College Library, No. 2276/10]. On both maps, the islands are designated also in the same color as the Iranian coast.

11. For details, *see* Mirfendereski, *"The Tamb Islands Controversy, 1887-1971,"* pp. 176-178.

12. F.O. 371/13721 (1929), Arabia E982/52/91: F.S. to G.I., letter no. F160-N/28 New Delhi, 29 January 1929, enclosure 3, envelope no. 1: Translated purport of a letter from Shaikh Yusuf, Governor of Lingeh, to Muhammad Hassan Khan, Governor-General of Bandar Abbas, 24 Jamadi-ul-aval 1302 (1885).

13. For details, *see* Mirfendereski, *"The Tamb Islands Controversy, 1887-1971,"* pp. 183-187.

14. Lauterpacht, H., *Oppenheim's International Law,* Vol. 1, 6th ed. (London: Longmans Green & Co., 1947), p. 407. *See also Island of Palmas,* p. 111.

15. A useful discussion of the nationality principle as source of title is contained in J. B. Moore, *Digest of International Law,* Vol. I (Washington, D.C.: Government Printing Office, 1906), p. 17; Rivier, A., *Principes du Droit des Gens,* Vol. I (Paris: Arthur Rousseau, 1896), p. 49; Pradier-Fodéré, P., *Traité de Droit International Public: Européan & Américain,* Vol. I (Paris: G. Pedone-Lauriel, 1885), pp. 121-144.

16. Rivier, *Principes du Droit des Gens.*

17. *See,* for example, Vincent, W., *The Voyage of Nearchus from the Indus to the Euphrates* (London: Cadell & Davis, 1797), reprinted in Vincent, W., *The Commerce and Navigation of the Ancients in the Indian Ocean* (London: Cadell & Davis, 1807), pp. 357 (fn. 122) (Gumbad-e Bousurg and Gumbad-e Kutcheek); Morier, J., *A Second Journey through Persia, Armenia, and Asia Minor, to Constantinople between the Years 1810 and 1816* (London: Longman & Co., 1818), p. 30 (Gumbuz); Curzon, G.N., *Persia and the Persian Question,* Vol. II (London: Longmans Green & Co., 1892) (London: Frank Cass & Co., 1966), p.448 (Tomb, Gumbaz); Kiepert, J. S. H., *Arabien* (Weimar, 1857)[Harvard College Library No. 2306/10](Kleine and Grosse Gumboz).

18. Ramusio, G. B., "La Navigatione Di Nearcho" (1550), in G.B. Ramusio, *Navigationi et Viaggi,* Vol. I (1550)(Amsterdam: Theatrum Orbis Terrarum, 1970), p. 270.

19. Dames, M. L., trans. and ed., *The Book of Duarte Barbosa: An Account of the Countries bordering on the Indian Ocean and their Inhabitants,* Vol. I (written by Duarte Barbosa and completed in 1518) (London: Hakluyt Society, 1918), p. 80.

20. For a detailed discussion of the etymological history of the Tonb Islands, including other lesser known appellations, *see* Mirfendereski, Guive, "The Typonomy of the Tonb Islands," in *Journal of Iranian Studies,* Vol. 30 (1-2) (forthcoming, 1996).

21. F.O. 371/19979 (1936), Arabia E2902/2902/91, Baggallay's minutes, 25 July 1936; Walton (I.O.) to J. C. Sterndale Bennette (F.O.), P.Z.3422/36, 29 June 1936.

22. *See* F.O. 371/21831 (1938), E1154/1154/91: Admiralty to Baggallay (F.O.), M06555/37, 26 February 1936 (Farsi, Arabi, and other islands "should be

annexed by one of our four Arab clients and not by either Persia or Saudi Arabia"); Baggallay (F.O.) to Gibson (I.O.), No. 1154/1154/91, 11 April 1938. For more details, *see* Mirfendereski, *"The Tamb Islands Controversy, 1887-1971,"* at pp. 196-203.

23. The term in Persian is *savabegh-e mossalam-e tarikhi.*

24. *Blitz,* 24 June 1971, interview with the Shah, reprinted in *Kayhan International* (Tehran), 26 June 1971.

25. *Kayhan International* (Tehran), 23 October 1971, interview with the Shah. A more popular expression of Iran's historical title to the Tonbs speaks of the islands being Iran's from time immemorial (*az rooz-e azal*: meaning from the dawn of time). In support of Iran's repossession of the islands, Iran's representative stated to the Security Council in December 1971: "The Iranian title to the islands is both long-standing and substantial. It has not been developed recently to justify the measures now taken. These are only the present reflection of historic title which could not remain physically unasserted upon the removal from the Persian Gulf of the British presence." U.N.S.C.O.R., par. 211.

26. F.O. 371/13010 (1928), Arabia E4266/421/91: [Confidential India Office Memorandum, I.O. B397, P4512/28], *Status of the Islands of Tamb, Little Tamb, Abu Musa, and Sirri,* by J.G. Laithwaite, 24 August 1928 (hereinafter cited as "Laithwaite Memorandum"), Part II, par. 7.

27. U.N.S.C.O.R., par. 161.

28. For an analysis of the history of the eastern region of the Persian Gulf in the period from 546 B.C. to 1750, *see* Mirfendereski, *"The Tamb Islands Controversy, 1887-1971,"* pp. 207-310.

29. Minorsky, V., trans. and ed., *Hudud al-'Alam* (ca. 982 A.D.)(London: Luzac & Co., 1937), p. 58. *See also* Playfair, J. *System of Geography,* Vol. V, (Edinburgh: Peter Hill, 1813), 321-322 (islands westward of Qishm "merit no description").

30. Arrian (d.180 A.D.), *Historia Indika,* Book VII, ch.37, in E.I. Robson, trans., *Arrian: History of Alexander and India* (London: W. Heinmann, 1949)(Loeb Classical Library), Vol. II, pp. 414-417; Vincent, W., *The Voyage of Nearchus and Periplus of the Erythraean Sea* (Oxford: Oxford University Press, 1809), pp. 58-59.

31. Claudius Ptolemaeus (d.168 A.D.), *Geographia,* Book VI (published in Venice in 1511) (Amsterdam: Theatrum Orbis Terrarum, 1969), ch. IV. Depicted on the *Sixth Map of Asia,* Tabiana is most likely the Tonbs. *See* Mirfendereski, *"The Tamb Islands Controversy, 1887-1971,"* Annex I, pp. 674-683.

32. Ferguson, J. H., *Manual of International Law for the Use of Navies, Colonies, and Consulates* (London: W.B. Whittington & Co., 1884), p. 100.

33. *Wheaton's Elements of International Law,* 8th ed., R.H. Dana, Jr., ed. (Boston: Little, Brown & Co., 1866), note 107.

34. Herodotus, *Persian Wars,* Book III.93, in F.R.B. Godolphin, ed., *The Greek Historians,* Vol. I (New York: Random House, 1942), p. 204. The empire consisted of the Iranian coast, the opposite continent and islands such as Qishm, Hormuz, Larak, Hengam, Bahrain, and Muharraq. *See* Rennell, J., trans. and ed., *The Geographical System of Herodotus,* Vol, I (London: Bulmer & Co., 1800), pp. 290-293.

35. *See* the sections dealing with the history of the Persian Gulf in the following sources: Malcolm, J., *The History of Persia* (London: John Murray, 1829); Sykes, P., *History of Persia* (London: Macmillan & Co., 1951); Cottrell, A., ed., *The Persian Gulf States* (Baltimore: John Hopkins University Press, 1980); Wilson, A. T., *The Persian Gulf* (Oxford: Clarendon Press, 1928); Curzon, *Persia and the Persian Question,* Vol. II.

36. *See* Mirfendereski, *"The Tamb Islands Controversy, 1887-1971,"* pp. 214-218.

37. Wilkinson, J. C., "A Sketch of the Historical Geography of the Trucial Oman Down to the Beginning of the Sixteenth Century," in *The Geographical Journal,* 130 (1964), pp. 340-342; Wilkinson, J. C., "The Origins of the Omani State," in Hopwood, D., ed., *The Arabian Peninsula* (London: Allen & Unwin, 1972), pp. 73-74.

38. *See generally* Ibn Razik, Salil, *History of the Imams and Seyyids of Oman,* P. Badger, trans. and ed. (London: Hakluyt Society, 1871), pp. 29-35; Miles, S. B., *The Countries and Tribes of the Persian Gulf,* Vol. I (London: Harrison & Sons, 1919), pp. 102-128. For a detailed description and analysis of the place of islands in the scheme of Buyids' naval and merchant marine presence in the eastern Persian Gulf, *see* Mirfendereski, *"The Tamb Islands Controversy, 1887-1971,"* pp. 228-236.

39. For a general history of the eastern Persian Gulf in the Seljuq period, ibid., pp. 236-248.

40. For a history of Kish Island, *see generally* Wilson, *The Persian Gulf.*

41. Le Strange, G., and Nicholson, R. A., eds.(London: Luzac & Co., 1921).

42. Ibid., p. 141 (English text) and p. 151 (Persian text). Ibn al-Balkhi's name for Tonb may be read as either Dam or Zam. For a detailed study of Ibn al-Balkhi's depiction of the islands of the Persian Gulf, *see* Mirfendereski, *"The Tamb Islands Controversy, 1887-1971,"* at Appendix I, Section 2.a.

43. *See,* for example, Yakut al-Rumi, *Mudjam al-Buldan,* (w.1224 A.D.) Vol. IV (Beirut: Dar Sader, 1955), p. 422. Yakut wrote of Kish Island that "diving for pearls was carried out here and in the neighboring islands and all these belonged to the owners of Kish, which was the residence of the ruler of the sea." Ibid.

44. *See generally* Sinclair, W. F., and Ferguson, D., trans. and eds., *The Travels of Pedro Teixeira* (London: Hakluyt Society, 1902), Appendix A (*A Short Narrative of the Origin of the Kingdom of Hormuz* based on

Shahnameh (w.1347-1378) by Turan-Shah, King of Hormuz); Aubin, J., "Les Princes D'Ormuz de XIII au XV Siècle," in *Journal Asiatique,* 241 (Paris: La Société Asiatique, 1953).

45. Sinclair and Ferguson, *The Travels of Pedro Teixeira,* pp. 169-181.

46. Hamdallah Mustawfi al-Kazvini, *Nuzhat al-Qulub* (ca. 1340 A.D.), Guy Le Strange, ed. (Leyden: E.J. Brill, 1913).

47. Ibid., pp. 171, 186, 234. Mustawfi's name for Tonb may read as Kand, Kond, Gand, or Gond. For a detailed analysis of Mustawfi's treatment of the islands of the Persian Gulf, including the identification of islands by their present day names, *see* Mirfendereski, *"The Tamb Islands Controversy, 1887-1971,"* Appendix I, Section 2.b.

48. *See generally* Sinclair and Ferguson, *The Travels of Pedro Teixeira;* Aubin, "Les Princes d'Ormuz de XIII au XV Siècle"; and Wilson, *The Persian Gulf.*

49. *See* D'Albuquerque, Braz, *The Commentaries of the Great Afonso D'Albuquerque,* Vol. I (1744), W. de Gray Birch, ed. (London: Hakluyt Society, 1872-1884), ch.24, pp. 83-84.

50. Dames, *The Book of Duarte Barbosa,* Vol. II, pp. 68-82. Barbosa's name for Tonb is Fomon (later in Spanish, as Tomon).

51. Curzon, *Persia and the Persian Question,* Vol. II, p. 419; Lorimer, J. G., *Gazetteer of the Persian Gulf, Oman, and Central Arabia,* Vol. I, *Historical* (Farnborough: Irish University Press, 1970) (first published in 1915), pp. 29-37; Miles, *The Countries and Tribes of the Persian Gulf,* Vol. I, pp. 191-193; Wilson, *The Persian Gulf,* pp. 153-157, 161-162; Manoel da Faria e Sousa, *Asia Portuguesa,* Isabel Ferreira, ed. (Pôrto: Biblioteca Histórica/Livraria Civilização, 1945), Vol. VI, Pt. III, ch. 8, par. 23.

52. Salmon, T., *Modern History or the Present State of All Nations* (1729) (3rd ed.)(London: Longman, 1744), Vol. I, p. 327.

53. *See generally* Mirfendereski, *"The Tamb Islands Controversy, 1887-1971,"* pp. 296-309.

54. *See generally* Lockhart, L., *Nadir Shah* (London: Luzac & Co., 1938); Lockhart, L., "The Navy of Nadir Shah," in *Proceedings of the Iran Society,* Vol. 1 (London: The Iran Society, 1936); Salil Ibn Razik, *History of the Imams and Seyyids of Oman,* pp. 100-155; Miles, *The Countries and Tribes of the Persian Gulf,* Vol.I, pp. 254-261.

55. *See* Lockhart, *Nadir Shah,* pp. 144-147, 183-184, 212-215; Lockhart, *Proceedings,* pp. 10-13.

56. The Tonbs straddle the inbound and outbound sea lanes of communication in the eastern Persian Gulf, as well as overlooking the shipping lanes between points on the Iranian coast and the eastern lower gulf. Due to its position, Great Tonb has offered haven to the distressed, itinerants, and smugglers. In 1835, the British sloop the *Elphinstone* engaged the main piratical squadron

of the Bani Yas tribe (Abu Dhabi) and routed it off Great Tonb. *See* Kelly, J. B., *Britain and the Persian Gulf* (Oxford: Clarendon Press, 1968), pp. 355-356. In 1925-1929, the Iranian government concluded that Tonbs were being used by smugglers plying the Dubai-Lingeh route, while the British government concluded that weather was the reason for boats seeking shelter at the Tonbs. For details, *see* Mirfendereski, *"The Tamb Islands Controversy, 1887-1971,"* pp. 142-151. Similarly, Iran's arguments in 1968-1971 favoring return of the Tonbs to Iranian control evoked images of the island being used to obstruct or interfere with oil and other shipping in the Persian Gulf. For details, ibid., 157-164.

57. DePando, J., *Elementos del Derecho Internacional,* 2nd ed. (Madrid, 1843), Sec. LIX, p. 103.

58. For details regarding the impact of these and other events on the eastern Persian Gulf in general and the status of the Tonbs in particular, *see generally* Mirfendereski, *"The Tamb Islands Controversy, 1887-1971,"* pp. 312-390.

59. Laithwaite Memorandum, Part II, par. 6-7.

60. *See* Mirfendereski, *"The Tamb Islands Controversy, 1887-1971,"* pp. 312-360.

61. Lorimer, *Gazetteer of the Persian Gulf,* Vol. I, pp. 34, 91-95, 98-102, 107-110, 135, 408-422, 434, 631-674, 689-698, 755-759, 1059-1060, 1667-1670, 1824-1825, 1837-1853, 1872, 1930, 2095; Malcolm, *The History of Persia,* Vol. II, ch. XVI; Sykes, *History of Persia,* Vol. II, ch. 72; Wilson, *The Persian Gulf,* at ch. XIII and pp. 192-212; Kelly, *Britain and the Persian Gulf,* ch. X and pp. 19, 99-166, 200-201; Eqbal A., *Motala'ati dar Bab-e Bahrain va Jazayer-o Savahel-e Khalij-e Fars* (Tehran: Chapkhaneh-e Majlis, 1948/49), pp. 116-118; Movahed, J., *Bastak va Khalij-e Fars* (Tehran: 1970), pp. 37-43; Minorsky, V., "Linga," in *Encyclopaedia of Islam,* Vol. III (Houtsma et al. eds.) (London: Luzac & Co., 1936), p. 28; Burrell, R. M., "Britain, Iran and the Persian Gulf: Some Aspects of the Situation in the 1920s and 1930s," in Hopwood, *ed., The Arabian Peninsula* (London: Allen and Unwin, 1972), pp. 172; Salil ibn Razik, *History of the Imams and Seyyids of Oman,* pp. 156-213, 238-240; Miles, *The Countries and Tribes of the Persian Gulf* Vol. I, pp. 318, and Vol. II, pp. 265-288, 302-321; Busse, H., *History of Persia under Qajar Rule* (translated from the Persian of Hassan Fassai's *Farsnama-ye Naseri,* ca. 1883)(New York: Columbia University Press, 1972), pp. 101-103, 134-135, 144-145, 153-155; Moyse-Bartlett, H., *The Pirates of Trucial Oman* (London: MacDonald, 1966), pp. 3-34, 42-62.

62. F.O. 371/14535 (1930), Persia 5935/143/34: Robert Clive (Teh.) to A. Henderson (F.O.), no. 520, 22 October 1930, no. 1, enclosure 3. *See also* Curzon, *Persia and the Persian Question,* Vol. II, p. 409.

63. For the proceedings of the Al Bu Samait in this period, *see* Lorimer, *Gazetteer of the Persian Gulf,* Vol. I, p. 1672; Saldanha, J. A., *Précis of Correspondence on International Rivalry and British Policy in the Persian Gulf: 1872-1905* (Secret) (Calcutta: Government of India, 1906), pp. 86-87; F.O. 371/

13721 (1929), Arabia E840/52/91: Letter no. 536, the Residency Agent at Shargah to the Political Resident, 10 November 1928, enclosure: Ahmad ibn Abdullah ibn Salim's deposition, dated 23 October 1928.

64. F.O. 371/13721 (1929), Arabia E982/52/91: Letter no. F. 160-N/28, Foreign Secretary (G.I.) to India Office, 29 January 1929, enclosure: Extract from translation of a letter from Shaikh Khalifa-Bin-Saiyid, Chief of Lingeh, to the Chief of Ras el-Khaimah, 12 Ramadhan 1289 A.H.

65. F.O. 371/13721 (1929), Arabia E840/52/91: Letter no. 536, the Residency Agent at Shargah to the Political Resident, 10 November 1928, enclosure; Copy of a letter of Sheikh Khalifah bin Said, Ruler of Lingeh, to Sheikh Humaid bin Abdullah, Ruler of Ras el-Kaimah, 20 Ramadhan 1289.

66. Morsy Abdullah, M., *The United Arab Emirates* (London: Croom Helm, 1978), pp. 235-236.

67. *See generally* Mirfendereski, *"The Tamb Islands Controversy, 1887-1971,"* pp. 350-390.

68. F.O. 371/13721 (1929), Arabia E982/52/91: Letter no. F.160-N/28, Foreign Secretary (G.I.) to India Office, 29 January 1929, enclosure 3: Extract from translation of a letter from Shaikh Ali-Bin-Khalifa to the Chief of Ras-el-Khyma, 13 Moharram 1294. Another but differing translation of this letter is found in ibid., enclosure no. 1: Translation of letter written in 1877 by Shaikh Ali-Bin-Khalifah, of Lingeh, to Sheikh Hamyed-Bin-Abdullah, Chief of Ras-el-Khaimah.

69. Ibid., enclosure 3: Translated purport of a letter from the Residency Agent at Shargah to the Political Resident, no. 3, 18 January 1888, and enclosure thereto: Extract from translation of a letter from Sheikh Yusuf, Chief of Lingeh, to Sheikh Hamid-Bin-Abdullah, Chief of Ras-el-Khyma, 1 Jamad 1301.

70. To limit further the acts of piracy and depredation by the maritime tribes of the lower Persian Gulf, including the Qawasim of Sharjah and Ras al-Khaimah, in 1835, the British government established a restrictive line above which the boats of the Trucial sheikhs could not cruise. In the eastern Persian Gulf, the line passed through Abu Musa and Sirri Islands, while the Tonbs remained in the middle of the "neutral" maritime highway. Following the British encounter with a "piratical" vessel off Great Tamb and the reports of Abu Musa and Sirri being "notorious pirate liars," in 1836, the British Government moved the restrictive line to the south of Abu Musa and Sirri Islands. *See* Lorimer, *Gazetteer of the Persian Gulf,* Vol. I, pp. 694-696; Kelly, *Britain and the Persian Gulf,* pp. 354-360; Jenab, M. A., *Khalij-e Fars: Ashenaii ba Amarat-e An* (Tehran: Entesharat-e Padideh, 1970), p. 317. In 1864, the Indo-European Telegraph line connecting British India with other points in the Middle East and beyond was laid four miles southward of Great Tonb, as the British government extracted promises from the Qasimi sheikhs in the lower Persian Gulf to guard the line against interference by their subjects. *See* Lorimer, *Gazetteer of the Persian Gulf,* Vol. I, Appendix J (pp. 2408-2411);

Kelly, *Britain and the Persian Gulf,* pp. 555-563. Beginning in as early as the 1820s British officers resorted to Great Tonb for recreation. *See* Kempthorne, G. B., "Notes on a Survey along the Eastern Shores of the Persian Gulf in 1828," in *The Journal of the Royal Geographical Society* (London), Vol. V (1835), p. 280; Whitelock, H. H., "Description of the Islands and Coasts Situated at the Entrance of the Persian Gulf, in *The Journal of the Royal Geographical Society* (London), Vol. III (1838), p. 81; Curzon, *Persia and the Persian Question,* Vol. II, p. 448. Furthermore, at this time, Britain extracted from the Qawasim and other tribes of the lower Persian Gulf a series of undertakings aimed at curtailing the slave traffic, which apparently plied the waters near the Tonbs. *See* Lorimer, *Gazetteer of the Persian Gulf,* Appendix L; Kelly, *Britain and the Persian Gulf,* ch. X; Wilson, *The Persian Gulf,* ch. XVIII; Farrant (Teh.) to Viscount Palmerston, 12 November 1847, enclosure: Report on the Slave Trade of the Persian Gulf, reprinted in *British and Foreign State Papers,* Vol.36 (London: Foreign Office, 1847-1848), pp. 711-712. For a discussion of larger geostrategic and political interests of Britain in Iran and the Persian Gulf, *see* Kazemzadeh, F., *Russia and Britain in Persia: 1865-1914* (New Haven: Yale University Press, 1968).

71. For details, *see* Lorimer, *Gazetteer of the Persian Gulf,* Vol.I, pp. 289, 737, 920, 2047-2048, 2065-2066; Curzon, *Persia and the Persian Question,* Vol. II, pp. 409-410.

72. Laithwaite Memorandum, Part III: Occupation of Sirri by Persia 1887, par. 12.

73. Ibid.

74. F.O. 371/13721 (1929), Arabia E982/52/91: Letter no. F160-N/28, 29 January 1929, from Foreign Secretary (G.I.) to India Office, enclosure 3: Brief purport of five letters written by Shaikh Yusuf-Bin-Muhammad to Muhammad Hassan Khan, Governor of Bunder Abbas and Lingeh, envelope No. 1: letter dated 25 Jemadi-u-Aval 1302.

75. Ibid., envelope no. 2, letter dated 5 Jemadi-us-Sani 1302.

76. Ibid., envelope no. 3: letter dated 15 Jemadi-u-Sani 1302. It is not revealed in the British documents what was "that Tamb business."

77. Ibid., envelope no. 4: letter dated 28 Jamad-us-Sani 1302.

78. Morsy Abdullah, *The United Arab Emirates,* p. 234.

79. Ibid., pp. 235-236.

80. Ibid., p. 236.

81. Ibid., pp. 236-237.

82. Foreign Office Map Room, no. 2699. F.O. 371/18917 (1935), Arabia E2145/653/91: A.E. Lambert's minutes, 29 May 1935. *See* discussion below.

83. F.O. 371/18917 (1935), Arabia E2145/653/91: A.E. Lambert's minutes, 29 May 1935. (Hereinafter cited as "F.O., Lambert's minutes".)

84. F.O. 371/13009 (1928), Arabia E4152/421/91: Parr (Teh.) to Foreign Office, telegram no. 254, 20 August 1928; Foreign Office to Parr, no. 181, 25 August 1928; F.O. 371/18917 (1928), Arabia E2145/653/91: C.W. Baxter's minutes, 23 August 1928. (Hereinafter cited as "F.O., Baxter's minutes".)

85. Ibid.

86. Laithwaite Memorandum, Part III, pars. 15-16.

87. Ibid., par. 11, citing Political Resident to G.I., telegram, 15 November 1887.

88. Ibid., par. 15; Morsy Abdullah, *The United Arab Emirates,* pp. 238 and 242.

89. F.O., Lambert's minutes; F.O. Map Room, no. 2723, no. 2084 (Foreign Office Records 925/4650: *Survey of India: Map of Persia*), and no. 4640. A portion of Curzon's map (1891) is reproduced in Appendix 2, at p. 2, and a portion of *Map of Persia* (1897) is reproduced in Appendix 2, p. 3.

90. *The Temple of Preah Vihear* (1962)(Cambodia v. Thailand), Merits, Judgment of 15 June 1962, *ICJ Reports* (1962), pp. 23, 27-31 and the dissenting opinion of Sir Gerald Fitzmaurice, p. 55. *See also Costa Rica-Nicaragua Boundary Dispute,* Arbitral Award of 1886, in Moore, J. B., *International Arbitrations, to which the United States was a Party,* Vol. II, (Washington DC: Government Printing Office, 1898), p. 1945 ("the Government of Nicaragua was silent when it ought to have spoken, and so waived the objection now made.") For a list of cases where silence or inaction has been construed as giving rise to territorial sovereignty, *see* Mirfendereski, *"The Tamb Islands Controversy, 1887-1971,"* pp. 424-425.

91. McNair, A. D., *The Law of Treaties* (Oxford: Clarendon Press, 1961), p. 485. For the various forms of estoppel, *see Blacks's Law Dictionary,* 4th ed., pp. 648-651.

92. *I.C.J. Statute,* art. 38(1)(c).

93. *See generally* Lauterpacht, H., *Private Sources and Analogies of International Law* (London: Longmans Green, 1927), pp. 203-211; Bowett, D.W., "Estoppel before International Tribunals and its Relation to Acquiescence," in *The British Year Book of International Law,* Vol. 33 (1957), p. 176; MacGibbon, I. C., "Estoppel in International Law," in *International & Contemporary Law Quarterly,* Vol. 7 (1958), p. 468; Blum, Y. Z., *Historic Titles in International Law* (The Hague: Martinus Nijhoff, 1965), ch. III; Jennings, R. Y., *The Acquisition of Territory in International Law* (Manchester University Press, 1963), pp. 41-45; McNair, *The Law of Treaties,* pp. 485-489.

94. *The Temple of Preah Vihear,* p. 63 and the *dissenting opinion* of Judge Wellington Koo, p. 97.

95. McNair, *The Law of Treaties,* p. 485.

96. *Fur Seals Arbitration Award* (1893) (Great Britain v. United States), in *British and Foreign State Papers,* Vol. 95 (1901-1902), p. 1185; Moore, *International Arbitrations,* Vol. I, p. 755.

97. McNair, A. D., "The Legality of the Occupation of the Ruhr," in *British Year Book of International Law*, Vol. 5 (1924), p. 35.

98. *Temple of Preah Vihear, supra* note 90, pp. 39-51, 62-64, 70, 97; Schwarzenberger, Georg, "The Fundamental Principles of International Law, in *Hague Receuil de Cours*, Vol. 87 (1955), pp. 312 *et seq.*

99. The first concept in Persian is *zedd va naqiz guyi* and the second is *adam-e enkar ba'd az eghrar.*

100. F.O. 371.13009 (1928), Arabia E4152/421/91: Parr (Teh.) to Foreign Office, telegram no. 254, 20 August 1928; Foreign Office to Parr, no. 181, 25 August 1928; F.O., Baxter's minutes.

101. Laithwaite Memorandum, Part III, par. 15; Morsy Abdullah, *The United Arab Emirates*, pp. 238, 242.

102. Laithwaite Memorandum, Part XI, section 36.

103. F.O., Baxter's minutes.

104. F.O. 371/18917 (1928), Arabia E2145/653/91: Lord Cushendon's minutes, 24 August 1928.

105. Ibid., Lascelles, D.W., Memorandum on Persian Claim to Tamb and Abu Musa, 4 September 1934, pars. 2-3.

106. F.O., Lambert's minutes; F.O. Map Room, no. 2723.

107. Ibid., no. 2084.

108. In the mid-1880s, Curzon became a friend of the Marquis of Salisbury, whose influence helped elect Curzon to Parliament in 1886, the same year as the issue of the *Map of Persia* by the admiralty. At about the same time as the time of compilation and issue of Curzon's *Map of Persia, Afghanistan, and Baluchistan* and the reissuance of the 1886 *Map of Persia* by the war office, in 1891, Curzon became undersecretary of state for India. He was installed as viceroy of India in 1899. He bore no particular fondness for Iran: While Secretary for Foreign Affairs, in 1923, he scolded the British minister in Tehran for suggesting that the issue of Iran's claim of sovereignty over Bahrain be referred to international arbitration. He wrote: "It is repugnant that Great Britain should be brought to an arbitration on a question of sovereignty by a third class power like Persia . . [It] is dangerous to entrust such important interests to the risks of arbitration by a single individual." F.O. 371/11442 (1926), Arabia E419/419/91: P. Loraine (Teh.) to Austen Chamberlain (F.O.), 30 September 1925, citing passages from an earlier correspondence from Lord Curzon to P. Loraine, Telegram no. 88, 1 May 1923. Lord Curzon's admonition was used later in 1926 to dissuade the new Secretary for Foreign Affairs, Austen Chamberlain, from agreeing to submit the Tonbs issue to arbitration. Ibid.

109. F.O. Records 925/2084: Explanatory Note, Parts I and II.

110. *Persia and the Persian Question,* Vol. II, p. 448.

111. F.O. Records 925/4640, *Survey of India: Map of Persia.* F.O. Map Room, no. 4640. *See also* Lambert's minutes. Compiled in the drawing office of the Government of India at Simla, this map relied on the war office's 1886 and 1891 editions of the *Map of Persia* and on Curzon's Map.

112. *The Alaskan Boundary Dispute* (1903) (Great Britain/United States), in P. Cobbett, *Leading Cases on International Law,* Vol. I, 3rd ed., (London: Stevens & Haynes, 1909), p. 103.

113. Ibid.

114. Ibid.

115. *Title to the Islands in the Passamaquody* (1794), in Moore, J. B., *International Adjudications,* Vol. VI (New York: Oxford University Press, 1933), p. 213.

116. *Island of Palmas,* in Scott, *The Hague Court Reports,* pp. 108-110.

117. Ibid., pp. 108-110.

118. *See,* for example, *Walker's International Atlas* (Philadelphia: H. B. Walker, 1890), map plate designated "Persia" (the Tonbs and Iran are in pink) Levasseur, P. E., *Grand Atlas de Géographie Physique et Politique* (Paris: Librairie Ch. Delagrave, 1891), map plate designated "Asie occidentale" (Tonbs and Iran are in yellow); *The Times Atlas* (London: The Times Publishing Co., 1895), map plate designated "Asia Minor & Persia" (Tonbs and Iran are in pink), a 1900 reproduction of this map appears in Appendix 2, p. 4.

119. For details, *see generally* Mirfendereski, *"The Tamb Islands Controversy, 1887-1971,"* pp. 441-455.

120. *See* Lorimer, *Gazetteer of the Persian Gulf,* Vol. I, Appendix O (pp. 2594-2597, 2602-2607). *See also* Kazemzadeh, *Russia and Britain in Persia,* ch.5; Sykes, *History of Persia,* Vol. II, ch.80.

121. F.O. 371/310 (1907), Persia 34/41755, no.1: [F.O.] Memorandum Respecting the Persian Gulf Islands of Abu Musa, Tamb, and Sirri, by Alwyn Parker, 17 December 1907 (Hereinafter cited as the "Parker Memorandum"), Part I; Laithwaite Memorandum, Part IV, par. 18.

122. Parker Memorandum, Part I; Laithwaite Memorandum, Part IV, pars. 17-18; Lorimer, *Gazetteer of the Persian Gulf,* Vol. I, p. 745; Morsy Abdullah, *The United Arab Emirates,* p. 244.

123. Parker Memorandum, Part I; Laithwaite Memorandum, Part IV, par. 20. *See also* Lorimer, *Gazetteer of the Persian Gulf,* Vol. I, pp. 745-746.

124. Parker Memorandum, Part I.

125. Ibid.

126. Ibid.

127. Iranian Foreign Ministry, Letter from Muzaffar al-Din Shah to Minister of Foreign Affairs, Moshir al-Dawleh, 22 Rabi-al-Aval 1323 (11 June 1904).

128. Parker Memorandum, Part I; Laithwaite Memorandum, Part IV, par. 20.

129. Iranian Foreign Ministry, Moshir al-Dawleh, minutes, 29 Rabi al-Aval 1323 (15 June 1904). The reference to the other location is to Abu Musa Island, on which Iranian customs also hoisted a flag in March 1904.

130. Ibid., digest of British Legation's Reply-Note to the Foreign Minister, June 22, 1904.

131. Lauterpacht, H., *Oppenheim's International Law,* Vol. I, 8th ed. (New York: David McKay Co., 1967), p. 555 ("belongs to no state"); *Subject of Difference Relative to the Sovereignty over Clipperton Island* (France/ Mexico), Arbitral Award of His Majesty Victor Emmanuel, The King of Italy, 28 January 1931, translated and reprinted in *The American Journal of International Law,* 26 (1932), pp. 391-393 ("not belonging to a state"); Moore, *Digest of International Law,* Vol. I (1906), p. 258 ("not occupied by a civilized power"); Cobbett, *Leading Cases on International Law,* Vol. I, p. 110 ("territory not belonging to any civilized state"); Hackworth, G. H., *Digest of International Law,* Vol. I (1940), p. 401 ("not under the sovereignty of any state"); Schwarzenberger, G., *A Manual of International Law,* 5th ed. (New York: Frederick A. Praeger, 1967), p.122 ("not under the jurisdiction of any subject of international law"); *The Boundary Between the Colony of British Guiana and the United States of Brazil,* Arbitral Award of His Majesty the King of Italy, 1904, printed in *British and Foreign State Papers,* Vol. 99 (1905-1906), p. 930 ("not in the dominion of any State"); *Islands of Palmas,* in Scott, *The Hague Court Reports,* p. 101 ("without a master").

132. Lauterpacht, *Oppenheim's International Law,* Vol. I, 8th ed., pp. 555-563.

133. The leading international law case prior to World War II on the relevance of the status of native societies in territories considered *terra nullius* by European colonizers is *Legal Status of Eastern Greenland* (Denmark v. Norway)(1933), Permanent Court of International Justice, Series A/B, no. 53), in which the Court dealt with the status of Eskimo natives of Eastern Greenland in the context of the Danish "occupation" of their territory as far back as the tenth century A.D. For the opinion of publicists on the subject, *see* Lauterpacht, *Oppenheim's International Law,* Vol. I, 8th ed., p. 555. For a survey of the treatment of the native societies by the colonial powers of Europe, *see* A. S. Keller, et al., *Creation of Rights of Sovereignty Through Symbolic Acts: 1400-1800* (New York: Columbia University Press, 1938) and M. F. Lindley, *The Acquisition and Government of Backward Territory in International Law* (London: Longmans Green & Co., 1926).

134. *Black's Law Dictionary,* 5th ed., 1979, p. 1065.

135. *See generally* ibid.

136. *See generally* Lauterpacht, *Opppenheim's International Law,* Vol. I, 8th ed., pp. 554-558, 575-581; Blum, *Historic Titles in International Law,* pp. 6-37; Johnson, D. N. H., "Acquisitive Prescription in International Law," in *British Year Book of International Law,* Vol. 27 (1950); Waldock, C. H. M., "Disputed Sovereignty in the Falkland Islands Dependencies," in *British Year Book of International Law,* Vol. 25 (1948), pp. 334-337; *Island of Palmas,* in Scott, *The Hague Court Reports,* pp. 92 and 100-101; *Eastern Greenland,* p. 46; Hill, N., *Claims to Territory in International Law and Relations* (London: Oxford University Press, 1945), pp. 148-149; *Minquiers and Ecrehos* (United Kingdom/France), Judgment of 17 November 1953, *ICJ Reports* (1953), pp. 65-71.

137. Parker Memorandum, Part I, citing Major Percy Cox (P.R.) to India Office, 20 September 1904. And when Iran repossessed Great Tonb in November 1971 "the inhabitants prayed for the health of the Shahinshah." Tehran Radio Home Service, broadcast at 10:30 GMT, 30 November 1971.

138. For details surrounding these events and activities, *see* Mirfendereski, *"The Tamb Islands Controversy, 1887-1971,"* pp. 512-523.

139. For details regarding these events and activities, *see* ibid., pp.536-541. Iranian Foreign Ministry: Digest of Moshir al-Dawleh's note to the British Legation (Tehran) 1 Rabi al-Sani 1323 (20 June 1904) (Iran's protest against the sheikh's second hoisting of flag); Digest of British Legation's Reply-Note to the Foreign Ministry, 22 June 1904; Digest of Events (1905) (regarding rumor about building houses); Digest of Events (1912-1913); Summary of Moaqqar al-Dawleh (Bushehr) to Daryabegi (Tehran) (October 1912) (regarding the lighthouse); Summary of Moazed al-Sultan's discussions with the British Minister (February 1913). The dates in parentheses here and also those in notes 140, 143 and 145 below are approximations ascertained by the author in 1977 and reported in Mirfendereski, "The Tamb Islands Controversy, 1887-1971."

140. For details, *see* Mirfendereski, *"The Tamb Islands Controversy, 1887-1971,"* pp. 541-573. Iranian Foreign Ministry: Digest of Events, 1308 (1929-1930) (regarding news of British flag on Tonb); Proceedings of the year 1313 Shamsi (1933-1934), the *Palang*'s visit to Tonb (regarding Iranian naval visits).

141. F.O. 371/18901 (1935), Arabia E712/4/91: Political Resident to H.M.'s Minister (Teh.), no. 23, 30 January 1935; Arabia E3204/4/91: Knatchbull-Hugessen (Teh.) to G. W. Rendel (F.O.), 3 May 1935; Arabia E3204/4/91: G.W. Rendel (F.O.) to H. Knatchbull-Hugessen, 29 May 1935.

142. For details, *see* F.O. 371/23264 (1939): Persia E3026/3026/34, Persia E3365/3026/34, Persia E5742/3026/34. *See also,* Mirfendereski, *"The Tamb Islands Controversy, 1887-1971,"* pp. 575-577.

143. For details, *see* Iranian Foreign Ministry: Ministry of the Treasury to Foreign Ministry, no. 342, 8 Day 1319 (29 December 1940) and Joint Chiefs of Staff (War Ministry) to Foreign Ministry, no. 31134, 27 Bahman 1319

(16 February 1941) (regarding the toll collector); Ministry of the Treasury to Council of Ministers, 11 Ordibehesht 1327 (2 May 1948); Foreign Ministry to Council of Ministers, no. 3723, 10 Mehr 1325 (2 October 1948); Foreign Minister to Iranian Ambassador (London), 24 Amordad 1328 (15 August 1949); Foreign Ministry to War Ministry, no. 3612, 24 Amordad 1328 (15 August 1949); Foreign Ministry to British Embassy (Teh.), 27 Amordad 1328 (18 August 1949); British Embassy (Teh.) to Foreign Ministry, no. 1013, 2 Shahrivar 1328 [24 August 1949]; Navab to Foreign Minister, 1 Mehr 1328 (23 September 1949); Foreign Minister to Prime Minister, no. 6125, 22 Aban 1328 (13 November 1949); Foreign Minister to Prime Minister, 15 Farvardeen 1329 (4 April 1950); Foreign Ministry to Prime Minister, 1 Ordibehesht 1332 (21 April 1953); Foreign Ministry to Prime Minister, no. 1035, 21 Ordibehesht 1332 (14 May 1953); Foreign Ministry to Swiss Embassy (Teh.), no. 1207, 29 Ordibehesht 1332 (19 May 1953); Swiss Embassy to Foreign Ministry, no. 2/m/k, 11 July 1953; Interior Ministry to Foreign Ministry, no. 2/13892/12975, 14 Azar 1332 (5 December 1953). For a synthesis of the contents of the afore-cited documents, *see* Mirfendereski, *"The Tamb Islands Controversy, 1887-1971,"* pp. 579-584.

144. Mossaheb, Gholam-Hossein, *Dayarat ol-Ma'aref-e Farsi,* Vol. I, *Tonb* (Tehran: Franklin Publications, 1345/1966-67).

145. *See* Iranian Foreign Ministry: Savak to Foreign Ministry, no. 3370, 11 Khordad 1339 (1 June 1960); Minutes of Political Undersecretary (Afshar)(not dated); British Embassy to Foreign Ministry, no. 1084/61, 23 Shahrivar 1340 (14 September 1961); Foreign Ministry to British Embassy, no. 3052, 30 Shahrivar 1340 (21 September 1961); British Embassy to Foreign Ministry, no. 1084/62, 23 Day 1340 (13 January 1962), and Foreign Ministry to British Embassy, no. 5724, 30 day 1340 (20 January 1962) (regarding Iranian helicopter landing); Savak to Foreign Ministry, 3 Azar 1344 (25 November 1965); Foreign Ministry to Prime Minister, 20 Azar 1344 (12 December 1965); Interior Ministry to Foreign Ministry, 7 Day 1346 (28 December 1967); Foreign Ministry to Prime Minister, 7 Day 1346 (28 December 1967), minutes of interdepartmental meeting (closed session) of 16 Day 1346 (6 January 1968); Foreign Ministry to British Embassy, 17 Day 1346 (7 January 1968) and Foreign Ministry to Iranian Ambassador (London), 17 Day 1346 (7 January 1968) (regarding the reporting of Anglo-Arab activities and Iranian protests); Minutes of meeting between Political Director-General and the British Charge d'Affaires, at the Foreign Ministry, Tehran, 22 Day 1346 (11 January 1968); Foreign Ministry to Iranian Ambassador (London), 23 Day 1346 (12 January 1968); Foreign Ministry to British Embassy, 14 January 1968, Imperial Navy to Foreign Ministry, 24 Day 1346 (14 January 1968); Imperial Navy to Foreign Ministry, 25 Day 1346 (15 January 1968); Imperial Navy to Foreign Ministry, 26 Day 1346 (16 January 1968); and Iranian Ambassador (London) to Foreign Ministry, 3 Bahman 1346 (23 January 1968) (regarding Iranian naval presence in Tonb waters and vicinity); Minutes of the interdepartmental meeting of 15 Bahman 1346 (4 February

1968) (regarding Iran contemplating to haul down the sheikh's flag on Great Tonb). For a synthesis of the materials contained in the afore-cited documents, *see* Mirfendereski, *"The Tamb Islands Controversy, 1887-1971,"* pp. 564-591.

146. *See* Lauterpacht, *Oppenheim's International Law,* Vol. I, 8th ed., pp. 557-558; Lindley, *The Acquisition and Government of Backward Territory,* pp. 159; Waldock, "Disputed Sovereignty," pp. 335-336; *Island of Palmas,* in Scott, ed., *The Hague Court Reports,* pp. 94, 126-129; *Clipperton Island,* pp. 390-394; *Eastern Greenland,* p. 43; *Minquiers and Ecrehos,* pp. 65-71.

147. Waldock, "Disputed Sovereignty," p. 335.

148. Lauterpacht, *Oppenheim's International Law,* Vol. I, 8th ed., pp. 576-577; Blum, *Historic Titles,* pp. 155-160, Johnson, "Acquisitive Prescription," pp. 343-347. In *Venezuela-British Guiana Boundary Case,* Arbitral Award of 1899, cited in Blum, *Historic Titles,* p.161, the tribunal agreed with Venezuela's argument that her protests against the British usurpation had been constant and emphatic, and they were enforced by "all the means practicable for a weak power to employ in its dealings with a strong one, even to the rupture of diplomatic relations." Similarly, in *Chamizal Arbitration Award* (United States/Mexico) (1910), reported in *United Nations Reports of International Arbitral Awards* (Vol. XI), reprinted in *The American Journal of International Law ,* Vol. 5 (1911), pp. 782, 803, the tribunal found the United States' possession of Chamizal from 1848 until 1895 to have been challenged effectively by Mexico's mild protests communicated through diplomatic channels. By contrast, Britain at times has argued that in order for protest to prevent acquisitive prescription the objecting party must press its claim by other available means as well. *See Anglo-Norwegian Fisheries* (United Kingdom v. Norway) (1951), *ICJ Pleadings, Oral Arguments, Documents,* Vol.II, p. 654; *Corfu Channel Case* (United Kingdom/Albania) (1949) *ICJ Pleadings, Oral Arguments, Documents,* Vol.II, p. 277; *Minquiers and Ecrehos* (United Kingdom/France) (1953), *ICJ Pleadings, Oral Arguments, Documents,* Vol. I, p. 554. Ironically, when Argentina followed up her years of paper protests against British occupation of the Falklands with military action, in 1982, Britain protested the action as illegal and waged war against Argentina. *See* United Nations Security Council, *Provisional Verbatim Record,* meetings of 1-3 April 1982 (Doc.S/PV.2345-S/PV.2350). It was precisely the discouragement of recourse to violence that moved the arbitral tribunal in the *Chamizal Case,* p. 803, to find the fact of mere paper protests sufficient to challenge physical possession of territory. More "drastical" measures, the tribunal found, would have provoked violence and then Mexico, the author of such measures, would have had to carry the blame for not resorting to a "reasonable and milder form of protest." Ibid.

149. *Stielers Hand-Atlas,* zehnte Auflage Hundertjahr-Ausgabe, herausgegeben unter Leitung von Prof. Dr. H. Haack (Gotha: Justus Perthes, 1938), Plate 67: Iran-Turan and Plate 66: Arabien.

150. *Columbia Lippincott Gazetteer of the World,* Leon Seltzer, ed. (New York: Columbia University Press, 1952), p. 1959.

151. For details, *see* Mirfendereski, *"The Tamb Islands Controversy, 1887-1971,"* pp. 601-603.

152. Vadala, R., *Le Golfe Persique,* Annex I, *Ports Persans* (Iranian Ports) (Paris: Librairie Arthur Rousseau, 1920), p. 85. He referred to Little Tonb simply as an uninhabited island.

153. *The World Atlas* (compiled by Chief Administration of Geodesy and Cartography under the Council of Ministers of the U.S.S.R.) (Moscow: 1954), Plate: Iran, Afghanistan, and West Pakistan.

154. *The World Atlas* (compiled by Chief Administration of Geodesy and Cartography under the Council of Ministers of the U.S.S.R.) (Moscow: 1967), Plate no. 143-144: Iran, Afghanistan, and West Pakistan.

155. *Hammond's Modern Atlas of the World* (New York: C.S. Hammond & Co., 1909), Map Plate, p. 96: Persia, Afghanistan, Baluchistan.

156. *Rand McNally's Cosmopolitan World Atlas,* Centennial Edition: 1856-1956 (Chicago: Rand McNally & Co., 1956), Index, p. 157A.

157. *Varldatlas* (Bonniers Stora, edition)(Stockholm: A. Bonniers Forlag, 1951), Map Plate: Irak, Persien (Iran) och Afghanistan.

158. *Atlas International Larousse* (politique et économique), I. De Janchy, and S. Rado, eds. (Paris: Librairie Larousse, 1965), Map Plate no. 13A: Southwest Asia, index p. 3.

159. *Atlante Internazionale* (de Touring Club Italiano), 8th ed. (Milan: Touring Club Italiano, 1968), Map Plate no. 92: Iran, Afghanistan, West Pakistan.

160. Ibid., Map Plate no. 91: Arabiyah and Misr el-Bahri.

161. Jackson, W., *Persia: Past and Present* (London: Macmillan & Co., 1909), containing W. A. K. Johnston's *Map of Persia* (Edinburgh).

162. *See,* for example, *Persia, Afghanistan and Baluchistan* (London: 1920) (Harvard College Library, 2275/1920A) (The Tonbs are shown in the same grey color as Iran); *Philip's Travelling Maps: Persia* (London: George Philip & Sons, 1922) (Harvard College Library 2276/22) (Tonbs and Iran are colored in grey); *Persia, Afghanistan, and Baluchistan* (London: 1922) (Harvard College Library 2276/22) (Tonbs and Iran are depicted in purple).

163. *The Times Survey Atlas of the World* (London: The Times Publishing Co., 1922), Gazetteer/Index, p. 237. Little Tonb is not mentioned.

164. *The Times Atlas of the World,* Vol. II, *South West Asia & Russia,* Mid-Century Edition, J. Bartholomew, ed. (Boston: Houghton Mifflin Co., 1959), Index/Gazetteer, pp. 1, 5, 42, 44.

165. *The Times Index-Gazetteer of the World* (London: The Time Publishing Co., 1965), p. 832.

166. *Islands of Palmas,* in Scott, ed., *The Hague Court Reports,* pp. 128-129.

167. *Eastern Greenland,* p. 46.

168. Ibid., pp. 67-72.

169. Fitzmaurice, Gerald, "The Law and Procedure of the International Court of Justice, 1951-1954: Points of Substantive Law, Part II," in *British Year Book of International Law,* Vol. 32 (1955-56), p. 35.

Appendices

APPENDIX 1: "ANGLO-IRANIAN MEMORANDUM

OF UNDERSTANDING" 1971

and the exchange of notes among various parties in relation thereto (official documents provided by the Ministry of Foreign Affairs, the Islamic Republic of Iran).

MEMORANDUM OF UNDERSTANDING

Neither Iran nor Sharjah will give up its claim to Abu Musa nor recognise the other's claim. Against this background the following arrangements will be made:

1. Iranian troops will arrive on Abu Musa. They will occupy areas the extent of which have been agreed on the map attached to this memorandum.

2(a) Within the agreed areas occupied by Iranian troops, Iran will have full jurisdiction and the Iranian flag will fly.

(b) Sharjah will retain full jurisdiction over the remainder of the island. The Sharjah flag will continue to fly over the Sharjah police post on the same basis as the Iranian flag will fly over the Iranian military quarters.

3. Iran and Sharjah recognise the breadth of the island's territorial sea as twelve nautical miles.

4. Exploitation of the petroleum resources of Abu Musa and of the seabed and subsoil beneath its territorial sea will be conducted by Buttes Gas and Oil Company under the existing agreement which must be acceptable to Iran. Half of the governmental oil revenues hereafter attributable to the said exploitation shall be paid directly by the company to Iran and half to Sharjah.

5. The nationals of Iran and Sharjah shall have equal rights to fish in the territorial sea of Abu Musa.

6. A financial assistance agreement will be signed between Iran and Sharjah.

Foreign and Commonwealth Office

London S.W.1

24 November, 1971

ly dear Colleague

I enclose a copy of a letter addressed to
Her Majesty's Government from the Ruler of
Sharjah, in which the Ruler asks for confirmation
that the Iranian Government accepts the arrangements
for Abu Musa set out in the Annex to his letter.
I would be grateful for confirmation that the
Iranian Government accepts the arrangements.

Yours sincerely

(ALEC DOUGLAS-HOME)

His Excellency
    Dr. Abbas-Ali Khalatbari.
        Minister for Foreign Affairs, Iran.

Khalid bin Mohamed Al Qasmi
Ruler of Sharjah & Its Dependencies

خالد بن محمد القاسمي
حاكم الشارقة وملحقاتها

Date 18 November 1971

التاريخ

The Secretary of State for
  Foreign and Commonwealth Affairs,
The Foreign and Commonwealth Office,
London.

After Greetings,

With reference to our discussions about the arrange-
ments between Sharjah and Iran on the Abu Musa question,
I confirm that I accept the arrangements set out in the
Memorandum of Understanding annexed to this letter. I
should be grateful for confirmation that the Iranian
Government for its part accepts the arrangements.

Finally, please accept our highest regards and respects.

KHALID BIN MOHAMMED AL-QASIMI
Ruler of Sharjah and Its Dependencies

IMPERIAL MINISTRY
OF FOREIGN AFFAIRS

Tehran, 25th November, 1971.

No. M/21282

Your Excellency,

I confirm that my Government accepts the arrangements for Abu Musa as set out in the enclosure to your letter of 24th November, 1971.

A copy of the Memorandum of Understanding in which the arrangements are set out is annexed to this letter.

Abbas Ali Khalatbari
Minister for Foreign Affairs

The Principal Secretary of State
for Foreign and Commonwealth Affairs,
London.

IMPERIAL MINISTRY
OF FOREIGN AFFAIRS

Tehran, 25th November, 1971.

No. M/21284

Your Excellency,

With reference to my letter No. M/21282
of today's date and in reply to yours of 24th November,
1971, I am instructed by my Government to inform you
that Iran's acceptance of the arrangements relating to
Abu Musa set out in the enclosure to your aforesaid
letter is given on the understanding that nothing in
the said arrangements shall be taken as restricting the
freedom of Iran to take any measures in the Island of
Abu Musa which in its opinion would be necessary to
safeguard the security of the Island or of the Iranian
forces.

I would be grateful for confirmation
that this understanding has been conveyed to the Ruler
of Sharjah.

Abbas Ali Khalatbari
Minister for Foreign Affairs

The Principal Secretary of State
for Foreign and Commonwealth Affairs,
London.

Foreign and Commonwealth Office

London S.W.1

26 November, 1971

My dear Colleague

With reference to your letter
number M/21284 of 25 November, 1971 I have taken note
of the understanding on which your government's
acceptance of the arrangements relating to
Abu Musa is given and have conveyed that
understanding to the Ruler of Sharjah.

Yours sincerely

(ALEC DOUGLAS-HOME)

His Excellency
    Dr. Abbas-Ali Khalatbari.
        Minister for Foreign Affairs, Iran.

CABLE
BUTTESOAK
TELEX
336-467
TWX
910-366-7038

BUTTES GAS & OIL CO.

1970 BROADWAY
OAKLAND, CALIFORNIA 94612
(415) 839-1600

MAILING ADDRESS
P. O. BOX 2071
OAKLAND, CALIFORNIA
94604

November 26, 1971

Dr. M. Eghbal
Chairman of the Board and
  General Managing Director
National Iranian Oil Company
Post Office Box No. 1863
Tehran, Iran

Your Excellency:

1. The Buttes Gas & Oil Co. understands that certain arrangements have been made relating to Abu Musa and its territorial sea, which provide, inter alia, that:

   A. Neither Iran nor Sharjah would give up its claim to Abu Musa and its twelve mile territorial sea, nor recognize the other's claim;

   B. Exploitation of the petroleum resources of Abu Musa and of the sea-bed and subsoil beneath its territorial sea will be conducted by Buttes Gas & Oil Co. under the existing agreement which must be acceptable to Iran. Half of the governmental oil revenues hereafter attributable to the said exploitation shall be paid directly by the Company to Iran.

2. The Company hereby agrees to make the payment under paragraph 1(B) above directly to the Government of Iran, and has taken the necessary measures in accordance with the preceding paragraph.

3. The Company further agrees that the terms of the Tehran Oil Price Agreement of February 14, 1971 will be adhered to.

4. Our Company would be grateful for confirmation that National Iranian Oil Company on behalf of the Government of Iran accepts that, pursuant to the acceptance of the arrangements, our Company or its subsidiaries can proceed with operations under the terms of this letter.

Yours sincerely,

John Boreta
President

JB:cw

NATIONAL IRANIAN OIL COMPANY

ADD·NAFTMELLI
P.BOX NO.1863
TEL.NO.6151
TELEX 2516

CENTRAL OFFICE
AVE.TAKHTE.JAMSHID
TEHRAN

Tehran,27 Nov. 1971

Gentlemen

       Pursuant to the acceptance of certain arrangements with respect to Abu Musa and its territorial sea, I confirm that National Iranian Oil Company on behalf of the Government of Iran accepts that your company or its subsidiaries can proceed with operations under the terms of your letter of 26 November 1971.

Dr. Eghbal
Chairman of the Board

Buttes Gas and Oil Company

IMPERIAL MINISTRY
OF FOREIGN AFFAIRS

Tehran, 30th November, 1971

Your Highness,

        I have the honour, on behalf of the Imperial
Iranian Government, and in accordance with the agreed
mutual intention of Iran and Sharjah to develop and strengthen their relations to the benefit of each State in as
many fields as possible, to make the following proposals in
relation to 'financial assistance.

a. The Imperial Iranian Government will assist Your Highness
    by making semi-annual contributions of £ 750,000 Sterling
    on 21st April and 21st October of each year, beginning
    in 1972, provided that

      (i). such a contribution shall not be made in any
          period of six months in which the revenue received
          by Your Highness from the commercial exploitation
          of oil, gas or mineral deposits on the Island of
          Abu Musa and beneath its territorial waters
          exceeds £1.5 million Sterling, or

      (ii) in any period of six months in which the revenue
          received by Your Highness from the commercial
          **exploitation of oil, gas or mineral deposits on
          the Island of Abu Musa and beneath its territorial
          waters** is less than £1.5 million Sterling but
          exceeds £ 750,000 Sterling, the contribution shall

IMPERIAL MINISTRY
OF FOREIGN AFFAIRS

- 2 -

be reduced by the amount of that excess.

b. If this Agreement enters into force before 21st April,
    1972, the Imperial Iranian Government will make to
    Your Highness on the date on which this Agreement enters
    into force an additional contribution equal to a total
    of as many monthly contributions of £125,000 Sterling
    as could be made on the 21st day of each month between
    the date of such entry into force and the first contri-
    bution under paragraph (a) above.

c. The provisions of paragraph (a) above shall remain in
    force for an initial period of nine years beginning
    21st April, 1972. At the end of the eighth year the
    provisions shall be reviewed and it will be open to
    either the Imperial Iranian Government or Your Highness
    to give notice that the provisions shall be terminated
    at the end of the ninth year.

d. The sum mentioned under (a) above shall be payable, at
    the choice of Your Highness, in United States of America
    Dollars or in Federal Germany's Deutche Marks instead
    of Pounds Sterling, in which case the amount payable
    shall be calculated according to the parity prevailing
    on the date when this agreement enters into force.

IMPERIAL MINISTRY
OF FOREIGN AFFAIRS

- 3 -

   If the foregoing proposals are acceptable
to Your Highness, I have the honour to suggest that the
present Note and Your Highness's reply to that effect
shall be regarded as constituting an agreement between
the Imperial Iranian Government and Your Highness in this
matter which shall enter into force on the date of Your
Highness's reply.

         Abbas Ali Khalatbari
         Minister for Foreign Affairs

His Highness
Sheikh Khalid Bin Mohammed
Al-Qasimi,
Ruler of Sharjah.

IMPERIAL MINISTRY
OF FOREIGN AFFAIRS

Tehran, 30th November, 1971.

Your Highness,

      I have the honour to refer to the Agreement
constituted by the exchange of letters between us dated
30th November, 1971 and in this connection I am instructed
to state that:-

a. The Imperial Government of Iran will regard itself
    as entitled to terminate or suspend payments under
    the said Agreement if Your Highness takes any action
    inconsistent, in Iran's view, with friendly relations
    between Iran and Sharjah.

b. The present letter constitutes an integral part of
    the said Agreement.

                        Abbas Ali Khalatbari
                    Minister for Foreign Affairs

His Highness
Sheikh-Khalid Bin Mohammed
Al-Qasimi,
Ruler of Sharjah.

Khalid bin Mohamed Al Qasmi
Ruler of Sharjah & Its Dependencies

خالد بن محمد القاسمي

حاكم الشارقة وتوابعها

Date 1st December 1971.

Your Excellency,

I have the honour to acknowledge receipt of Your
Excellency's letter of the 30th November 1971, the text of which
is as follows:

" I have the honour, on behalf of the Imperial
Iranian Government, and in accordance with the agreed mutual
intention of Iran and Sharjah to develop and strengthen their
relations to the benefit of each State in as many fields as
possible, to make the following proposals in relation to financial
assistance.

a.   The Imperial Iranian Government will assist Your
Highness by making semi-annual contributions of
£ 750,000 Sterling on 21st April and 21st October
of each year, beginning in 1972, provided that

(i) such a contribution shall not be made in any
period of six months in which the revenue received
by Your Highness from the commercial exploitation
of oil, gas or mineral deposits on the Island of
Abu Musa and beneath its territorial waters exceeds
£1.5 million Sterling, or

(ii) in any period of six months in which the revenue
received by Your Highness from the commercial exploitation of oil, gas or mineral deposits on the Island of
Abu Musa and beneath its territorial waters is less
than £1.5 million Sterling but exceeds £ 750,000 Sterling,
the contribution shall be reduced by the amount of that excess.

b.   If this Agreement enters into force before 21st April,
1972, the Imperial Iranian Government will make to Your
Highness on the date on which this Agreement enters
into force an additional contribution equal to a total
of as many monthly contributions of £ 125,000 Sterling
as could be made on the 21st day of each month between
the date of such entry into force and the first contribution under paragraph (a) above.

c.   The provisions of paragraph (a) above shall remain in
force for an initial period of nine years beginning
21st April, 1972. At the end of the eighth year the
provisions shall be reviewed and it will be open to
either the Imperial Iranian Government or Your Highness
to give notice that the provisions shall be terminated
at the end of the ninth year.

- 2 -

d.   The sum mentioned under (a) above shall be payable, at
the choice of Your Highness, in United States of America
Dollars or in Federal Germany's Deutche Marks instead
of Pounds Sterling, in which case the amount payable
shall be calculated according to the parity prevailing
on the date when this agreement enters into force.

     If the foregoing proposals are acceptable to Your Highness,
I have the honour to suggest that the present Note and Your Highness's
reply to that effect shall be regarded as constituting an agreement
between the Imperial Iranian Government and Your Highness in this matter
which shall enter into force on the date of Your Highness's reply".

     I have the honour to inform Your Excellency that the
statement in Your Excellency's letter is acceptable to me and hence
that Your Excellency's letter and this reply shall be regarded as
constituting an agreement between Iran and myself in this matter
which shall enter into force on to-day's date.

Khalid bin Mohamed al Qasimi.

His Excellency, Mr. Abbas Ali Khalatbari,
Minister for Foreign Affairs,
Imperial Ministry of Foreign Affairs,
Iran.

APPENDIX 2: MAPS

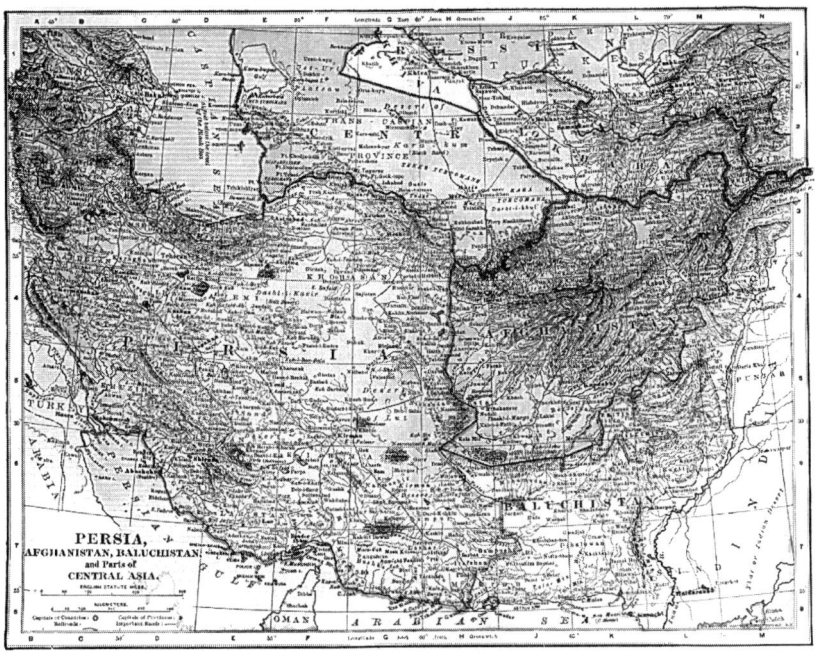

Map 1 *Persia, Afghanistan and Beluchistan,* 1891. Compiled under the supervision of G. Curzon M. P. by Wm Joe Turner. Longmans, Green and Co., London and New York.

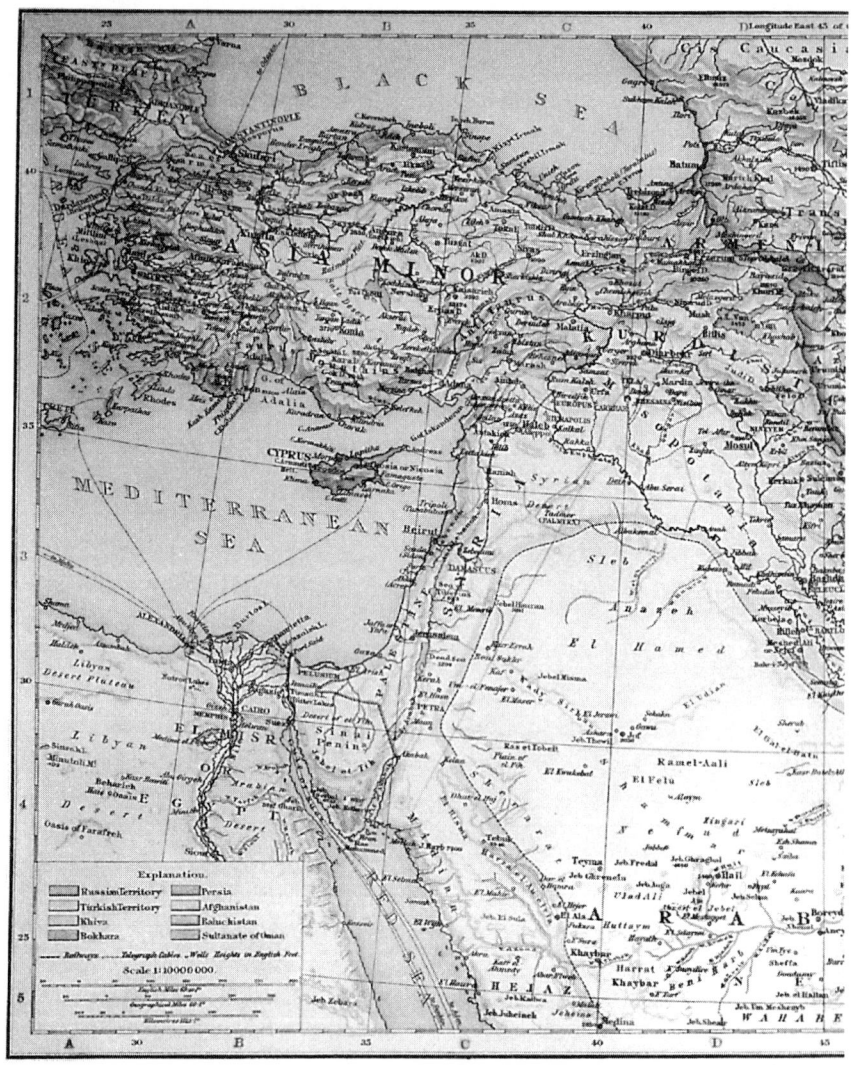

Map 2 Asia Minor and Persia, 1900. From *The Times Atlas*. The Office of the Times.
The boxed area of this map appears in detail in map 3.

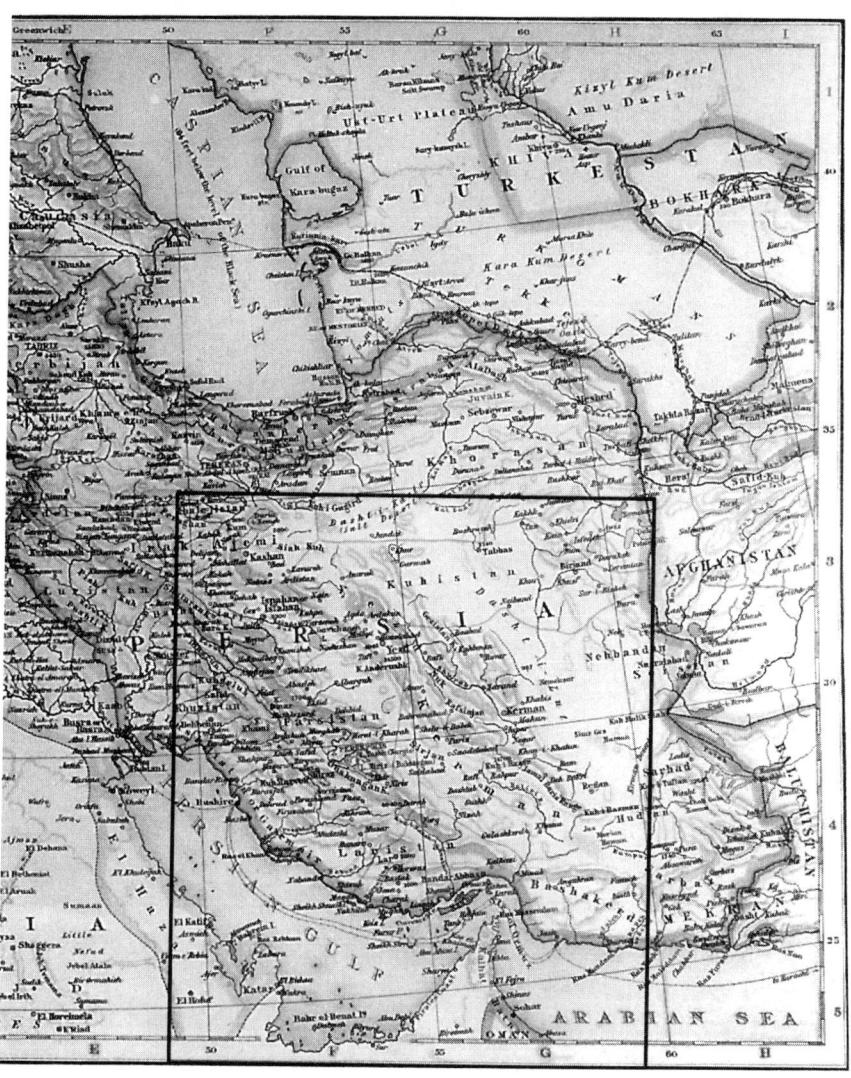

Map 3 Asia Minor and Persia, 1900. (Area of detail from map 2.) From *The Times Atlas*. The Office of the Times.

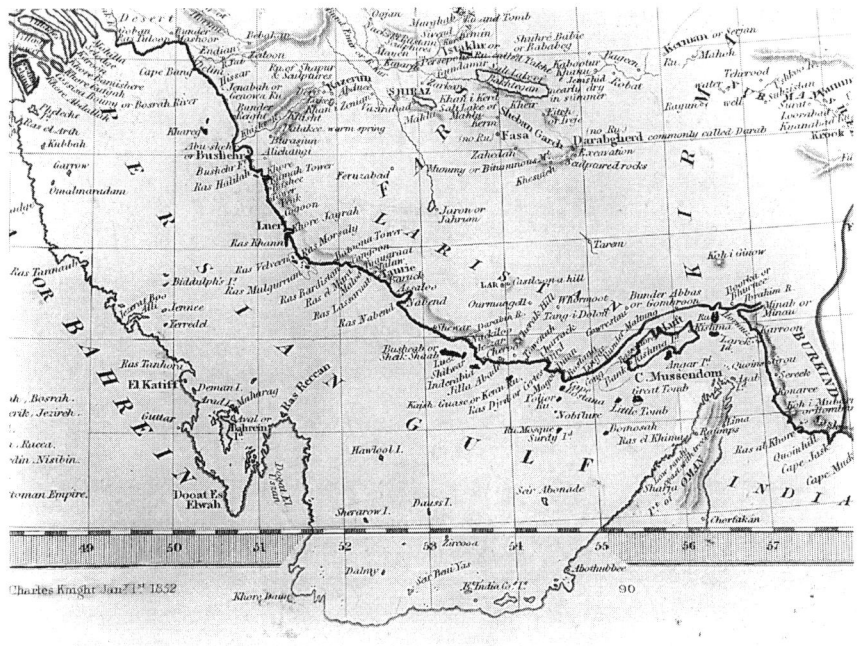

Map 4 *Persia with Part of the Ottoman Empire,* 1831, by G. Long. Published under the Superintendence of the Society for the Diffusion of Useful Knowledge. [London, Charles Knight. Jan. 1st 1852].

Bibliography

A. DOCUMENTS: IRAN
1. Ministry of Foreign Affairs

Imperial Government's Relations with the Countries within the Jurisdiction of the Ninth Political Department. Tehran, 1976.

Memorandum of Understanding, signed by the Iranian Minister of Foreign Affairs on behalf of Iran and the Principal Secretary of State for Foreign and Commonwealth Affairs, dated 25 November 1971, and enclosure no. M/21284, dated 25 November 1971.

Selection of Persian Gulf Documents. Tehran: Ministry of Foreign Affairs of the Islamic Republic of Iran's Institute of Political and International Studies, 1989. Publication no. 91.

Siasat-e Khareji. Vol. VI (Foreign Policy). Tehran: Ministry of Foreign Affairs of the Islamic Republic of Iran's Institute of Political and International Studies, 1993.

Gozida-ye Asnad-e Khalij-e Fars (Selected Documents on the Persian Gulf). Tehran: Vahed-e Nashr-e Asnad, Ministry of Foreign Affairs of the Islamic Republic of Iran's Institute of Political and International Studies, 2nd print: 1372 (1994).

2. Miscellaneous

Collection of Iranian Government Documents, Tehran.

B. DOCUMENTS: GREAT BRITAIN
1. Admiralty

The Persian Gulf Pilot, including the Gulf of Omman, Captain C.G. Constable and Lieutenant A.W. Stiffe. London: Hydrographic Admiralty, 1864.

The Persian Gulf Pilot, including the Gulf of Omman, Captain C.G. Constable & Lieutenant A.W. Stiffe. 2nd ed. London: Hydrographic Admiralty, 1870.

Persian Gulf Pilot, 11th ed. London; Hydrographer of the Navy, 1967.

2. Foreign Office Records

F.O. 60, 78 (1880-1881), 371 (1906-1909, 1913, 1926, 1928-1930, 1934-1936, 1938-1939) 368 (1909), 416, 925, 45507, 157031 and 163032.

3. India Office Records

Annual Administration Reports of the Persian Gulf Residency and Muscat Political Agency (1875-1876). Calcutta.

Bombay Selections (*see below* at *Selections*) *Collection of Treaties, Engagements and Sunnuds.* Vol. I. Compiled and edited by C.U. Aitchinson. Calcutta, 1876.

Gazetteer of the Persian Gulf, Oman, and Central Arabia. Compiled and edited by J. G. Lorimer. (3 vols.) Volume I: *Historical* (reprinted from an original in the India Office Library), Calcutta: Government of India, 1915 and Volume II: *Geographical and Statistical* (reprinted from an original in the India Office Library), Calcutta: Government of India, 1908. Farnborough: Irish University Press, 1970.

Marine Miscellaneous [Bombay], 1836.

Précis of Correspondence on International Rivalry and British Policy in the Persian Gulf: 1872-1905. Compiled and edited by J.A. Saldanha. Simla: Government of India, 1906.

Précis on Commerce and Communication in the Persian Gulf, 1801-1905. Compiled and edited by J.A. Saldanha. Simla: Government of India, 1906.

Selections from the Records of the Bombay Government, New Series no. 24. Compiled and edited by R. Hughes Thomas, Bombay, 1856.

4. Maps

Map of Persia, 1886, War Office [Foreign Office Map Room, no. 2699].

Map of Persia, 1891, War Office [Foreign Office Map Room, no. 2723].

Map of Persia, Afghanistan, and Baluchistan, 1891, London: Royal Goegraphical Society [Foreign Office Map Room, no. 2084].

The Persian Gulf, Captain C.B.S. St. John. Bombay, 1876.

Survey of India: Map of Persia, 1897, Government of India [Foreign Office Map Room, no. 4640].

5. Marine Surveys

Brucks, Commander (H.C. Marine) George B., "Trigonometrical Survey made by order of the Honorable Court Directors of the United East Indian Company," in *Bombay Selections* [1830], above.

Kemball, Lt. A.B., "Observations on the Past Policy of the British Government towards the Arab Tribes of the Persian Gulf," in *Bombay Selections* [1844], above.

Kemball, Captain A.B., "Statistical and Miscellaneous Information Connected with the Possessions, Revenues, Families of Imam of Muskat, the Ruler of Bahrein, Chiefs of the Maritime Arab States in the Persian Gulf," in *Bombay Selections* [1854], above.

Kempthorne, G.B., "Notes on a Survey along the Eastern Shores of the Persian Gulf in 1828," in *The Journal of the Royal Geographical Society*, V (London: 1835).

McCluer, John, *An account of Navigation between India and the Persian Gulf* (London: 1786).

Pelly, Lt.-Col. Lewis, "Remarks on the tribes, trade and resources around the shore line of the Persian Gulf," in *Transactions of Bombay Geographical Society*, 17 (1863).

Taylor, Lt. Col. Robert, "A List of Names of Positions of the Persian Gulf," in *Marine Miscellaneous* [1836] above.

Whitelock, H.H., "Description of the Islands and Coasts Situated at the Entrance of the Persian Gulf, in *The Journal of the Royal Geographical Society*, III (London: 1838).

6. Miscellaneous

British and Foreign State Papers. London: Foreign Office. Vols. 36 (1847-1848), 95 (1901-1902), 99 (1905-1906)

C. DOCUMENTS: UNITED NATIONS

Document A/47/516: Resolution 5223/98/3. September 13, 1992.

Security Council, *Provisional Verbatim Record*, meetings of 1-3 April 1982 (Doc. S/PV.2345-S/PV.2350).

Security Council, *Official Records*, 26th year, 1610th meeting, 9 December 1971.

UN Monthly Chronicle, IX (1)(January 1972): Record of the Month of December 1971.

D. INTERVIEWS

Amir Khosro Afshar, by Pirouz Mojtahed-Zadeh, in London, April 10, 1994.

Amir Khosro Afshar, by Pirouz Mojtahed-Zadeh, in London, January 2, 1991.

E. NEWS & INFORMATION

Al-Ahram (Cairo), November 10, 1968; December 8, 1971,

Arab Report & Record (London), September 16-30, 1971.

BBC Radio, *Persian Service News Bulletin,* 25 August 1992.

BBC Summary of World Broadcasts: The Middle East ME/1573/A/7, 29 December 1992.

The Boston Globe, April 3, 6, 1995, March 1- 3, 6-7, 14-15, 19, 22-23, 1995, October 1, 1992, September 29, 1992.

ClariNet Electronic News Service, February 14, 1995, February 9, 1995, December 5, 1994, October 4, 1994, October 1, 1994, September 18-19, 1994.

Echo of Iran (London), XXX, XXXX.

The Economist, December 1, 1979, December 22, 1979 (letter to editor), and November 6, 1992 (letter to editor).

Ettelaat (Tehran), June 27, 1971; November 30, 1971.

Foreign Broadcast Information Service, FBIS-NES-92-076, April 20, 1992.

Iran Almanac (Tehran), 1972.

Iran Focus, November 1992.

Kayhan (Tehran), February 20, 1971; June 25, 1971; November 30, 1971; October 8, 1992.

Kayhan International (Tehran), 26 June 1971 (English edition).

Middle East Economic Survey (London), 11 January 1993.

The New York Times, December 27, 1992, September 20, 1992, September 17, 1992, September 13, 1992, April 16, 1992.

The Times (London), September 22, 1992, November 18, 1971.

The Scotsman, September 7, 1962.

United Arab Emirates, *Press Release* (London, October 1992).

The Washington Post, September 25, 1992.

F. LEGAL MATERIALS

1. Cases

Anglo-Norwegian Fisheries (United Kingdom v. Norway) (1951), *ICJ Pleadings, Oral Arguments, Documents.* Vol. II.

Alaskan Boundary Dispute (1903) (Great Britain/United States), in P. Cobbett, *Leading Cases on International Law.* Vol. I. 3rd ed. London: Stevens & Haynes, 1909.

Boundary Between the Colony of British Guiana and the United States of Brazil, Arbitral Award of His Majesty the King of Italy, 1904, printed in *British and Foreign State Papers.* Vol. 99 (1905-1906).

Chamizal Arbitration Award (United States/Mexico) (1910), reported in *United Nations Reports of International Arbitral Awards.* Vol. XI, reprinted in *The American Journal of International Law.* Vol. 5 (1911).

Clipperton. See *Subject of Difference Relative to Sovereignty.*

Corfu Channel Case (United Kingdom/Albania) (1949) *ICJ Pleadings, Oral Arguments, Documents.* Vol. II.

Eastern Greenland. See *Legal Status of Eastern Greenland.*

Fur Seals Arbitration Award (1893) (Great Britain v. United States), in *British and Foreign State Papers.* Vol. 95 (1901-1902).

Island of Palmas (United States/Netherlands). Permanent Court of Arbitration at The Hague, Award of 4 April 1928, reprinted in J.B. Scott, ed., *The Hague Court Reports* (2nd ser., 1932).

Legal Status of Eastern Greenland (Denmark v. Norway) (1933), Permanent Court of International Justice, Series A/B, No. 53 (1933).

Minquiers and Ecrehos (United Kingdom/France), Judgment of 17 November 1953, *ICJ Reports* (1953).

Minquiers and Ecrehos (United Kingdom/France) (1953), *ICJ Pleadings, Oral Arguments, Documents.* Vol. I.

Palmas. See *Island of Palmas.*

Subject of Difference Relative to the Sovereignty over Clipperton Island (France/ Mexico), Arbitral Award of His Majesty Victor Emmanuel, The King of Italy, 28 January 1931, translated and reprinted in *The American Journal of International Law.* Vol. 26 (1932).

Temple of Preah Vihear (1962)(Cambodia v Thailand), Merits, Judgment of 15 June 1962, *ICJ Reports* (1962).

Title to the Islands in the Passamaquody (1794), in J.B. Moore, *International Adjudications.* New York: Oxford University Press, 1933). Vol. IV.

Venezuela-British Guiana Boundary Case, Arbitral Award of 1899, cited in Blum. *See* Blum.

Costa Rica-Nicaragua Boundary Dispute, Arbitral Award of 1886, in J.B. Moore, *International Arbitrations to which the United States was a Party.* Vol. II. Washington, D.C.: Government Printing Office, 1898.

2. Treatises

Albaharna, Husain M., *The Arabian Gulf States,* 2nd ed. Beirut: Librairie du Liban, 1975.

Bavand, Davoud H., *The Historical, Political and Legal Bases of Iran's Sovereignty over the Islands of Tunb & Abu Musa.* New York: Internet Concepts Incorporated, 1994.

Bavand, Davoud H., "Bar-rasi-e Mabani-e Tarikhi va Hoquqi-e Jazayer-e Irani-e Tonb va Abu Musa," in *Jame-eh Salem*, II (7) (Tehran: December 1992– January 1993).

Black's Law Dictionary. St. Paul: West Publishing Co., 4th ed., 1968; 5th ed., 1979.

Bledsoe, Robert L. & Boczek, Boleslaw A., *International Law Dictionary*. Santa Barbara: ABC-CLIO, 1987.

Blum, Y. Z., *Historic Titles in International Law*. The Hague: Martinus Nijhoff, 1965.

Bowett, D.W.,"Estoppel before International tribunals and its Relation to Acquiescence," in *The British Year Book of International Law*, Vol. 33 (1957).

Cobbett, P., *Leading Cases on International Law*, 3rd ed. London: Stevens & Haynes, 1909. Vol. I.

DePando, J., *Elementos del Derecho Internacional*, 2nd ed. Madrid, 1843.

Ferguson, J. H., *Manual of International Law for the Use of Navies, Colonies, and Consulates*. London: W.B. Whittington & Co., 1884.

Fitzmaurice, G., "The Law and Procedure of the International Court of Justice, 1951-1954: Points of Substantive Law, Part II," in *British Year Book of International Law*, Vol. 32 (1955-56).

Hackworth, G.H., *Digest of International Law*, Vol. I (1940).

Hill, N. *Claims to Territory in International Law and Relations*. London: Oxford University Press, 1945.

Jennings, R.Y., *The Acquisition of Territory in International Law*. Manchester University Press, 1963.

Johnson, D. N. H., "Acquisitive Prescription in International Law," in *British Year Book of International Law*, Vol. 27 (1950).

Keller, A.S., *et al.*, *Creation of Rights of Sovereignty Through Symbolic Acts: 1400-1800*. New York: Columbia University Press, 1938.

Lauterpacht, H., *Private Sources and Analogies of International Law*. London: Longmans Green, 1927.

Lauterpacht, H., *Oppenheim's International Law*. Vol. I. 6th ed. London: Longmans Green & Co., 1947.

Lauterpacht, H., *Oppenheim's International Law*. Vol. I. 8th ed. New York: David McKay Co., 1967.

Lindley, M.F., *The Acquisition and Government of Backward Territory in International Law*. London: Longmans Green & Co., 1926.

MacGibbon, I.C., "Estoppel in International Law," in *International & Contemporary Law Quarterly*, Vol. 7 (1958).

McNair, A.D., "The Legality of the Occupation of the Ruhr," in *British Year Book of International Law,* Vol. 5 (1924).

McNair, A.D., *The Law of Treaties.* Oxford: Clarendon Press, 1961.

Mirfendereski, G., *The Tamb Islands Controversy, 1887-1971: A Case Study in Claims to Territory in International Law.* Ph.D. diss. Fletcher School of Law and Diplomacy, Tufts University, Medford, Massachusetts, USA (1985).

Moore, J.B., *Digest of International Law.* Washington, D.C.: Government Printing Office, 1906. Vol. I.

Pradier-Fodéré, P., *Traité de Droit International Public: Européan & Américain.* Vol. I. Paris: G. Pedone-Lauriel, 1885.

Rivier, A., *Principes du Droit des Gens.* Vol. I. Paris: Arthur Rousseau, 1896.

Schwarzenberger, G. "The Fundamental Principles of International Law, in *Hague Receuil de Cours,* Vol. 87 (1955).

Schwarzenberger, G., *A Manual of International Law,* 5th ed. New York: Frederick A. Praeger, 1967.

Waldock, C.H.M., "Disputed Sovereignty in the Falkland Islands Dependencies," in *British Year Book of International Law,* Vol. 25 (1948).

Wheaton, W., *Elements of International Law,* 8th ed., R.H. Dana, Jr., ed. Boston: Little, Brown & Co., 1866.

G. CARTOGRAPHICAL WORKS AND GAZETTEERS

Arabien. Weimar: J.S.H. Kiepert, 1857 [Harvard College Library No.2306/10].

Atlas International Larousse (politique et economique), I. De Janchy and S. Rado, eds. Paris: Librairie Larousse, 1965.

Atlante Internazionale (de Touring Club Italiano), 8th ed. Milan: Touring Club Italiano, 1968.

Carte du Golphe Persique. Paris: French Foreign Ministry, 1764.

Charte von Persien. Prague, 1811 [Harvard College Library, No.2276/10].

Columbia Lippincott Gazetteer of the World, Leon Seltzer, ed. New York: Columbia University Press, 1952.

D'Anville, *Map of the Empire of Persia,* 1770 and 1794.

Grand Atlas de Géographie Physique et Politique, P. E. Levasseur. Paris: Librairie Ch. Delagrave, 1891.

Hammond's Modern Atlas of the World. New York: C. S. Hammond & Co., 1909.

Map of Persia. Edinburgh: Johnston, W.A.K., in Jackson. *See* Jackson, below.

Mossaheb, G. H., *Dayarat ol-Ma'aref-e Farsi.* Vol. I. Tehran: Franklin Publications, 1345/1966-67.

Persia, Afghanistan and Baluchistan. London: 1920 [Harvard College Library, 2275/1920A].

Persia, Afghanistan, and Baluchistan London: 1922 [Harvard College Library, 2276/22].

Persien. 1804 [Harvard College Library, 2276/8].

Philip's Travelling Maps: Persia. London: George Philip & Sons, 1922 [Harvard College Library 2276/22].

Rand McNally's Cosmopolitan World Atlas. Centennial Edition: 1856-1956. Chicago: Rand McNally & Co., 1956.

Stielers Hand-Atlas, Dr. H. Haack, ed. Gotha: Justus Perthes, 1938.

Times Atlas. London: The Times Publishing Co., 1895.

Times Atlas of the World. Vol. II. Mid-Century Edition. J. Bartholomew, ed. Boston: Houghton Mifflin Co., 1959. Vol. II.

Times Index-Gazetteer of the World. London: The Time Publishing Co., 1965.

Times Survey Atlas of the World (Gazetteer/Index) London: The Times Publishing Co., 1922.

Varldatlas. Bonniers Stora, ed. Stockholm: A. Bonniers Forlag, 1951.

Walker's International Atlas. Philadelphia: H.B. Walker, 1890.

World Atlas. Compiled by Chief Administration of Geodesy and Cartography under the Council of Ministers of the U.S.S.R. Moscow: 1954.

World Atlas Compiled by Chief Administration of Geodesy and Cartography under the Council of Ministers of the U.S.S.R. Moscow: 1967.

H. HISTORY, GEOGRAPHY, AND POLITICS

Alikhani, A., ed. *Confidential Diary of Alam.* Vol. I. Persian edition, 1992.

Alikhani, A. ed. *The Shah and I: Confidential Diary of the Royal Court of Iran by Amir Assadollah Alam.* London: I.B. Tauris, 1991.

Amirahmadi, H., and Hooglund, E., *US-Iran Relations: Areas of Tension and Mutual Interest.* Washington, D.C.: The Middle East Institute, 1994.

Amirahmadi, H., "The Spiraling Gulf Arms Race," in *Middle East Insight* 10 (2) (January-February, 1994).

Amirahmadi, H., and Entessar, N., *Iran and the Arab World.* New York: St. Martin's Press, 1993.

Amirahmadi, H., ed., *The United States and the Middle East: A Search for New Perspective.* Albany: State University of New York Press, 1993.

Amirahmadi, H., and Bill, J. A., *The Clinton Administration and the Future of U.S.-Iran Relations.* Policy Report No. 3. Washington, D.C.: Middle East Insight, 1993.

Amirahmadi, H., "Economic Destruction and Imbalances in Post-Revolutionary Iran," in Amirahmadi, H., and Entessar, N., eds., *Reconstruction and Regional Diplomacy in the Persian Gulf.* London: Routledge, 1992.

Amirahmadi, H., *Revolution and Economic Transition: The Iranian Experience.* Albany: The State University of New York Press, 1990.

Amirahmadi, H., "Economic Reconstruction of Iran: Costing the War Damage," in *Third World Quarterly* 12 (1) (January 1990), pp. 26-47.

Arab Research Centre, *Proceedings of the Round Table Discussion on the Disputed Gulf Islands,* Arab Research Centre, London, November 18, 1992. London: Arab Research Centre, January 1993.

Arrian, *Historia Indika. See* E.I. Robson.

Aubin, J., "Les Princes D'Ormuz de XIII au XV Siècle," *in Journal Asiatique,* 241 (Paris: La Société Asiatique, 1953).

Badger, P., trans. and ed., *Salil Ibn Razik's History of the Imams and Seyyids of Oman.* London: Hakluyt Society, 1871.

Bandar-Abbasi, Mohammad Ali Khan (Sadeed al-Sultana), *Sarzaminha-ye Piramun-e Khalij-e Fars Va Darya-ye Omman.* Tehran: Entesharat-e Jahan-e Mo'aser, 1371(1993).

Barbosa, Duarte. *See* Dames.

Burrell, R.M., "Britain, Iran and the Persian Gulf: Some Aspects of the Situation in the 1920s and 1930s," in Hopwood. *See* Hopwood.

Busch, Briton C., *Britain and the Persian Gulf: 1894-1914.* Berkeley: University of California Press, 1967.

Busse, H., *History of Persia under Qajar Rule* (translated from the Persian of Hassan Fassai's *Farsnama-ye Naseri,* ca.1883. New York: Columbia University Press, 1972.

Chubin, S., and Zabih, S., *The Foreign Relations of Iran.* Los Angeles: University of California Press, 1974.

Cottam, R.W., *Iran and the United States: A Cold War Case Study.* Pittsburgh: University of Pittsburgh Press, 1988.

Cottrell, A., ed., *The Persian Gulf States.* Baltimore: John Hopkins University Press, 1980.

Curzon, George N., *Persia and the Persian Question* (1892) London: Cass & Co. 1966. 2 volumes.

Dabiri, Mohammad Reza, "Abu Musa Island; A Binding Understanding or A Misunderstanding," in *Iranian Journal of International Affairs,* V (3/4) (Fall/ Winter, 1993/94).

D'Albuquerque, B., *The Commentaries of the Great Afonso D'Albuquerque* (1744), W. de Gray Birch, ed. London: Hakluyt Society, 1872-1884. Vol. I.

Dames, M. L., trans. and ed. *The Book of Duarte Barbosa: An Account of the Countries bordering on the Indian Ocean and their Inhabitants.* Vol I (written by Duarte Barbosa and completed in 1518). Hakluyt Society, London, 1918. Vol. I.

Eqbal, A., *Motala'ati dar Bab-e Bahrain va Jazayer-o Savahel-e Khalij-e Fars.* Tehran: Chapkhaneh-e Majlis, 1948/49.

Faria e Sousa, Manoel da, *Asia Portuguesa.* Vol. I. Isabel Ferreira, ed. Pôrto: Biblioteca Histórica/Livraria Civilização, 1945.

Fassai, H., *Farsnama-ye Naseri* (ca. 1883). *See* Busse.

Godolphin, F.R.B. ed., *The Greek Historians.* Vol. I. New York: Random House, 1942.

Hawley, Donald, *The Trucial States.* London: George Allen & Unwin, 1970.

Hay, Rupert, *The Persian Gulf States.* Washington, D.C.: The Middle East Institute, 1959.

Herodotus, *Persian Wars. See* F.R.B. Godolphin.

Hopwood, D., ed., *The Arabian Peninsula.* London: Allen & Unwin, 1972.

Hudud al-'Alam (ca. 982). *See* Minorsky.

Hunter, S.T., *Iran and the World: Continuity in a Revolutionary Decade.* Bloomington: Indiana University Press, 1990.

Ibn al-Bakkhi, *Farsnama* (ca. 1111). G. Le Strange, and R. A. Nicholson, eds. London: Luzak & Co., 1921.

Ibn Hawqal, Abul-Qasem, *Surat al-Ardh* (written in A.H. 367). 2nd ed. London, 1988.

Ismael, T.Y., and Ismael, J.S., eds., *The Gulf War and the New World Order: International Relations of the Middle East.* Gainesville: University Press of Florida, 1994.

Jackson, W., *Persia: Past and Present.* London: Macmillan & Co., 1909.

Jenab, M.A., *Khalij-e Fars: Ashenaii ba Amarat-e An.* Tehran: Entesharat-e Padideh, 1970.

Karim-Zadeh Tabrizi, Mohammad-Ali, ed., *Asnad va Faramin-e Montasher Nashodeh-e Qajari.* London, 1989.

Kazemzadeh, F., *Russia and Britain in Persia: 1865-1914*. New Haven: Yale University Press, 1968.

Kazwini, Hamdallah Mustawfi al, *Nuzhat al-Qulub* (ca. 1307). G. Le Strange, ed. Leyden: E.J. Brill, 1913; 2nd ed., 1928.

Kelly, J.B., *Britain and the Persian Gulf 1795-1880*. Oxford: Clarendon Press, 1968.

Kelly, J.B., *Eastern Arabian Frontiers*. London: Faber & Faber, 1964.

Kinneir, John Macdonald, *A Geographical Memoir of the Persian Empire*. London: 1813.

Lissan al-Molk, Mirza Mohammad Taqi, *Nasekh at-Tavarikh*. Vol. I (reports of events of early nineteenth century in and around Iran). Tehran: Mohammad Baqer Behbudi, 1974.

Lockhart, L., "The Navy of Nadir Shah," in *Proceedings of the Iran Society*. Vol. 1. London: The Iran Society, 1936.

Lockhart, L., *Nadir Shah*. London: Luzac & Co., 1938.

Malcolm, J., *The History of Persia*. London: John Murray, 1829.

Malone, J.J., *The Arab Lands of Western Asia*. Englewood Cliffs: Prentice Hall, 1973.

Maqdasi, *Ahsan at-Taqasim Fi Marefat al-Aqalim*, 2nd ed. Liden, 1906.

Massoudi, A., *Khalije Fars dar Doran-e Sarbolandi va Shokouh*. Tehran: Ettela'at Publications, 1973.

Massoudi, A., *The Persian Gulf: In the Light of International Rivalries & Provocations* (text of a speech at the Rotary Club of Iran on July 17, 1972).

McMunn, J.D., *Great Britain's Withdrawal from the Persian Gulf: An Analysis of Policy and the Process,* an unpublished master's thesis on file at Georgetown University, Washington, DC, 1974).

Miles, S.B., *The Countries and Tribes of the Persian Gulf*. London: Harrison & Sons, 1919. 2 vols.

Minorsky, V., "Linga," in *Encyclopaedia of Islam*. Vol. III. Houtsma et al., eds. London: Luzac & Co., 1936.

Minorsky, V., trans. and ed., *Hudud al-'Alam* (A.D. w.982). London: Luzac & Co., 1937.

Mirfendereski, G., and Meshkati, N., "America's Undertow, Iran's Achilles' Heel in the Persian Gulf," in *US-Iran Review* 1 (Commentary) (April, 1993), p. 6.

Mojtahed-Zadeh, P., *Countries and Boundaries in the Geopolitical Region of the Persian Gulf*. Tehran: IPIS Publications, 1993.

Mojtahed-Zadeh, P., *Evolution of Eastern Iranian Boundaries*. Ph.D. diss. London University, 1993.

Mojtahed-Zadeh, P., *The Changing World Order and the Geopolitical Regions of Caspian Central Asia and the Persian Gulf*. London: Urosevic Foundation, 1992.

Mojtahed-Zadeh, P., et al., "Special Report on Abu Musa," in *San'at-e Haml-o Naghl* (Transport Industry Monthly), 1474 (Tehran: November, 1992).

Mojtahed-Zadeh, P., *Political Geography of the Strait of Hormuz*. Joint Geography Department & Middle East Centre Publication of the School of Oriental and Asian Studies. London: London University, 1990.

Mojtahed-Zadeh, P., *Joghrafiay-e Tarikhi-e Khalij-e Fars*. Tehran: Tehran University Press, 1975.

Mojtahed-Zadeh, P., *Sheikh Neshinhay-e Khalij-e Fars*. Tehran: Ataei Publications, 1970.

Morier, J., *A Second Journey through Persia, Armenia, and Asia Minor, to Constantinople between the Years 1810 and 1816*. London: Longman & Co., 1818.

Morsy Abdullah, M., *The United Arab Emirates*. London: Croom Helm, 1978.

Movahed, J., *Bastak va Khalij-e Fars*. Tehran: 1970.

Moyse-Bartlett, H., *The Pirates of Trucial Oman*. London: MacDonald, 1966.

Mustawfi. *See* Kazwini.

Nateq, Homa, *Iran dar Rah-yabi-e Farhangi, 1834-1848*. London: Payam Publications, 1988.

Nuzhat al-Qulub (ca. 1340). *See* Kazwini.

Playfair, J., *System of Geography*. Vol. I. Edinburgh: Peter Hill, 1813.

Ptolemaeus, C., *Geographia* (published in Venice in 1511). Amsterdam: Theatrum Orbis Terrarum, 1969.

Ramazani, R., *Iran's Foreign Policy: 1943-1973*. Charlottesville: University of Virginia Press, 1975.

Ramusio, G.B., "La Navigatione Di Nearcho" (1550), in G.B. Ramusio, *Navigationi et Viaggi* (1550). Vol. I. Amsterdam: Theatrum Orbis Terrarum, 1970.

Razik, S. ibn. *See* Badger.

Rennell, J., trans. and ed., *The Geographical System of Herodotus*. Vol. I. London: Bulmer & Co., 1800.

Robson, E.I., trans., *Arrian: History of Alexander and India*. Vol. II. London: W. Heinmann, 1949. Loeb Classical Library.

Rohroborn, Klaus-Michael, *Provinzen und Zentralgewalt Persiens* (Persian edition) Kaykavous Jahandari, trans. Tehran: B.T.N.K, 339, 1978.

Round Table. *See* Arab Research Centre.

Salmon, T., *Modern History or the Present State of All Nations* (1729). Vol. I. 3rd ed. London: Longman, 1744.

Savory, Roger M., "A.D. 600-1800," in Cottrell, Alvin J., ed., *The Persian Gulf States.* Baltimore: John Hopkins University Press, 1980.

Schofield, R.N., *Territorial Foundation of the Gulf States.* London: UCL Press, 1994.

Shammas, Pierre, *Border Disputes in the Greater Middle East,* a paper presented to the Royal Institute of International Affairs, Chatham House, London, February 17, 1993.

Sheikh al-Eslami, Javad, *Qatl-e Atabak.* Tehran: Kayhan Publications, 1988.

Sinclair, F.W., and Ferguson, D., trans. and eds., *The Travels of Pedro Teixeira.* London: Hakluyt Society, 1902.

SIPRI, *SIPRI Yearbook 1994, World Armaments and Disarmament.* Oxford: Oxford University Press, 1994.

Swift, R., *Project Norouz.* New York: Tower Books, 1982.

Sykes, P. *History of Persia.* London: Macmillan & Co., 1951.

Tabari, Mohammad Ben Jarir, *Tarikh Tabari.* Vol. II. (Persian translation by Abol-Qasem Payandeh). Tehran: Bongah-e Tarjomeh va Nashr-e Ketab, 1973.

Teixeira, P., *A Short Narrative of the Origin of the Kingdom of Hormuz.* based on the *Shahnameh* by Turan-Shah, King of Hormuz, 1347-1378. *See* Sinclair and Ferguson.

Vadala, R., *Le Golfe Persique.* Paris: Librairie Arthur Rousseau, 1920.

Vadiei, K., *Joghrafiya-ye Ensani-e Iran.* Tehran: Tehran University Press, 1974.

Vincent, W., *The Voyage of Nearchus from the Indus to the Euphrates.* London: Cadell & Davis, 1797.

Vincent, W., *The Commerce and Navigation of the Ancients in the Indian Ocean.* London: Cadell & Davis, 1807.

Vincent, W., *The Voyage of Nearchus and Periplus of the Erythraean Sea.* Oxford: Oxford University Press, 1809.

Wilkinson, J.C., "The Origins of the Omani State," in Hopwood. *See* Hopwood.

Wilkinson, J.C., *Water and Tribal Settlement in South-East Arabia.* Oxford Research Studies in Geography. Oxford: Clarendon Press, 1977.

Wilkinson, J.C., "The Julanda of Oman," in *Journal of Oman Studies,* 1 (1975).

Wilkinson, J.C., *Arab Settlement in Oman.* Ph.D. diss. Oxford University, 1969.

Wilkinson, J.C., "A Sketch of the Historical Geography of the Trucial Oman Down to the Beginning of the Sixteenth Century," in *The Geographical Journal,* 130 (1964).

Wilson, A.T., *The Persian Gulf.* Oxford: Clarendon Press, 1928.

Wright, Denis, "Ten Years in Iran: Some Highlights," in *Asian Affairs* XXII (October, 1991).

Wright, Denis, *The English Amongst the Persians.* London: Heinemann, 1977.

Yaqut al-Rumi, *Mudjam al-Buldan* (ca. 1224). Vol. V. Beirut: Dar Sader, 1955.

Index

Entries with *n* refer to note numbers.
Entries in **boldface** refer to maps.